PARAGUAY

PARAGUAY

The Personalist Legacy

Riordan Roett
and Richard Scott Sacks

Westview Press
BOULDER • SAN FRANCISCO • OXFORD

Westview Profiles / Nations of Contemporary Latin America

The U.S. Department of State does not necessarily endorse the views and opinions expressed in this book.

Unless otherwise indicated, photographs are by Richard Scott Sacks. Maps and charts are by Drake Roberts.

Published in 1991 in the United States of America by Westview Press, Inc., 5500 Central Avenue, Boulder, Colorado 80301, and in the United Kingdom by Westview Press, 36 Lonsdale Road, Summertown, Oxford OX2 7EW

Library of Congress Cataloging-in-Publication Data
Roett, Riordan, 1938–
   Paraguay : the personalist legacy / Riordan Roett and Richard Scott Sacks.
      p. cm.—(Westview profiles. Nations of contemporary Latin America)
   Includes bibliographical references and index.
   ISBN 0-86531-272-9
   1. Paraguay—Civilization. 2. Paraguay—Politics and government—20th century. I. Sacks, Richard Scott. II. Title. III. Series.
F2670.R63 1991
989.2—dc20   90-45813
                                                                                    CIP

Printed and bound in the United States of America

The paper used in this publication meets the requirements of the American National Standard for Permanence of Paper for Printed Library Materials Z39.48-1984.

10   9   8   7   6   5   4   3   2   1

To Domingo Rivarola and Graziella Corvalán
with grateful thanks for their
initial support and enduring patience
—RR

And for Glynis Ann and Jared Maurice,
without whose love and understanding
this book would never have been written
—RSS

Paraguay is not a country—it is an obsession.
—Juan Carlos Herken Krauer

Contents

Tables and Illustrations

Foreword

Until almost the end of the 1980s, Paraguay and General Alfredo Stroessner were perceived as virtually synonymous in the minds of a whole generation. Indeed, this dictator often eclipsed the small, inland South American country over which he ruled for more than a third of a century. Yet, in the long run, the most important events in Paraguay occurred before Stroessner came to dominate the scene. Two of the hemisphere's most significant wars were fought chiefly in Paraguay— one in the 1860s and the other during the 1930s. The former, often called the War of the Triple Alliance, pitted Paraguay against Brazil, Argentina, and Uruguay in an epic struggle that could have had but one outcome—the eventual defeat and occupation of Paraguay. The more recent Chaco War (1932–1935) was fought against Bolivia, with Paraguay enjoying the home field advantage. Yet if the result could be termed a victory for Paraguay, it was a costly one that brought no advantages with it. Moreover, a good look at nineteenth-century Paraguay shows that the roots of the Stroessner phenomenon were planted deeply in Paraguay's national life from the time of independence.

Riordan Roett and Richard Sacks have joined efforts to do full justice to a country and a people who are seeking to build a better future on the very questionable foundation of the Stroessner legacy. They show that the long-lived Stroessner dictatorship was no aberration, but rather a logical link in Paraguay's almost unbroken tradition of essentially authoritarian to downright despotic rulers: Indeed, José Gaspar Rodríguez de Francia, Carlos Antonio López, and Francisco Solano López become highly understandable in the context of the nineteenth-century Paraguay effectively described by the authors. Solano's battlefield death in 1870 left a long-term vacuum, and instability à la Bolivia replaced strongman rule. In the aftermath of the Chaco War, the military's political role expanded, and the 1947 civil war set the stage for Stroessner's rise and subsequent 35-year hold on power.

Although Paraguay's economy is quite limited, it is far from simple subsistence. Economic growth was high during the 1974–1981 period, yet that growth was not sustainable once the great hydroelectric project at Itaipú—a Brazilian initiative—was completed. Roett and Sacks argue persuasively that the potential for renewed growth exists as Paraguay enters the 1990s. Even more important and original than their concise and competent treatment of the economy, however, is their elucidation of Paraguayan culture, centering upon the role of Guaraní as the true national language in this most mestizo of all Latin American countries. Within their analysis of society, they give special and sensitive attention to the changing roles of women and Indians.

The ousting of Stroessner in February 1989 and the subsequent election of General Andrés Rodríguez occurred too recently for their long-run effects to be clear. Roett and Sacks do, however, provide a systematic analysis of the structures and forces involved in the evolving political processes and clearly portray the environment in which these function. They help the reader understand Paraguay's very tentative and incomplete transition from authoritarian rule, a transition that is not yet, in important ways, one clearly headed toward real democracy. In this respect, their careful and insightful assessment of external factors and Paraguay's international position adds an important dimension.

The reader with a preexisting interest in Paraguay will find answers in this book to just what this country is, how it has reached its present state, and where it may be going. Individuals interested in broadening their comparative understanding of Latin America will be rewarded with a text that clears away persistent myths and misconceptions about this little-known country lying between Brazil, Argentina, and Bolivia. They will find that Paraguay is far from being simply the other side of the Uruguayan coin—a Southern Hemisphere Albania to that more advanced and fortunate little country's shining Switzerland. Beyond this, the Paraguayan case provides a link, via Bolivia, between the heavily European Southern Cone nations of South America and the highly Indian Andean countries.

Ronald M. Schneider

Preface

The shots fired during the early morning hours of February 3, 1989, at the Asunción headquarters of the presidential escort battalion presented the planet with its first blood-and-steel evidence that the year would be recorded, like 1848, as one of universal human liberation. The deposed government of Alfredo Stroessner had held power in Paraguay for close to 35 years, a political longevity then surpassed only by Bulgaria's Todor Zhivkov, North Korea's Kim Il-song, and Jordan's King Hussein.

The new president, Stroessner's second-in-command and close associate, Andrés Rodríguez, immediately announced that his government would work to establish a political system that would guarantee the full exercise of human rights in Paraguay. Rodríguez wasted no time in calling and carrying out elections on May 1, 1989, arguably the freest elections ever held in Paraguay. For once, by presaging what was to come in Eastern Europe later in the year and by showing the world that absolute dictators would soon become as rare as mastodons, Paraguay was in sync with the rest of humankind.

As news reports from this country in the center of South America disappeared from the front pages of the Western press, Paraguay faded once again into the shadows. It is an odd place, this Guaraní outpost squeezed on three sides by its enormous neighbors, Argentina and Brazil. A landlocked island of distinct historical and political tradition surrounded by the continental land mass, Paraguay had never known anything but dictatorship. Cynics were not surprised when Rodríguez received close to 75 percent of the vote in the May 1 presidential election.

Buoyed, as it were, by the dead weight of the country's peculiar past, detractors of the new regime were soon qualifying the February coup that catapulted Rodríguez into power as nothing more than a palace revolution. Some even suggested, in a remarkable example of Paraguayan paranoia (also much in keeping with tradition, bred of isolation and the anxiety of being surrounded on all sides), that the coup was not a coup at all but merely an elaborate piece of theater staged to provide Stroessner with a convenient exit. Optimists brusquely dismissed the doubters, claiming that the Paraguayan ship of state had experienced a fundamental change in course.

To his credit, some 16 months after the February 1989 coup, President Rodríguez was piling obstacles in the path of any Paraguayan, including himself, who might attempt to return to the bad old ways of Paraguay under Stroessner. For example, Rodríguez told delegates to the June 4, 1990, Organization of American States (OAS) general assembly in Asunción that democracy and respect for human rights were now irreversible realities in Paraguay. Rodríguez defined Paraguay's task— and his own—as undoing the effects of centuries of absolutism.

Over the years, the Paraguayan political pendulum often has oscillated between the poles of despotism and civil war. If Rodríguez fulfills his stated promise to step down as president after one term, and if Paraguayans can prepare themselves to cope with the tensions and responsibilities of democracy without submitting once more to the national bane—one-man rule—then the country really may start to dismantle the legacy of its personalist past.

Richard Scott Sacks

Acknowledgments

We wish to acknowledge our debt to the many people whose cooperation and contributions made this work possible. In particular, we are grateful to Martin Andersen, Esteban Caballero, Gerry Cooney, Garland Dennett, Jim Dinsmoor, Dennis Hanratty, Jack Martin, Manuel Romano, Jorge Seall, Clyde Taylor, and Thomas Whigham, who read the manuscript or portions of it. We also thank Line Bareiro, Melissa Birch, Paul Dax, Benjamín Fernández, Alfredo Forti, Maria T. Gutierrez, Fernando Masi, Diane Monash, Alan Rogers, and Antonio Segovia for their time, patience, advice, and invaluable assistance in helping to organize the research.

Riordan Roett
Richard Scott Sacks

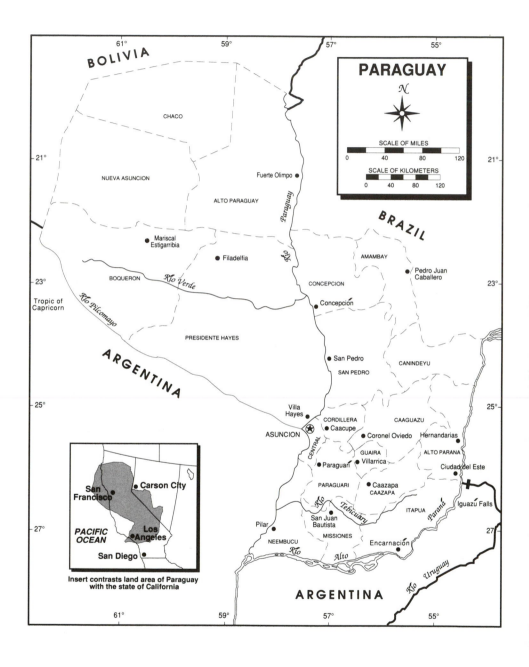

PARAGUAY

N

SCALE OF MILES

0   40   80   120

SCALE OF KILOMETERS

0   40   80   120

BOLIVIA

CHACO

NUEVA ASUNCION

Fuerte Olimpo

ALTO PARAGUAY

BRAZIL

Mariscal
Estigarribia

Filadelfia

AMAMBAY

Pedro Juan
Caballero

BOQUERON

Rio Verde

CONCEPCION

Concepción

Tropic of
Capricorn

Rio Pilcomayo

PRESIDENTE HAYES

San Pedro

SAN PEDRO

CANINDEYU

ARGENTINA

Villa
Hayes

CORDILLERA

Caacupe

CAAGUAZU

ASUNCION

CENTRAL

Coronel Oviedo

Hernandarias

GUAIRA

ALTO PARANA

San Francisco

Carson City

Paraguari

Villarrica

Ciudad del Este

PACIFIC
OCEAN

Los
Angeles

PARAGUARI

Caazapa

CAAZAPA

Iguazú Falls

San Diego

Pilar

San Juan
Bautista

Tebicuary

ITAPUA

Paraná

Parana

NEEMBUCU

MISSIONES

Encarnación

Rio

Alto

Rio Uruguay

Insert contrasts land area of Paraguay
with the state of California

ARGENTINA

Paraguay

Rio

1

Introduction

The waters of the Upper Paraná alone are said to equal those of all European rivers. . . . As for the Paraguay, from its source, As Sete Lagoas (The Seven Lagoons) in the central sierra of South America, to this confluence it flows some 1,200 miles; from here to the sea another 950. . . .

The forest—this has happened suddenly—has become jungle. Temperature has risen, there is a change in vegetation, which is thicker, brilliantly lit by flowers, white, violet, scarlet. At the rim of this dark violent chaos lie huge rotting trees, half in, half out of the muddy water. The choking confusion of vegetation, the thickset trees, lianas, creepers are seen to be components of a wall; its very impenetrability excites one to try it.
—Gordon Meyer, The River and the People

On February 3, 1989, Paraguay emerged from almost thirty-five years of one-man rule—a modern record for Latin America—when a rival general overthrew General Alfredo Stroessner in a bloody coup. The general who overthrew Stroessner, Andrés Rodríguez, was one of Stroessner's closest associates. Rodríguez had invested much personal capital in Stroessner's regime and had benefited unabashedly from his rule. As this book was being written, Rodríguez had become the constitutional president of the republic. He was elected three months after the coup to fill out the term of his predecessor, just as Stroessner had been elected in 1954 to fill out the term of the deposed Federico Chaves.

With the most dubious of credentials as a democrat, Rodríguez nonetheless claimed to be putting the Paraguayan republic on the road to democratic government, vowing to step down when his term expires in 1993. Newspapers that Stroessner had banned were again on the streets. Many leading figures of the regime's last years were behind bars or cleaning out cavalry stables. For the first time in history, mayors were about to be chosen by local, direct election instead of being appointed by the central power of the state.

Most important, Paraguayans were universally relieved that Stroessner was gone and were beginning to lose their fear of the police. Although

One of Stroessner's ubiquitous signs. Most of these signs disappeared within days of the February 3, 1989, coup.

Rodríguez is accused by many of being involved in drug trafficking in earlier years, he nonetheless promised to wage a crusade against the drug lords, whose influence was spreading everywhere in South America during the 1980s. As the man who got rid of an increasingly odious dictatorship, Rodríguez was enjoying a prolonged political honeymoon. Paraguay, under Rodríguez, was finally getting ready to enter the political twentieth century.

As president of a country that had never had a democratic system, Rodríguez was saying and doing some unusual things during his first year in power. But there is little about Paraguay that is not extraordinary. Paraguay's population of 4 million is probably the most homogeneous on the continent, both racially and culturally. Unlike some of its neighbors, Paraguay has no racially based caste system: Virtually every Paraguayan is of mestizo ancestry. Nearly all Paraguayans speak the same language; their common national tongue is not Spanish but Guaraní, an Indian language. No other Western country affords an indigenous language such wide currency.

Paraguay is paradoxical. The first independent nation in South America, it has been one of the least free. The country never has had what Westerners would call a "clean" election; it has been run by

President Andrés Rodríguez before a Monday, February 6, 1989, news conference, three days after he seized power from President Alfredo Stroessner.

dictators almost continuously since the Spaniards left. Approximately the size of California, the country is completely landlocked, yet it is a regional trading capital. Paraguay is nearly devoid of valuable natural resources with one exception: The world's largest electricity-producing dam, Itaipú, is located on the Paraguay-Brazil border. Another huge dam, with one-quarter Itaipú's capacity, is scheduled for completion by 1995 at Yacyretá, on the Argentine frontier.

There is no compelling reason that Paraguay did not become an exotic but remote province of Argentina or Brazil. The country's sixteenth-century birth was accidental: A handful of Spanish adventurers who had survived a brutal passage in their quest for gold found no riches, only a poor, godforsaken place at the ends of the earth. Paraguay became, for a short time, the focal point of Spanish colonial ambitions in southern South America, until would-be immigrants began to shun the colony for its lack of exploitable wealth. Under colonial rule, Paraguay was one of the least accessible places in the world. It soon became little more than a buffer province that the relentlessly expanding Portuguese in Brazil never ceased nibbling at.

Sometime during the eighteenth century, Paraguay became a place where time stood still; it was rural, poor, fearfully hot during most of the year, and almost as isolated and inaccessible as Tibet. Only now is it starting to emerge from this state. The tradition—or better, the habit—of personalist rule that began in colonial times has not yet died out in Paraguay. Independent institutions that may reflect independent thinking and produce independent agendas have never flourished. Attempts at independent action or thought have always inconvenienced those who monopolized state power. Whether ruled by Spaniards, dictators, or civilian or military oligarchs, Paraguayans never were asked their opinion about how they should be governed. Decisions are made, traditionally, not by consensus but by the man at the top.

The dictatorial tradition has done nothing to impede Paraguayan nationalism. Paraguayans have often been called on to defend their nation on the battlefield, and they have not shirked from the task. Independence was won when Paraguayan arms defeated an Argentine invasion. Paraguay underwent two major wars after independence. The first, the Triple Alliance War (1864–1870), was a holocaust that halved Paraguay's population, leaving only one-tenth of the original male population alive. The second was the Chaco War (1932–1935) against Bolivia, which killed 80,000 soldiers on both sides but left Paraguay in possession of most of the contested area. Paraguay has proved that it possesses a national cohesion that is unrivaled in Latin America.

For such a small, out-of-the-way place, Paraguay has always attracted attention, if not notoriety, from abroad. In *Candide*, Voltaire took a gibe at the Jesuits in Paraguay who, during the seventeenth and eighteenth centuries, with the blessing of the Spanish kings, had organized at least 100,000 Indians on communal settlements far from the control of the colonial governor. Thomas Carlyle and Richard Burton, both English writers of the nineteenth century, recognized Paraguay as a bizarre place that reveled in its isolation and oddities by building a "Chinese wall" around itself. Indeed, from about 1816 until 1840, Paraguay resembled a "mousetrap": No one was permitted to leave. Paraguayans who left were not allowed to return. Even foreigners who entered were forced to stay.

Although Paraguay achieved independence from Spain early, in 1811, the dictators who held power until 1870 were virtual kings who called themselves presidents. Paraguayans have been conditioned to follow; their leaders have gotten used to wielding absolute power. This habit was reinforced after 1947, when a brutal civil war prostrated the country, exiled a third of the population, and paved the way for the Stroessner dictatorship. With the overthrow of Stroessner in 1989, Paraguay was only just beginning to adopt the political practices of twentieth-century multiparty democracies.

Predictably, Paraguay's dictators (Higínio Morínigo and Alfredo Stroessner, in particular) have felt attracted to people of like mind. In Asunción in 1989, one could still walk along a street named for Francisco Franco or view a statue of Anastasio Somoza García, the Nicaraguan dictator. Ironically, Somoza's dictator son, Anastasio Somoza Debayle, was blasted to pieces by Argentinian guerrillas in Stroessner's capital shortly after fleeing Nicaragua's revolutionary forces in 1979.[1] Jozef Mengele, the Auschwitz concentration camp doctor known as the "Angel of Death" for, among other things, his hideous experiments on 1,500 sets of twins, was issued a Paraguayan passport sometime in 1960. He was rumored to have worked briefly as a physician in the Chaco region[2] before moving to Brazil, where he drowned in 1985.

Even if we assume that Rodríguez's intentions are good, there are still limits to what he can accomplish easily, given Paraguay's past. The slowness of the regime in bringing corrupt officials and torturers to trial indicates that the Colorado party–military–government ménage upon which the presidency rests will not tolerate any threats to its existence. Some internal dispute within the Colorado party or between the Colorado party and the military, as yet unforeseen, may cause the current alignment to disintegrate. What would replace it is unclear. Order has been a precious commodity in Paraguay, where pacific regime changes are unknown. Paraguay could easily descend again into the chaos that characterized the 1948–1954 period, when Asunción (Paraguay's capital) was a no-man's land and then-Colonel Alfredo Stroessner once arrived at the Brazilian Embassy in the trunk of a car to seek asylum.

Gradual change will be in the interests of most, and perhaps Rodríguez and his (we hope, civilian) successors will be able to find the right mix of stability and change that would cause a true revolution in Paraguayan political life. Modernization is the order of the day, not so much of buildings and roads as of the thought patterns of the people and their leaders, of society and its institutions, and of political practices and methods. The 1989 coup gave Paraguayans an opportunity. It will be up to them to transform this opportunity into accomplishments.

*   *   *

Slightly smaller than California, slightly larger than Zimbabwe, Paraguay has a surface area of 157,047 square miles, or 406,752 square kilometers. The 1988 population was estimated at slightly over 4 million, with most Paraguayans living within a few dozen miles to the east and south of the capital, Asunción (see Table 1.1). The country has common boundaries with Argentina, Brazil, and Bolivia and is completely land-locked. It is cut into two unequal portions by the Paraguay River, which

TABLE 1.1   Paraguay—Vital Statistics

Area	
km²	406,752
mi²	157,047
Population (1988—40.9% urban; 59.1% rural)	4,039,000
Annual population growth rate (percent, 1970–1988)	3.2
Population per km²	9.9
Birth rate (per 1,000, 1980–1985)	35.8
GDP per capita in dollars (1988)	1,557.00
Mortality (per 1,000, 1980–1985)	6.8
Infant mortality (per 1,000 live births, 1980–1985)	53.0
Life expectancy (at birth, in years, 1980–1985)	66.4

Source: Interamerican Development Bank figures.

flows north to south from Brazil to its confluence with the Paraná River in the extreme south of Paraguayan territory.

There are probably few places where a river divides less similar habitats. The western region, called the Chaco, with about 60 percent of Paraguay's territory but less than 2 percent of the population, is a vast, virtually flat, and unpopulated thorn and palm forest abounding in game and tropical birds. The average altitude in the Chaco is 130 meters (426 feet) above sea level. Near the Paraguay River, the Chaco is typically under water for much of the year, but it becomes an arid semidesert in the western portion near the Bolivian border. Paraguay's portion constitutes the greatest part of the Chaco, which also extends into Argentina and Bolivia.

Temperatures are higher in the Chaco than elsewhere in Paraguay, averaging 24–25 degrees Celsius (75–77 degrees Fahrenheit) throughout the year (Map 1.1).

Rainfall in the western Chaco (500 millimeters, or 19.7 inches a year) is less than one-third the annual total for the extreme eastern end of Paraguay (1,700 millimeters, or 66.9 inches per year) (Map 1.2). Nonetheless, agriculture in the Chaco is not negligible. The Mennonite farmers around Filadelfia have prospered despite the intense heat and uncertain rainfall and have developed techniques uniquely suited to the local ecology. Until the 1950s, however, the most important product coming out of the Chaco was quebracho extract, used for tanning leather.

On the east bank of the Paraguay River lies Paraguay proper, where the bulk of the population lives and the climate is much more amenable to human settlement and agriculture. The altitude varies from 50 to 830 meters (164 to 2,722 feet) above sea level. Most of the eastern region is green and fertile, with rolling hills and low-altitude rock outcroppings in some areas and plains in others, especially in the southeast. Traditionally, the core of the Paraguayan nation has been located within a

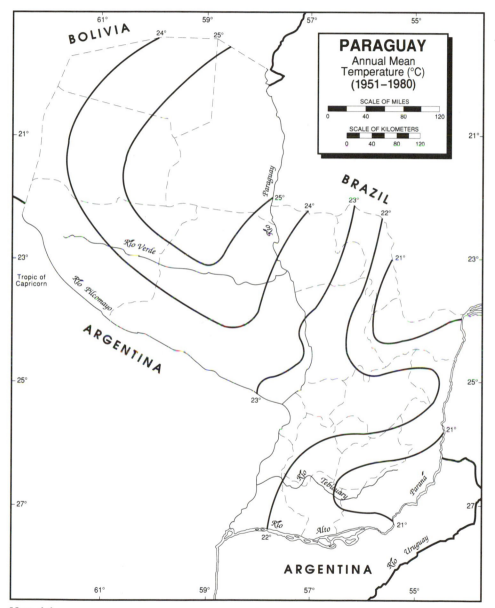

Map 1.1

8

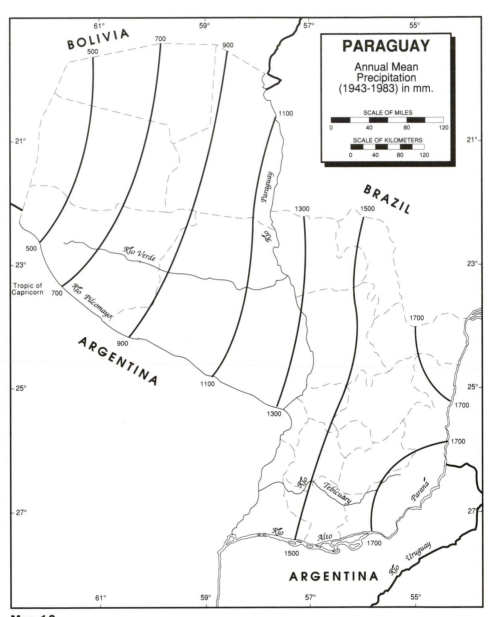

PARAGUAY

Annual Mean
Precipitation
(1943-1983) in mm.

SCALE OF MILES

0   40   80   120

SCALE OF KILOMETERS

0   40   80   120

BOLIVIA

BRAZIL

ARGENTINA

ARGENTINA

Rio Verde

Rio Pilcomayo

Rio Paraguay

Rio Tebicuáry

Rio Alto Paraná

Rio Uruguay

Tropic of
Capricorn

500

700

900

1100

1300

1500

1700

61°   59°   57°   55°

21°   23°   25°   27°

Map 1.2

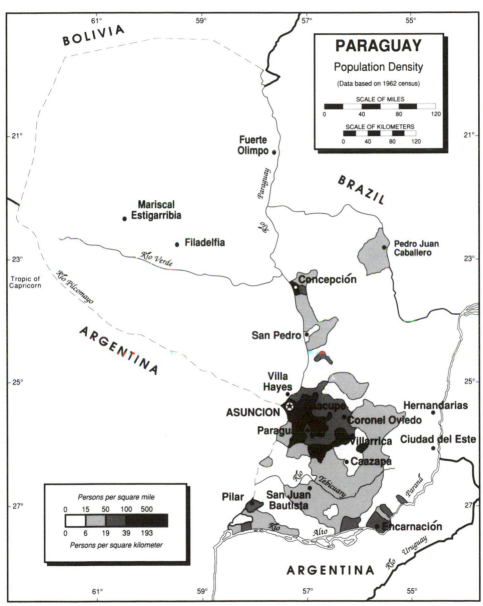

PARAGUAY

Population Density

(Data based on 1962 census)

SCALE OF MILES
0   40   80   120

SCALE OF KILOMETERS
0   40   80   120

BOLIVIA

BRAZIL

ARGENTINA

Fuerte
Olimpo

Mariscal
Estigarribia

Filadelfia

Río Verde

Río Pilcomayo

Tropic of
Capricorn

Pedro Juan
Caballero

Concepción

San Pedro

Villa
Hayes

ASUNCION

Paragu

Hernandarias

Coronel Oviedo

Villarrica

Ciudad del Este

Caazapá

Pilar

San Juan
Bautista

Encarnación

Río   Tebicuary

Paraná

Río   Alto

Río   Uruguay

ARGENTINA

Persons per square mile
0   15   50   100   500

0   6   19   39   193
Persons per square kilometer

Map 1.3

10

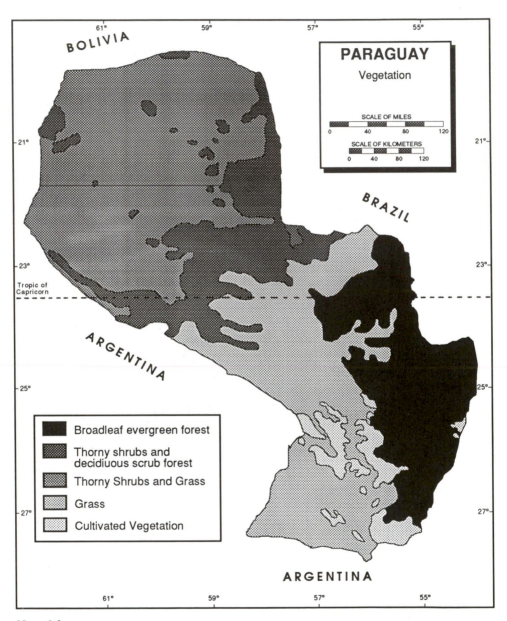

Map 1.4

few dozen miles to the west and south of the capital, Asunción (Map 1.3). This city of around 1 million people is 1,000 miles (1,600 kilometers) upriver from Buenos Aires and about the same distance from the Brazilian coast. One of the oldest cities in the New World, Asunción was founded in 1537.

Until the 1960s, the Paraguay-Paraná river system provided Paraguay with its only outlet to the rest of the world. With the completion of the Friendship Bridge over the Paraná River at Foz do Iguaçu–Ciudad del Este (previously known as Puerto Presidente Stroessner), an all-weather road from Asunción to the South Atlantic, and Brazilian-donated port facilities at Paranaguá, Paraguay in a sense has attained the status of a maritime power. Blockades by the Argentines at Buenos Aires are now a thing of the past.

Agriculture has always dominated the Paraguayan economy, but it has become even more important in recent years as a foreign exchange earner. Since the 1970s, Paraguay has become a significant exporter of cotton and soybeans (see Chapter 5). Beef production, important in the past, also has growing potential as an export commodity. Paraguay's potential as a producer of garden products and vegetables (see Map 1.4) will probably depend on the success of the regional integration schemes— which have been discussed for years—that would link the economies of Brazil, Argentina, Uruguay, and Paraguay. Wood production has also increased in recent years, threatening to destroy the fast-shrinking forest reserves near the Brazilian border. The Brazilians have long since cut down their own forests.

NOTES

1. Ironically, Somoza's assassination occurred on a street named for a famous dictator, the Avenida Generalissimo Franco.

2. Alex Shoumatoff, "The End of the Tyrannosaur," *Vanity Fair*, 52:9, September 1989, pp. 230–304.

2

Paraguayan History,
1524–1904

*Paraguay was perhaps the first nation in the Western Hemisphere to evidence
a collective awareness of nationalism, and it has carried that sense of national
uniqueness and identity through absurd heights. . . . The factors bearing upon
an early fruition of national sentiment . . . are three: race, geography, and a
well-grounded sense of threat. All interacted to produce a nationalism which
at times has bordered on the truly virulent.*
                              —John Hoyt Williams, "Race, Threat, and
                  Geography—The Paraguayan Experience of Nationalism"

EARLY EXPLORATION AND SETTLEMENT

Paraguay's recorded history began with the arrival of Europeans
looking for gold and silver. Portuguese explorer Aleixo Garcia was first,
traversing Paraguay during his 1524 raid on the Inca Empire in search
of the "White King." Garcia was the first European in Paraguay, the
first to cross the Chaco, the first to reach the Inca Empire, and probably
the first to see Iguazú Falls. His story shares the hallucinatory quality
of the exploits of the early conquistadores in Mexico and Peru, with
one difference: Garcia did not survive. A survivor of the ill-fated 1516
voyage of Juan Díaz de Solís to the yet-to-be-named Río de la Plata,
Garcia had been shipwrecked on Santa Catarina Island near the Brazilian
coast, where he learned Guaraní and heard about an incomparably
wealthy "White King" living in the interior. In 1524 Garcia set out with
several Europeans and Indians to locate the White King's empire. Near
the present site of Asunción, the local Guaraní clans gave him a 2,000-
man army. Garcia led his raiders across the Chaco—a harsh desert
wilderness of searing heat, floods, and storms—to the foothills of the
Andes. There they plundered the fringes of the Inca Empire, amassing
a considerable hoard of silver, but fierce attacks by Huayna Capac (the
reigning Inca) forced them to withdraw. On their way back to the Brazilian

Iguazú Falls. Until the Triple Alliance War (1864–1870), Iguazú was in Paraguayan territory. Now this natural wonder is on the border between Argentina and Brazil.

coast, Garcia and the other Europeans were murdered during an Indian rebellion (probably ending up as a meal for cannibals), and the silver hoard was dispersed. Garcia was the only European to penetrate the Inca Empire from the east. Many notable conquistadores in Paraguay's early history, such as Pedro de Mendoza, Juan de Ayolas, Alvar Núñez Cabeza de Vaca, and Domingo de Irala (see below), tried to duplicate Garcia's feat, but without success.[1]

When rumors that Garcia had found fabulous wealth reached Santa Catarina Island in 1526, they influenced the plans of Sebastian Cabot, who was then leading a voyage for Spain to the Orient. After hearing the stories about mountains of gold and silver in the interior, Cabot decided to explore the Paraná-Paraguay river system instead to look for a route to Peru. When he was far in the interior, Cabot sighted Indians with silver objects and named the river system "Río de la Plata" (River of Silver). The silver objects Cabot discovered probably were remnants of Garcia's trove.

On the strength of Cabot's report, Charles V of Spain in 1536 dispatched more than 1,000 men under Pedro de Mendoza to the river.[2] Cruel, sickly, and half-mad, Mendoza was a disastrous leader. He chose a desolate, windswept area with poor anchorage on the south coast of the Plata estuary as the site for the first Spanish fort in South America. On this treeless, inhospitable, dead-level plain, which was already inhabited by hostile Querandí Indians, Mendoza established the fort and named it Nuestra Señora del Buen Ayre (Our Lady of the Good Air, now known as Buenos Aires).

The settlement was doomed from the start. Resenting the Spanish intrusion, the Querandí laid siege to the tiny fort and soon reduced the Europeans to eating rats and the flesh of their deceased comrades. Then news arrived that Gonzalo de Mendoza and Juan de Salazar y Espinoza had built a fort at a good anchorage on the east bank of the Paraguay River a thousand miles upstream. The local Guaraní clans were rumored to be friendly. Most of the survivors at Buenos Aires promptly decamped upstream.[3] Gonzalo de Mendoza and Salazar had started building the fort on the Feast of the Assumption (August 15, 1537), so they called it Nuestra Señora Santa Maria de la Asunción.

The Guaraní welcomed the Spaniards with gifts of food and women, hoping the Europeans would help them subdue their enemies in the Chaco.[4] In fact, the Spaniards mounted some forays against the Chaco Indians, but they had no intention at that time of settling in Asunción. Instead, they wanted to use Asunción as a base to explore for gold and silver to the northwest. Ironically, the colony's future lay to the east, away from the inhospitable Chaco and inaccessible Peru. The history of Paraguay is the history of Asunción's eastward expansion.

A Basque soldier of fortune named Domingo de Irala emerged as governor after Juan de Ayolas, who had been Pedro Mendoza's second-in-command, failed to return from an expedition to find a way to Peru across the Chaco. Except for a two-year interruption by Alvar Núñez Cabeza de Vaca in 1542,[5] Domingo de Irala was Paraguay's governor until his death in 1556. Irala encouraged his men to marry Guaraní women to help guarantee the little colony's survival. His dominions were enormous because they had no boundaries. "La provincia gigante de los Indios," as Paraguay was called on the map, contained all of present-day Paraguay, Argentina, and Uruguay as well as large parts of Chile, Bolivia, and Brazil. The Spaniards searched in vain for gold and silver; Irala himself led an expedition into Bolivia in 1549, only to find the area already settled by Spaniards from Peru.[6]

As Elman Service has suggested, the early history of Paraguay can be divided into three periods: an *exploratory* phase (1537–1556), which was dominated by attempts to find gold and was characterized by informal relations between Spaniards and Guaraní; a *transitional* phase (1556–1580) that ended with permanent settlement and direct Spanish rule; and a *colonial* phase (after 1580), when administrative authority shifted from Asunción to Buenos Aires.[7] Two events marked the end of the exploratory phase. First, in 1553, Irala sent an armed group to the east (instead of to the west, the supposed direction of wealth) to ward off the attacking Tupí, who had Portuguese support. The second event was the imposition in Paraguay of the *encomienda*, an institution that allowed the Spaniards to subjugate and exploit the Indians. The *encomienda* assigned land and/or the Indians on it to an *encomendero*, who thus acquired rights to the Indians' labor.[8] Irala had resisted demands for grants of Indian slaves to villages until the year of his death, but finally he was forced to give in. As a result, each European received access to the services of about 60 Indians.[9]

A MONEYLESS PARADISE

The Spaniards soon realized that Paraguay was not El Dorado. Paraguay had no precious metals or mineral wealth of any kind. The Chaco and the Andes blocked the way to Peru, the focus of Spanish ambitions in South America. The route to Spain—down 1,000 miles of river to the South Atlantic and across 6,000 miles of ocean in fragile ships—was even more treacherous. Spanish ports were not allowed to trade with Paraguay. By order of the Crown, all trade first had to go to Panama, then overland across the isthmus. Once in Panama, cargos were loaded onto ships to Peru, then transferred to mules for the overland trip to Buenos Aires, where they were again loaded onto ships to Asunción. Paraguay's subsistence economy meant it had few means to pay for the goods it needed. It had no access to markets, and trade was almost nil.

Poverty and isolation had wide implications for Paraguay. The country became a poor, neglected colonial outpost where the lack of currency was so pronounced that all trade was by barter, the lack of markets perpetuated the poverty and subsistence agriculture of the Guaraní, and the settlers were free do as they pleased in their splendid isolation.

Paraguay confronted the Spaniards with difficult political choices. Fernando Cortes and Francisco Pizarro had conquered densely populated Indian nations of subservient peasants whose productive surplus gave their upper classes a comfortable existence. The Spaniards in Mexico and Peru replaced the defeated Indian lords at the top of a mostly intact social order, reserving the elite's privileges for themselves. Once the Indian masses accepted Christianity and Spanish suzerainty, they could be governed indirectly by local Indian rulers, who collected and delivered the tribute as specified by the terms of the *encomienda* grant.

No such situation existed in Paraguay, except that the Spaniards were seriously outnumbered. The Guaraní had no notion of government, no institutions, no upper class of kings and nobles, and no real unity. Instead, they had a loose clan structure based on hunting, gathering, and nomadic subsistence agriculture. The country had no ready-made political system that the Europeans could harness. In fact, the Spaniards themselves had brought the idea of government with them. The economic level of the Guaraní was low compared with the Indians of Mexico or Peru. The Spaniards could hardly collect tribute from this sparse population of hunters and gatherers.[10] Government was impossible outside of personal lines of authority based on kinship. The Spaniards found they had to marry into the Indian clans and accept a low standard of living or leave the country.

Intermarriage had its compensations. The Guaraní willingly offered their daughters to their Spanish soon-to-be kinsmen, whom they accepted as chiefs. Paraguay's European men had harems of 10–20 Guaraní wives and concubines apiece and sired biblical numbers of mestizo children.[11] This produced a prodigal number of mixed-race, culturally polyglot progeny that swamped the peninsular Spaniards. In one generation the mestizos had replaced the Spaniards as *encomenderos;* by the eighteenth century they outnumbered the Indians.[12]

Acculturation to Spanish ways was rapid, particularly as the Indian population began to decline due to miscegenation, warfare, and fatal epidemics of smallpox and measles. The small *encomiendas* speeded up the process of acculturation by bringing the Indians into much closer personal contact with Spanish ways than elsewhere in Latin America. These mestizos—Spanish in outlook, but speaking Guaraní—were the nucleus of the future Paraguayan nation. Possibly because their Spanish fathers were far too occupied with other matters to pay much attention to their upbringing, the mestizo younger generation had a pronounced rebellious streak. They looked down on Indians, yet they had no particular feelings of loyalty to Spain.

After a generation or two, the pattern of the modern Paraguayan nation was set. It was to be a poor, isolated nation with a unique culture amalgamated from Spanish and Guaraní influences and with few social distinctions to separate rulers from ruled. Its national pride was distorted by constant feelings of insecurity and paranoia. Hemmed in by warlike Chaco tribes to the west, aggressive Portuguese to the east, and arrogant residents of Buenos Aires to the south who controlled the outlet of the Paraná River, Paraguayans were under constant threat. In a country where authority was always exercised along personal rather than legal or institutional lines, these conditions tended to encourage Paraguayans to support strong national leaders who could ward off the foreign menaces.

BY THE SWORD OF THE WORD

The Church had played an exceedingly minor role in Paraguay's early history. Indians were not converted to Christianity; mestizos constantly scandalized the peninsular Spaniards with their lack of Christian moral standards. This omission finally attracted the notice of Spain's King Philip III and the Council of the Indies. Philip announced in 1610 that Paraguayan Indians would be subdued only "by the sword of the Word" and not by force. Although decrees were issued to restrict the local settlers' monopoly on Indian labor and their access to Indian women, these attempts were unrealistic. Without the *encomienda*, Spanish and mestizo colonists had a bleak future in Paraguay. The Church had to shift its focus from the area near Asunción to the eastern forests.

In 1609 the Jesuits began what was possibly the world's biggest experiment in cooperative living by organizing about 100,000 Indians in 20 communal settlements called *reducciones*[13] amid the huge pines and cedars in the wild Guayrá River region far to the northeast. For the next 150 years the Jesuits would control half of Paraguay. Their "empire within an empire" had the king's blessing, but Paraguayan settlers, whom these hardworking clergy were depriving of Indian labor, viewed the Jesuits with contempt, envy, and fear. The Indians felt differently because the Jesuits protected them from the Paraguayans and because the *reducciones* were the most prosperous Indian settlements in Spanish America.

The Jesuits quickly learned that they were within striking distance of *bandeirantes* (raiders) based in São Paulo. Also called *mamelucos*, these aggressive, mixed-race descendants of pirates and freebooters survived by selling slaves to Portuguese planters. Their first big raid on the *reducciones* in 1629 netted them about 15,000 captives. Led by Father Ruíz de Montoya, the Jesuits and their neophytes trekked hundreds of miles south to the area between the Paraná and Uruguay rivers (in present-day Argentina). At this time, Paraguay had no definite borders; the *mamelucos*, expanding westward from their base in São Paulo, pushed the Spanish frontier farther and farther inland. Only when the viceroy in Lima gave permission to arm the Indians in 1639 was the *mameluco* threat eliminated. But Spain had already lost a big chunk of territory because it failed to exploit the Jesuit outposts as buffers against the expanding Portuguese.[14]

By 1700, the *reducciones* had regained their previous population of 100,000. Neophyte labor was producing valuable exports such as linen, hides, tobacco, lumber, and *yerba maté*, a bitter Paraguayan tea. The Jesuits' growing wealth was a constant goad to the settlers—especially the exporting elite—who were also growing yerba and tobacco, but without benefit of the Jesuit near-monopoly on Indian labor.[15]

Trouble began in 1720, when the Lima viceroy reinstated a pro-Jesuit governor whom the settlers had deposed.[16] Instigated by the leading families of Asunción, the *comunero* revolt was the first serious challenge to Spanish colonial authority in the New World. The revolt soon attracted support from poor farmers in the interior and became radicalized. When the commoner army seized estates and drove the *hacendados* (estate owners) out of the countryside, the rich settlers took fright and begged the governor for protection. Ironically, only intervention by the Jesuit-led Indian armies saved Asunción from capture and broke the back of the revolt in 1735.

In the end, however, Jesuit paternalism was self-defeating. Indian converts were trained only to obey, not to think for themselves. When a royal decree banished the Jesuits in 1767, the wealth they had laboriously accumulated was stolen or destroyed. During the next few decades, their Indian followers scattered. Without protection from the Crown and Jesuit leadership, they were unable to maintain their former organization and prosperity. All that remained a century later were a vague memory and a few weed-choked ruins.

INDEPENDENCE

The revolt was symptomatic of the decline not just of Paraguay, but also of the entire Spanish colonial system. Although Charles III introduced sweeping administrative reforms in 1776, by the late 1700s the Spanish Empire was in irreversible decline.[17] The reforms put Asunción under *porteño* control,[18] making Paraguay, on paper at least, a mere outpost of Buenos Aires and even less a direct concern of Spain. Many

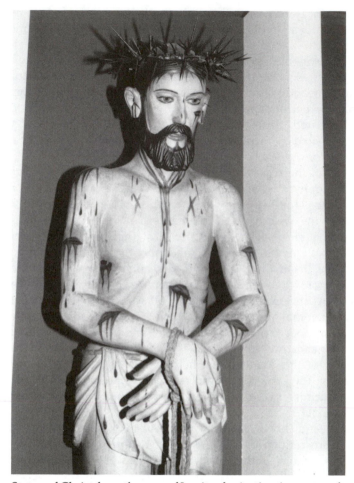

Statue of Christ from the area of Jesuit colonization (seventeenth century). The carving is probably the work of a Paraguayan Indian who did not speak Spanish.

problems remained unsolved. For example, conscription into colonial armies was causing a local labor shortage.[19] More importantly, decisions regarding Paraguay's economy were still being made far from Paraguay. For example, although the reforms tended to encourage exports, by allowing Paraguay to trade directly with Spain and other European countries, ruinous taxation threatened to price Paraguayan exports out of the market.[20]

Winds of change in Europe—in particular the French Revolution and the rise of Napoleon—finally blew the entire edifice to the ground.

Failure in war deprived Spain of its prestige and credibility among its colonial subjects. When the British attempted to seize Buenos Aires in 1806, they were driven out not by Spanish soldiers (there were none), but by a hastily assembled militia of the city's residents. In 1808 Napoleon deposed Ferdinand VII and put his own brother, Joseph, on the Spanish throne. This action destroyed the remaining legitimacy of the Spanish viceroys in the New World.

The *porteño cabildo* (Buenos Aires town council) deposed the viceroy on May 25, 1810, vowing to rule in Ferdinand's name until he could regain the throne. They immediately tried to extend their political control over the entire viceroyalty, including Paraguay, Banda Oriental (Uruguay), and Alto Perú (Bolivia), an attempt that would have far-reaching consequences. News from distant Europe had had little effect in Asunción, which after all was an intensely conservative colonial backwater, and Paraguayans made no move to depose their royal representative. Governor Bernardo de Velasco wrote to a contemporary in 1807 of "the blind obedience and great esteem and respect shown me by every class" and said that he was engaged daily in catching "monstrous fishes" from the riverbank behind the Government House.[21]

Although Paraguay barely noticed the changes that were sweeping Europe, the events in Buenos Aires stunned Asunción, where the thought of taking orders from the *porteños* was not pleasing. Owing to increased immigration from Spain during the eighteenth century, the Asunción *cabildo* was dominated by peninsular Spaniards, an urban class more royalist than the governor himself. Supreme in the local bureaucracy and commerce, the peninsular Spaniards had interests that were utterly incompatible with those of the rural Paraguayan creole elite. "Educated in the milieu of the Enlightenment, and deprived of all government positions,"[22] this Guaraní-speaking elite included officers in the local militia and ranchers who produced tobacco, yerba, and hides.[23]

Utter incompetence, arrogance, or both may explain why the *porteño cabildo* chose José Espínola y Peña to plead its case in Asunción. "Perhaps the most detested Paraguayan of his era," Espínola had been the henchman of the preceding governor, Lázaro de Ribera, an ambitious man with a controversial record whom the viceroy had relieved of his post in 1805.[24] Remembered as the man who had brutally impressed Paraguayans into military service for the disastrous 1807 defense of Buenos Aires and Montevideo against the British, Espínola barely escaped Asunción with his life.[25] In another ill-considered move, the *cabildo*, in December 1810, dispatched General Manuel Belgrano with 700 troops to force Paraguay into line.[26] Ordinary Paraguayans regarded Belgrano's army as a foreign invasion and flocked to the defense of their country. They feared, with reason, that the *porteños* wanted to use Paraguayan soldiers to subdue the rebels in Banda Oriental.

The fortunes of war rewarded Paraguay—creole-led Paraguayans beat the *porteños* twice, first at Paraguarí on January 19, 1811, and again at Tacuarí on March 9—but Spanish prestige took a beating. Fearing (incorrectly, as it turned out) that the day had been lost at Paraguarí, Governor Velasco and his general staff of *peninsulares* fled the battlefield. While the battle was being won by creole-led cavalry and troops, the governor and his Spanish officers were arriving, panic-stricken, in the capital. These victories had the effect of freeing the Paraguayans simultaneously from both *porteño* and Spanish control.

Despite his defeat, Belgrano carried on an effective correspondence with Paraguayan officers in the field and managed to convince many of them of the justice of the *porteño* crusade against Spain. The Paraguayan commander at Tacuarí allowed Belgrano and his army to slip across the Paraná before Velasco could arrive to accept his surrender. Worried by numerous anti-royalist plots and sensing that the incipient nationalism of his creole army would lead to rebellion, Velasco disarmed and demobilized his troops to prevent them from entering Asunción.

Although he could take no direct action against his victorious creole officers, who by then were national heroes, Velasco relieved many of them of their commands or posted them far from the capital, replacing them with the *peninsulares* who had lost their nerve at Paraguarí. Velasco also neglected to pay the disbanded army. By now a despised, ridiculed figure, Velasco turned increasingly to the ultra-royalist Asunción *cabildo* for support. The arrival in Asunción of José de Abreu, a Portuguese army lieutenant, fueled rumors that the *cabildo* was about to accept an offer of troops from Brazil, although Velasco in fact had already turned it down.[27] The rumors, in turn, sparked mutinies in the Asunción garrison on May 14 and 15, 1811. Feeling themselves at their last gasp, the royalists may have preferred Portuguese domination to a creole republic. Native-born Paraguayans, who had often defended their country against the Portuguese, saw this desperate move as treason. Independence from Spain and from Argentina was declared on May 17, 1811. Paraguay became the first independent nation in South America.[28]

THE RISE OF
JOSÉ GASPAR RODRÍGUEZ DE FRANCIA

Simply declaring independence, however, did not assure it. The *porteño cabildo* still considered Paraguay one of its provinces, and its need for Paraguayan conscripts became increasingly urgent in the face of numerous rebellions against its authority, particularly in Banda Oriental.

Many Paraguayans feared that union with Buenos Aires would expose Paraguay to the civil wars unleashed by the demise of Spanish power in southern South America. These disturbances were to soak the region in blood for over three decades. Yet Paraguay had little means aside from shrewd diplomacy to rebuff the *porteños* without risking another invasion. Realizing they lacked the skills for this subtle business, a group of Paraguayan military men turned to a theologian-turned-lawyer named José Gaspar Rodríguez de Francia.[29] Francia had been the highest ranking creole member of the Asunción *cabildo* and was to become Paraguay's first dictator.

One of three men named to lead the country temporarily after the events of May 14–17,[30] and one of five elected to the ruling junta[31] by a June 1811 assembly of delegates, Francia dominated Paraguayan politics by cultivating the myth of his indispensability. In a nation of politically immature, credulous peasants who knew little about events outside their own villages, where half-educated military men ran the government, this perhaps was an easier task than it might seem. As Francia would have such an enormous effect on the emerging country, it is worth devoting some space to his background and his character.

Francia belonged to a generation of native-born Latin American creoles who would have had no future in politics under Spanish rule but who rose quickly after independence. Francia's intelligence, education, honesty, reputation, and natural ability put him far ahead of his contemporaries. Born in 1766 to an aristocratic mother and a Brazilian tobacco expert, Francia was a doctor in theology trained at the College of Monserrat (at the University of Córdoba in present-day Argentina), an educational background that few Paraguayans could match. Oddly for one trained as a theologian, Francia detested the Church. When his anticlerical, anticolonial views undermined his position as professor of theology at Asunción's San Carlos Seminary, he turned to law.

As a lawyer, he built a reputation as a social activist by refusing dishonest clients and by defending the poor against the rich and powerful, often without pay. An admirer of the French Revolution, Francia had a library that was among the largest in Paraguay and included volumes by Jean-Jacques Rousseau, Voltaire, Denis Diderot, Comte de Volney, and the French Encyclopedists. His knowledge of languages, algebra, and astronomy set him completely apart: "In Paraguay, an acquaintance with French, Euclid's elements, equations, the mode of handling a theodolite, or with books prohibited by the Vatican, was . . . so much the exception to the general rule, that the man who had it . . . was deemed something between a magician and a demi-god."[32] The sight of Francia on his roof peering through a telescope was enough to convince many Paraguayans that he was a wizard who could predict the future.

Francia scored his first real success with a diplomatic victory over Buenos Aires in October 1811 by negotiating a treaty that granted de facto recognition to Paraguayan independence in return for vague promises of mutual aid. The treaty recognized Paraguayan territorial claims, abolished taxes paid to Buenos Aires, and forbade Buenos Aires from reimposing taxes on Paraguayan exports.[33] The outwitted *porteños* returned home essentially empty-handed. At the same time, by not pushing for official recognition of Paraguay's independence, Francia avoided polarizing the country into hostile nationalist and *porteñista* camps.

With Argentine hopes of absorbing Paraguay fading, the military felt less need to restrain its political ambitions. Francia resigned in December 1811 after complaining of military interference in his work. He was gambling that the bumptious, barely literate officers would have to beg him to return on his terms. He did not have to wait long. From his *chacra* (cottage) at Ybiray, Francia agitated ceaselessly against the military. Using the radical line of the French Revolution and its early triumph, the "Declaration of the Rights of Man and the Citizen," and its Rousseauean talk of the "General Will" in discussions with his many visitors, he accused the junta of betraying the revolution and leading the country to war and ruin.[34] Francia's propaganda was plausible because the junta quickly caused a crisis with Buenos Aires by extending aid to Uruguayan rebel José Artigas, which led to a virtual blockade of Paraguayan goods at the port city.[35] Meanwhile, Brazilian military probes in the north and Spanish naval activity on the rivers lent an air of impending doom. Francia took advantage of his freedom from state affairs during this period to recruit spies for his private intelligence service.

When the junta learned in November 1812 that *porteño* diplomat Nicolás de Herrera was on his way to Asunción, they begged Francia to return. They were panic-stricken at the thought of having to conduct a diplomatic negotiation. The stiff terms that they agreed to as the price for Francia's return to government revealed the depth of their insecurity. They gave Francia personal control of half the soldiers, arms, and munitions in the country until a new congress could meet the following year to decide the shape of Paraguay's government.

Herrera arrived in May 1813, intent on getting Paraguay to send a delegate to the upcoming Congress of the Provinces of the Río de la Plata. To his chagrin, he was informed that all decisions had to await the October congress in Asunción. Herrera was offered lodgings in an old customs shed, his movements were watched, and his visitors were screened. With Herrera under virtual house arrest, Francia prevailed on

junta members Pedro Juan Caballero and Fulgencio Yegros to expel two
junta members who were alleged to be *porteñista* sympathizers.[36] This
move left Francia as the only civilian junta member when the congress
convened on September 30.

With over 1,000 delegates chosen from throughout Paraguay, the
congress was certainly the first of its kind in Latin America. Perhaps
because he had spouted so much revolutionary republican rhetoric during
the period before the congress, Francia felt compelled to make it seem
that he had respected democratic forms in the selection of the delegates
and in the rules and procedures of the congress itself.[37] In fact, there
was nothing democratic about the manner in which the delegates were
chosen or in their work. Ironically, this "democratically" elected body
would set the stage for more than fifty years of dictatorship. Fired up
by patriotic speeches denouncing *porteñista* treachery (and perhaps
influenced by armed Francia partisans in the galleries), the delegates
quickly agreed that Paraguay would not attend the Congress of the
Provinces and cancelled the 1811 treaty. Herrera was not allowed in.

On October 12, the congress approved a plan—submitted by Francia
himself—that declared Paraguay an independent republic to be ruled
by two consuls, Francia and Yegros, who would alternate in power every
four months for a year until another congress could convene. Francia
would hold power during the first and the last four-month periods. On
October 13, prior to Herrera's departure for Argentina, Francia implied
to the envoy that Buenos Aires needed Paraguay more than Paraguay
needed the port. This was true. Aside from military action, Argentina's
only leverage over Paraguay was closing the river to Paraguayan traffic,
but that would not be enough to convince Francia to involve Paraguay
in Argentina's wars. The *porteños* had underestimated Francia. They
refused to believe that Paraguay could prefer isolation to an unequal
union or that Francia could make isolation work for Paraguay.

The politically astute soon realized that no force could stop Francia.
In effect, the consulship began the period of Francia's direct rule. Although
he represented the creole military elite, Yegros had no political ambitions
and was little more than a figurehead. Francia argued publicly for a
one-man dictatorship to replace the alternating two-man executive branch
and convinced the October 1814 congress to elect him to the post of
"supreme dictator of the republic" (El Supremo Dictador de la República)
for a five-year term. Another congress named him dictator for life in
1816.

Much has been made of the "class war" that Francia supposedly
waged against the Paraguayan elite on behalf of the masses of Paraguayan
peasants. True, to those who opposed him he must have appeared as
"the image of an avenging Archangel" intent on destroying them.[38] He

smashed the network of social bonds that defined the peninsular Spaniards as a class by criminalizing marriages between Europeans, forcing them, in effect, to marry mestizos, Indians, or mulattos. In the years after he became *El Supremo,* Francia arrested, exiled, jailed, or shot hundreds of Paraguay's Spanish and creole elite. In 1818, he closed Paraguay's borders to the contaminating influences of the outside world, allowing no one to enter or to leave without his permission.

Seeing clearly that the elite was the only force in Paraguay that could unseat him, Francia was selective in his retribution. He maintained good relations with elite citizens who proved loyal to him. Aside from the *peninsulares,* whom he mistrusted on principle, he jailed or executed only those members of the elite who opposed him. After the 1820 Good Friday conspiracy was uncovered, Francia arrested 180 citizens, executing Yegros and most of the military heroes of 1811.[39] The fines he levied subsequently on numerous elite familes amounted to expropriation. Firing squads executed about 70 people. The soldiers were given one ball per prisoner. If their aim was poor, they were ordered to finish their victims off with a machete or bayonet.[40] Caballero committed suicide in prison rather than submit to this fate.

Even by the bizarre standards of Latin America's postcolonial history, Francia stands apart. He was a solitary man who ruled harshly, "an implacable and vengeful enemy, who never forgot or forgave."[41] No detail of government was too trivial to escape his attention. His minister of finance and secretary of state were little more than glorified clerks.[42] Popular participation was not just not allowed; it was anathema. The army and the Church were placed under his exclusive control. Francia's spies were everywhere.[43] Arrested without charges and jailed without trial, Francia's opponents wound up in a special detention camp where they were "buried alive": shackled in underground dungeons, denied the use of toilet facilities and medical care, while they grew foot-long fingernails. The lucky ones died under torture in the "Chamber of Justice."

As fear destroyed free speech, Francia derived his power by crushing his elite opponents and by intimidating the Paraguayan masses. Peasants called him *Carai Guazú* (great lord) and regarded him as a savior. Concentrating all the reins of power in his hand, Francia ruled by using the state, which had become Paraguay's largest landowner. In fact, the common people probably gained considerably as the power of the traditional elites declined. Confiscated land was leased to peasants. Fines levied on the rich meant reduced taxes for everyone else. Some 45 state farms bred horses, cattle, and mules so quickly that the surplus was given away. Significantly, opposition to Francia surfaced only after he made the decision to close Paraguay and cut off trade with the outside world. But Francia retained the active or tacit support of other elite Paraguayans—not to mention that of the peasantry—whose way of life was hardly disrupted by his extreme measures. Many Paraguayans supported Francia because he kept the country at peace.

Some have portrayed Francia as a social revolutionary, a kind of Robespierre or Gracchus Babeuf intent on dispossessing the ruling landowning class and championing the interests of the Guaraní-speaking peasantry.[44] Though more research needs to be done on Francia, there is little evidence that he unloosed a period of social revolution on Paraguay. On the contrary, his rule was a period of personalist autocracy and intense social conservatism, not social transformation. Francia's quarrel with the elite was political, not ideological. His main imperative was to stay in power.

Francia was no socialist. In reshaping the Paraguayan state, he formed no class alliances with the masses, whom he considered unready for democracy and for whom he had contempt, calling them "pura gente idiota." He did practically nothing to educate the peasants, spending even less on education than the Spaniards had.[45] Paraguay under Francia experienced no agrarian reform; the state merely leased to the peasants the land it had confiscated.[46] Black slavery continued under Francia, and his government owned slaves. Francia's exclusive position as "first citizen" derived its legitimacy from the "Divine rights of kings" and its support from a population conditioned to obey. In a sense, Francia's rule simply perpetuated the Spanish monarchy.[47]

Political realities in Paraguay in large measure conditioned Francia's scope of action. Paraguay had no political parties—in fact, it had no institutions of any kind except a weak Catholic Church and a small military—few roads, few schools, and few opportunities for advancement. With the countryside sunk in an age-old torpor, educated people were Francia's main enemies. He judged, correctly, that they were likely to compromise Paraguayan sovereignty by inviting a union with Argentina that would help guarantee their wealth and social position. The travel ban hurt most those Paraguayans with ties or business in Buenos Aires, precisely the people who could conceivably lead a pro-*porteño* revolt. Without skilled administrators to carry out his instructions, Francia had almost no choice but to rule by himself. Democracy was not a possibility in independent Paraguay, but not only because Paraguay lacked people trained in government and administration. The country was surrounded by hostile neighbors; any government would have had to take strong measures to protect Paraguay's independence.

In many ways, Francia's rule set the pattern for postindependence Paraguayan governments, with one exception—though future rulers might be as cruel, as paranoid, and as despotic, none of them was more honest or competent. Francia took nothing from Paraguay for himself. The state coffers bulged with 36,500 pesos of his unspent salary when Francia died in 1840. Yet this frugal bachelor left no apparent heirs and no guidance on how he preferred Paraguay to continue without him.

CARLOS ANTONIO LÓPEZ

After Francia's death on September 20, 1840, came a period of coups and chaos, until a new congress of 500 delegates named Carlos Antonio López, a lawyer and landowner, as first consul in March 1841. In a country where showing exceptional ability could be fatal, López had wisely led an obscure life in the interior until Francia's death.[48] Another congress named him president of the Republic in 1844. Paraguay had its second dictator. López released most of Francia's 600 political prisoners, but free speech was still out of the question.

Although López continued a great many of Francia's policies, the two men could not have been more different. Francia was a dour, ascetic bachelor who dressed in black and lived in a modest household with four personal servants; López was extremely obese,[49] plundered Paraguay's state holdings for personal gain, and attempted to found a dynasty. He made his son, Francisco Solano López, a brigadier general at the age of eighteen, and sent him on a state mission to buy arms in Europe in 1853 at the age of twenty-seven.[50]

Yet the period of Carlos Antonio López's rule was a relatively happy time for Paraguay. López proved to be an enlightened despot who built roads and some 400 elementary schools. Secondary education was revived and state capital was used to finance industry, particularly textiles, paper, porcelain, ink, arms, and munitions manufacturing. Foreign educators, physicians, investors, and engineers were invited to Paraguay and encouraged to stay. The fall of Argentine dictator Juan Manuel de Rosas in 1852 removed a potential threat to López by opening the river to Paraguayan goods. Paraguay's trade tripled during the next ten years.

Under the rule of Carlos Antonio López, Paraguay began to acquire the reputation of being a progressive nation. As it had been with Francia, López's overriding aim was the defense of Paraguay, and the reforms he introduced contributed to this end. Foreign experts helped to build an iron factory that made guns and a railroad that could be (and would be) used to transport troops. Opening the country to trade also contributed to state revenue and gave López a chance to defend Paraguay's interests abroad, especially in Argentina, which still refused to recognize Paraguayan independence, and Brazil, which disputed Paraguay's northern border.

Foreign affairs began to loom large under López, who lacked Francia's skill for diplomacy. Francia had followed a rigid policy of absolute nonintervention in the affairs of foreign states. López was not so fastidious. In the words of historian Pelham Horton Box, López had "a fatal penchant for sowing the wind" and followed "curiously ill-advised and shifty policies" that brought trouble with Argentina, Brazil, the United States, and Great Britain.[51] By opening the country to trade and outside influence, López had to recognize the fact of Paraguay's geography and play a game of triangular diplomacy with Brazil and Argentina.

Francia had sought official contact with both countries but had been rebuffed (see Chapter 7). Although he "closed" Paraguay, he did allow minimal strategic trade, recognizing that Argentina was a bigger threat than Brazil. López ended Paraguay's isolation—an inevitable move—but was not adept at playing Brazil against Argentina. Triangular diplomacy had not been an issue until Paraguay established relations with both countries. Paraguay's existence checked the expansionist tendencies of both Brazil and Argentina, preventing them from fulfilling their ambitions regarding Paraguayan territory. As long as neither could expand at Paraguay's expense, both were disposed to tolerate the Paraguayan buffer. A Paraguayan triangular diplomat would avoid offending both nations simultaneously, never giving Brazil and Argentina a reason to unite against Paraguay. But López wooed both, offered little, avoided making tough choices and compromises, allowed controversies and border disputes to smolder, interfered in disputed areas, and angered Argentina and Brazil at the same time. His heir, López II, would reap the whirlwind.

THE TRIPLE ALLIANCE WAR

After Carlos Antonio's death in September 1862, another congress unanimously chose his thirty-six-year-old son, Francisco Solano López, as the next president of Paraguay. To assure his election, the younger López had arrested several dozen suspected oppositionists on the eve of the congress, and he did not stop arresting potential opponents until several months later when more than 400 were behind bars.[52]

Franciso Solano López is a controversial figure, mainly because of the role he played in the 1864–1870 war that pitted Paraguay against the Triple Alliance of Brazil, Argentina, and Uruguay. Since the nationalist revival of the 1930s, López is officially Paraguay's greatest hero, a patriot who mobilized the nation to fight its enemies to the death. His remains lie in a flag-draped casket in the Panteón, a white marble sepulchre in the center of Asunción. But others say López was a tyrant who used nationalism to disguise his megalomania, a man who was willing to

The Presidential Palace in Asunción, built by El Mariscal Francisco Solano López.

lead his country to death and destruction in his quest to become the "Napoleon of South America."[53] Many—including those who knew him—have accused López of unleashing the war that took over 200,000 Paraguayan lives and almost erased the country from the map.[54]

Using the ample treasury funds he inherited, López built up the Paraguayan military. Then, backed by an army strengthened by guns and conscripts and a populace united by Paraguay's peculiar paranoid racial-nationalist mixture, he set out to make Paraguay a power to be reckoned with. In particular, he wanted to forge a "third force": essentially, an alliance between Paraguay and Uruguay to keep Brazil and Argentina at bay and make them respect the rights of small powers.

This strategy turned out to be thoroughly wrong-headed. Uruguay— the scene of fractious civil war and upheaval for half a century after independence—was not a suitable partner. More to the point, Brazil and Argentina had largely recovered from their postindependence internal bickerings, and unity had brought them capabilities far beyond Paraguay's. Tiny Paraguay was in no sense prepared for a war against South America's two biggest countries. True, Paraguay's well-equipped, 30,000-man army was formidable, but not against Brazil, whose national guard alone outnumbered Paraguay's entire population of 450,000.[55] Even after conscripting every able-bodied male over the age of ten, López could not field an army as big as those of his rivals. The army had few reserves, its fighting units were undermanned, and its officer corps had been undertrained since the time of Francia to preclude the likelihood of coups. Paraguay lacked the population, industrial capacity, and technical ability to replace men, equipment, and materiel on its own, yet the country would have no access to outside aid after the outbreak of hostilities. Incompetence on a grand scale was to be López's hallmark.

López declared war on Brazil in 1864 after it ignored his warning to stop meddling in Uruguay. Despite their disadvantages, poor leadership being the most debilitating, the Paraguayans scored some early victories. Striking north at Mato Grosso, Paraguayan forces captured large stores of Brazilian armaments. Then López blundered. Instead of encouraging Argentine neutrality, he turned Brazil's natural rival into its ally. Aiming to attack southern Brazil, López sent his army into Argentina at Corrientes after permission to pass through Argentine territory had been denied. This cemented the alliance (signed on May 1, 1865) between Argentina, Brazil, and Brazil's puppet, Uruguay. In short order, Paraguay's navy was wiped out by Brazilian forces in a river engagement at Riachuelo in June 1865, and a portion of the army was cut to ribbons in September at Uruguayana. The Triple Alliance forces invaded Paraguay in 1866. After the disastrous battle of Tuyuty (May 2, 1866), in which most of Paraguay's remaining Spanish males were slaughtered, the war became a desperate struggle for survival.

López then sought to deny the Brazilian ironclads easy access to Asunción by fortifying a high point on the river called Humaitá. Situated on a bluff near the confluence of the Paraguay and the Paraná and surrounded by swamps, its batteries armed by 1867 with some 380 cannon and abundant ammunition,[56] Humaitá was well-nigh impregnable. It also was escape-proof, as its Paraguayan defenders soon learned. When the ironclads passed Humaitá on February 19, 1868, after Brazilian troops had occupied points north of it on the Paraguay River, Humaitá's defenders were isolated and cut off.

The courage and tenacity of Paraguay's soldiers postponed defeat but prolonged the suffering for several years. Not only were the scenes of war a horror, but also disease was rampant and probably took more lives than the actual fighting did. Some 60,000 soldiers had fallen or been captured by 1867, but 60,000 more were called up. As time went on, some units were formed exclusively of children under fourteen. Slaves were drafted; women were impressed for work behind the lines; and toothless, eighty-year-old men were sent to the front. Paraguayan troops went into battle semi-nude, with machetes or lances instead of guns. Even colonels went barefoot. Cavalry units charged the enemy on foot for lack of horses. Paraguayans in canoes were sent against

Brazilian ironclads. Thousands who managed to escape disease and enemy fire were massacred by López himself, who blamed his defeats on conspiracy. At the end of the war, only 28,000 Paraguayan males (including old men and children) remained alive.[57]

AFTERMATH OF A BLOODLETTING

Asunción was captured in 1869. López continued to conduct a guerrilla war in the remote north, but he finally died in battle in 1870. Paraguay was on the verge of disintegration. As gangs of vagabonds and criminals roamed the streets of Asunción, serious crimes occurred in broad daylight. Often the occupying forces were to blame. Public morality sank exceedingly low. One French botanist observed that there were 28 women for every man in the capital, noting that lovemaking was performed in the markets and "every place where there is a gathering of women."[58] Authorities eventually had to remove thousands of women with no obvious source of livelihood to the interior. As Brazil and Argentina gobbled huge chunks of territory, foreign speculators and con men descended on Asunción to feed off the Paraguayan corpse. Politics were chaotic and violent. Political assassination was widespread,[59] and corruption and fraud were rampant. Brazil and Argentina flagrantly interfered in Paraguay's internal affairs. Paraguay probably owed its continued existence to the reemergence of the natural rivalry between the two powers. The only bright spot was an arbitration by U.S. President Rutherford B. Hayes that resulted in the November 12, 1878, award to Paraguay of the area between the Verde and Pilcomayo rivers. Sovereignty over the area was transferred on May 14, 1879.

The Triple Alliance set up a provisional government soon after reaching Asunción and staffed it with Paraguayan legionnaires who had fought with the Argentines against López. The new government promulgated a constitution in 1870 patterned after those of Argentina and the United States and based on the ideals of laissez-faire liberalism then in vogue. No doubt its authors believed in its democratic ideals and its provisions for separation of powers, but the document was based on foreign ideas and was totally unsuited to Paraguay, which had known only dictatorship. The new constitution was never more than a scrap of paper.

Paraguay got a new political system, but it was founded under conditions of military defeat, foreign economic domination, and economic insecurity that would profoundly shape the country's future political life. The politically articulate coalesced into two groups—the Azules (Blues) or Gran Club and the Colorados (Reds) or Club del Pueblo. With many changes in personnel and political fortunes, these "clubs" were the respective precursors of the 1887 Centro Democrático, or Liberal party, and the Asociación Nacional Republicana (ANR), or Colorado party.[60]

Claiming to be the political heirs of López, the Colorados accused the Liberals of collaborating with the enemy and pointed with pride to their first president, General Bernardino Caballero, who had fought with López. The Liberals called López a tyrant and accused their opponents of being reactionaries. Despite the name calling, both parties adopted similar laissez-faire policies. Each party contained large numbers of *lopiztas* (former López supporters) and legionnaires. Family and personal loyalties and generational issues, rather than ideology, determined political preference. In general, the Colorado leaders had more political experience than the Liberals, who represented the "new" generation of political aspirants.

Opportunism was widespread, and people changed parties as circumstances shifted. Moreover, politics were not based on loyalty to ideologies or institutions but were personalist and paternalistic. Both parties lacked cohesion, because loyalty to a particular party *caudillo* (strong man) was all that assured an individual of his share of the spoils. Personal economic security could only be guaranteed by a patron. As a result, both parties constantly splintered into factions, whose competition often was more important than party rivalries. In 1874, a distinctly pro-Brazilian group[61] that would later found the Colorado party gained power after overthrowing pro-Argentina Benigno Ferreira. After the 1877 murder of President Juan Bautista Gill, this group continued in power under Cándido Bareiro, Bernardino Caballero, and Patricio Escobar. With his close associate and political advisor, the former legionnaire José Segundo Decoud, Caballero would make and unmake presidents until 1904.

Burdened by debt, the Paraguayan government had little choice but to sell state-owned lands to raise money. In fact, the politicians were eager to sell. These lands comprised about 95 percent of Paraguay's surface area and were the state's sole asset. Financial manipulation was rife, and the machinations of speculators, embezzlers, and thieving politicians plunged the country further into debt. During 1883–1887 the government sold vast tracts of land at low prices to foreigners who, along with Colorado party officials, acquired feudal fiefdoms in the countryside. Thousands of Paraguayan peasants were driven off the land they had farmed for generations. With nowhere to go, many faced extreme privation. Working conditions steadily grew worse, and for the first time many Paraguayans began to leave the country. Evidence of pervasive government corruption produced a tremendous outcry from the Liberals, who became bitter foes of the land sales, especially after Caballero blatantly rigged the 1886 election to ensure the election of his good friend General Patricio Escobar. Although they criticized the land sales once the measure became unpopular, the Liberals had initially advocated the same policies.

By 1900, 79 individuals owned 50 percent of the land. As politicians stole or squandered the money from land sales, Argentine, British, North American, French, and Italian business interests gained control of important segments of the manufacturing and processing industries. Problems caused by the war and the defeat were to plague Paraguay until well into the twentieth century.

NOTES

1. Charles E. Nowell, "Aleixo Garcia and the White King," *Hispanic American Historical Review*, 26:4, November 1946, pp. 450–466.

2. Few, if any, women accompanied this voyage, a fact that determined one social reality of early Paraguay: Because there were virtually no European women, the Spaniards married Indian women (see Chapter 5).

3. Mendoza meanwhile had decided to leave the Americas but probably died of syphilis on the return voyage to Spain. Buenos Aires was abandoned in 1541 and was not resettled until 1580.

4. The Chaco warriors were reputed to run so swiftly that they could catch deer with their bare hands.

5. Cabeza de Vaca's arrival brought the total European population to about 600 and was the only major reinforcement the colony received. Irala's men did not get along with the newcomers, whom they saw as interlopers. Irala finally arrested Cabeza de Vaca in 1544, held him in prison, and sent him in chains to Madrid two years later. By allowing them to choose their own governors, a 1537 decree had given Paraguayans relative independence from Spain. Paraguay was to exercise this right often.

6. These expeditions depleted the numbers of the Spaniards remaining at Asunción, who had to face attacks from hostile Indians. This was one reason that Irala's attempts at social leveling with the Guaraní made sense.

7. The "port," as Buenos Aires was known, was much too far removed to influence day-to-day decision making in Asunción. Real authority thus stayed in Paraguay. In 1617, the Provincia Gigante de los Indes, as Paraguay was then known, was divided in two, with Asunción the capital of an increasingly marginalized subprovince (Elman R. Service, *Spanish-Guaraní Relations in Early Paraguay*, Ann Arbor: University of Michigan Press, 1954).

8. Unlike in Peru or Mexico, where the *encomenderos* often exacted tribute, in Paraguay the *encomenderos* always exacted labor.

9. About 20,000 Indians were divided among the 320 surviving Europeans. Two types of *encomienda* sprang up: the *originario encomienda*, which consisted of year-round unpaid servitude at the Spaniard's household; and the *mitaya encomienda*, which exacted a labor tax or *mita* once a year from outlying Indian villages.

10. This is why the *encomienda* in Paraguay exacted labor and not goods.

11. According to accounts of the late sixteenth and early seventeenth centuries, Asunción contained about 10 women for every man.

12. The term *mestizo* is almost never used in Paraguay for the simple reason that nearly everyone has mixed blood.

13. The word *reducciones* comes from *reducir*, which means to reduce into settlements.

14. Between 1580 and 1640, Spain and Portugal were a united empire. During this period, Spanish administrators took little interest in quarrels between Spanish- and Portuguese-speaking settlers in this remote part of the South American empire. Because Spain and Portugal were nominally the same country, the Spanish administrators thought the Crown's interests would not be affected by the incursions of the Portuguese.

15. One reason for the Jesuit success in yerba cultivation was that, unlike the colonists to the north, the Jesuits planted yerba bushes in orderly rows on plantations rather than gathering leaves from wild stands.

16. The Crown had granted Paraguay unique permission in 1537 to choose its own governors whenever a governor died, which encouraged a tradition of revolt among the settlers when governors were imposed against their will.

17. Among other things, Buenos Aires was made the seat of a viceroyalty and allowed to trade directly with the outside world. It was Charles who expelled the Jesuits from Spanish dominions on July 22, 1767, hoping to use their wealth to finance his reforms and to add to royal power in Spanish America by ridding himself of an increasingly troublesome political liability. The 1767 inventory of the Jesuit holdings recorded over 700,000 head of cattle, more than 230,000 sheep, 45,000 oxen, 100,000 horses, 14,000 mules, and 7,500 donkeys.

18. The residents of Buenos Aires (which was commonly known as El Puerto) were called *porteños*.

19. Paraguay was forced to maintain a militia at its own expense to defend against Indian raids from the Chaco and Portuguese encroachments from Brazil because the Crown refused to garrison regular soldiers for this duty.

20. Paraguayan yerba exports regularly exceeded 200,000 *arrobas* (1 *arroba* = 25 pounds or 11.5 kilograms) annually, sometimes reaching 300,000 *arrobas*. Though this was not a negligible amount, it was far below the country's productive capacity. Paraguay had no incentive to produce more yerba for export because of the crippling taxes imposed on the product by practically every river port on its way to Buenos Aires and the outside world (John Lynch, *The Spanish American Revolutions, 1808–1826*, New York: W. W. Norton, 1973, p. 105).

21. John Hoyt Williams, *The Rise and Fall of the Paraguayan Republic: 1800–1870*, Austin: University of Texas Press, 1979, p. 3.

22. Jerry W. Cooney, "Paraguayan Independence and Dr. Francia," *The Americas*, 28:4, April 1972, p. 408.

23. Lynch, *Spanish American Revolutions*, p. 106.

24. Williams, *Rise and Fall of the Paraguayan Republic*, p. 24.

25. Cooney, "Paraguayan Independence," pp. 409–410.

26. Some accounts say that Belgrano had 1,100 troops. In any case, he faced a Paraguayan force numbering 5,000.

27. John Hoyt Williams, "Governor Velasco, the Portuguese, and the Paraguayan Revolution of 1811: A New Look," *The Americas*, 28:4, April 1972, pp. 441–449.

28. Buenos Aires did not declare independence until July 9, 1816.

29. At various times, on various occasions, Francia singed his name Dr. José Gaspar García Rodríguez de Francia; Dr. José Gaspar Rodríguez de Francia; Dr. Rodríguez de Francia; Gaspar de Francia; José Gaspar de Francia; Dr. Francia; Dictador Francia; and Francia, El Dictador. Also, Francia never used his patronymic "Rodríguez" by itself, as would be normal for Spanish speakers. Guido Rodríguez Alcalá takes Francia's ambivalence about his name as proof of an abnormal personality (Rodríguez Alcalá, *Ideología autoritaria*, Asunción: R. P. Ediciones, 1987, pp. 14, 60).

30. Velasco was retained temporarily as a third, nonvoting member of the triumvirate but was quickly dismissed. The second member was Colonel Juan Valeriano de Zevallos.

31. The junta included Francia, Fulgencio Yegros (who controlled the army), Pedro Juan Caballero, Dr. Juan Bogarín, and Fernando de la Mora.

32. George Pendle, *Paraguay: A Riverside Nation*, London: Oxford University Press, 1967, p. 16.

33. Cooney, "Paraguayan Independence," p. 420.

34. Rodríguez Alcalá, *Ideología autoritaria*, p. 11.

35. Williams, *Rise and Fall of the Paraguayan Republic*, p. 32.

36. The two members were Gregorio de la Cerda, an unofficial member of the junta who was exiled, and Fernando de la Mora, who was arrested and jailed (Williams, *Rise and Fall of the Paraguayan Republic*, p. 37).

37. Designing democratic wrappers for otherwise naked dictatorships became an art form in Paraguay, particularly under Alfredo Stroessner.

38. See Augusto Roa Bastos, *I, the Supreme*, New York: Alfred A. Knopf, 1986, pp. 188–189, who quotes Colonel José Antonio Zavala y Delgadillo's *Journal of Memorable Events*.

39. The 1820 conspiracy to assassinate Francia on Good Friday as he rode through the streets included the most prominent members of Asunción society. The plan might have succeeded except for the moral and religious scruples of one of the conspirators. This man, Juan Bogarín, revealed the plot to a priest at confession and followed the prelate's order to inform Francia.

40. Williams, *Rise and Fall of the Paraguayan Republic*, p. 53.

41. Lynch, *Spanish American Revolutions*, p. 110.

42. Ibid., p. 111.

43. A spy in Paraguay is called a *pyragüé*, literally "hairy footed one." A character out of Guaraní folklore, a pyragüé has hair all over his body—even on the soles of his feet—so that he can walk very quietly (Frederic Hicks, "Interpersonal Relationships and *Caudillismo* in Paraguay," *Journal of Inter-American Studies and World Affairs*, 13, 1971, p. 106). The use of the term *pyragüés* to mean "spy" first appeared under Francia.

44. See in particular Pelham Horton Box, *The Origins of the Paraguayan War*, New York: Russell & Russell, 1967, pp. 11–12; and Richard Alan White,

Paraguay's Autonomous Revolution, 1810–1840, Albuquerque: University of New Mexico Press, 1978.

45. Rodríguez Alcalá, *Ideología autoritaria*, pp. 25, 27.

46. This rent from the peasants became a handy source of income for a state that managed to retain its class independence for five decades (ibid.).

47. Ibid., p. 27.

48. Many accounts claim that Carlos Antonio's bride, Juana Paula Carillo, was pregnant by another man at the time of their marriage but that her parents bribed López with a large dowry to take her and spare them the embarrassment.

49. López was described as a "great tidal wave of human flesh; . . . a veritable mastodon," by one contemporary. Richard Burton wrote that he had "chops flapping over his cravat" (Burton, *Letters from the Battlefields of Paraguay*, London: Tinsley Brothers, 1870, p. 57).

50. During this expedition to the major capitals of Europe, Francisco Solano López met in Paris the woman who would be his lifelong mistress and would bear him five sons—Elisa Alicia Lynch. "La Lynch" returned to Paraguay after giving birth to their first son in Buenos Aires, moved into a palace (now a hotel) that López had built for her, and lived the life of a grande dame in Asunción. This strong-willed, charming, intelligent, attractive woman had enormous influence over Francisco Solano. She was later to bury him with her own hands and return to Europe, where she died penniless.

51. Box, *Origins of the Paraguayan War*, pp. 9–28.

52. Williams, *Rise and Fall of the Paraguayan Republic*, pp. 195–197.

53. British engineer George Thompson, who worked for Francisco Solano and served under him during the Triple Alliance War, called El Mariscal—the title López adopted—"a monster without parallel" in his book *The War in Paraguay*, which was published in London after the war (Pendle, *Paraguay: A Riverside Nation*, p. 20). The claim does not lack supporting evidence—López ordered the wartime executions of thousands of officers and soldiers and had two of his brothers shot and his mother and sisters flogged because he suspected them of conspiracy.

54. The number of casualties is often disputed because it is based on estimates and unreliable and/or nonexistent Paraguayan records.

55. Paraguay's population was no more than one-twentieth of the combined total of Argentina's and Brazil's 11 million.

56. Josefina Plá, *The British in Paraguay: 1850–1870* (translated by B. C. MacDermot), Richmond (Surrey): Richmond Publishing Co., 1976, p. 123.

57. Naturally, these figures are based on guesswork because Paraguay's population before the war is not known with any degree of precision.

58. Harris Gaylord Warren, *Paraguay and the Triple Alliance: The Postwar Decade, 1869–1878*, Austin: University of Texas Press, 1978, p. 153.

59. One sitting president and two (possibly three) former presidents were murdered during 1874–1887, while the suspected assassin, Juan A. Meza, as minister of the interior, controlled the police.

60. Over one hundred years old, these parties are among the oldest continuously functioning political organizations in the world.

61. Brazil had borne the brunt of the fighting and the expense in the Triple Alliance War, so it was natural that Brazil would overshadow Argentina for the time being in Asunción. According to estimates, Brazil suffered 150,000 dead and 65,000 wounded and spent over $200 million to defeat Paraguay.

3
Modern Paraguayan History: The Twentieth Century

The political parties are not compact and disciplined with a pretension to an ideology [but are] loose . . . factions of would-be officeholders, professing personal allegiance to their leaders but continually jockeying for greater power. . . . The absence of the old aristocracy, the lack of strength of the middle class, and the political inertness of the great mass of peasants result in a government without a following, unworried about public opinion, responsible to no large segment of the population, but in constant danger of being overthrown by an ephemeral coalition of other politicians. . . . Many of the politicians and officeholders, even occasional presidents, are ambitious men from the rural towns. . . . [Because] the presidents themselves may not complete their terms . . . , politicians are often the crudest adventurers, who expect to make their fortunes in one swoop on the public treasury. The ancient prototype of the politician, the backwoods caudillo, is still close to reality.
      —Elman R. and Helen S. Service, *Tobatí: Paraguayan Town*

LIBERAL PARAGUAY

In 1904 the Liberals overthrew the Colorado government with a successful invasion launched from Argentine territory. Led by General Benigno Ferreira, an ex-legionnaire, the invasion was the culmination of a Liberal party rebellion against Colorado rule that had begun in August 1904. After four months of fighting, on December 12, 1904, President Juan Antonio Ezcurra handed power to the Liberals and their allies in the military by signing the Pact of Pilcomayo aboard an Argentine gunboat.

Colorado factional bickering contributed to their 1904 defeat, but the Liberals were not immune to factionalism. The extreme political instability brought on by the 1870 defeat in the Triple Alliance War continued under Liberal rule. Before long, Liberal Paraguay descended into factional feuding, military coups, and finally a fourteen-month civil

39

war in 1922. In the thirty-five years they held power (1904–1940, aside from February 1936–August 1937), there were 21 Liberal administrations. From 1904 to 1922, Paraguay had 15 presidents. In 1916, Liberal president Eduardo Schaerer became the first Paraguayan politician since Juan B. Esgusquiza—and the only civilian—to complete his term in office.[1]

After Ezcurra resigned, Juan B. Gaona and then Cecilio Báez completed the 1902–1906 presidential term. The Liberal strongman, General Ferreira, was elected chief executive in 1906. But Ferreira failed to end the factional rivalries within the Liberal party and the armed forces and was himself displaced by a military revolt in July 1908. Ferreira's vice-president, Emiliano González Navero, completed the term in 1910. Manuel Gondra and Juan B. Gaona were elected president and vice-president in 1910 but succumbed to military intrigue in January 1911, when Gondra's minister of war, Colonel Albino Jara, seized power. But another revolt, initiated by loyalists of President Manuel Gondra, replaced Jara in July of the same year with Liberato Rojas. Rojas survived until February 1912, when Dr. Pedro P. Pena, a momentary compromise candidate among the warring Liberal factions, succeeded him as provisional president. The leader of the National Republican Abstentionist faction (PNRA) of the Colorado party, Pena soon followed his predecessors into history when Liberal leader Emiliano González Navero, one of the period's grand "survivors," was designated president.

Eduardo Schaerer, a Liberal strongman, became chief executive in August 1912. Schaerer led one of the major Liberal factions in the decades that preceded the outbreak of the Chaco War in 1932; former president Manuel Gondra led the faction that opposed the "Schaeristas." Schaerer was known as an action-oriented politician, Gondra as a manipulator and cabinet politician. They and their followers competed for power and, in so doing, destroyed any hope of a stable, democratic political order. Outwardly, their battles were based on abstruse programmatic differences; actually, they were based on machismo and charisma. Manuel Franco and José P. Montero, compromise candidates chosen to create a "breathing space" between the two primary factions, were elected on the Liberal ticket in 1916; when Franco died in June 1919, Montero completed his term.

The 1920s were likewise a time of mayhem for the Liberals. Manuel Gondra returned as president in August 1920, with Félix Paiva as his vice-president. Gondra appointed three of the new generation of leaders in the party to his cabinet: José P. Guggiari, Eusebio Ayala, and Eligio Ayala. The combative leader of the Radical Youth, the strongly anti-Schaerista Guggiari was the most controversial appointment. Gondra and Paiva were forced to resign in November 1921 because of factional fighting and were succeeded by Eusebio Ayala as provisional president.

Factional fighting finally produced a civil war. Although Schaerer supported Ayala, he and his followers opposed Ayala's cabinet appointments and blocked his program in the Congress. The Schaeristas and the Colorados passed a law calling for new presidential elections to force Eusebio Ayala to resign; instead, Ayala vetoed the law. In response, the Congress passed new legislation stating that the president had no power to veto an electoral law. In the resulting impasse, the Schaeristas turned to the army, and President Ayala called on Guggiari, the party youth, and loyal Liberal military officers to defend his administration. The hastily formed Constitutionalist "Army," loyal to President Ayala, drove back the Schaeristas when they attacked the capital on June 9, 1922, but on July 10, 1922, the Schaeristas defeated the Constitutionalists in a bloody counterattack.

But the civil war did not end Paraguay's perennial factionalism. In the years preceding the Chaco War, the ruling party was to splinter further. The post-1922 calm was superficial. Opposition Colorados refused to participate in elections they had no chance of winning, yet the Liberals hardly felt secure. Leftist Liberal factions criticized the government for tolerating the foreign economic interests that were reducing peasants to debt peonage. Eligio Ayala, the finance minister, replaced Eusebio Ayala when the latter resigned as president in April 1923. After being selected as the party's next presidential candidate, Eligio Ayala stepped down as chief executive in March 1924 to allow Luis A. Riart to serve the remainder of the term. Eligio Ayala and Manuel Burgos then took office on August 15, 1924.

An adherent of Manuel Gondra's faction, Ayala managed to evade the Schaeristas, complete his term of office, and replace Manuel Gondra as the faction leader. In a hotly debated decision, Eligio Ayala imposed José P. Guggiari as the 1928 Liberal candidate. One of the more combative Liberal party caciques, Guggiari had served as leader of the party's Radical Youth and as president of the Chamber of Deputies (lower house of the Paraguayan Congress) from 1923 to 1928, where he was a gadfly of the Schaeristas. A distinguished and relatively neutral but ineffective Liberal leader, Emiliano González Navero, was given the vice-presidency.

The Liberals constituted a traditional party with paternalistic, clientilistic links to ordinary Paraguayans in the countryside (see Chapter 6); as a result, the Liberal governments after 1904 did not install democracy but merely replaced the strong rule of military men (which had been the system under the Colorados) with the weak rule of a civilian oligarchy.[2] Because many Liberal leaders were wealthy and had foreign connections, they were vulnerable to the charge of serving foreign interests. This vulnerability was compounded by the Liberal failure to introduce social reforms, which the lower classes desperately needed. The Liberals never gained popular support and made few gestures toward the mass of poor, ignorant peasants in the countryside. The Liberals' fatal error was underestimating the appeal of nationalism, which became important in the 1930s.

During the 1920s, the Liberal leaders—Eusebio Ayala and Eligio Ayala (no relation), Félix Paiva, Luis A. Riart, and others—were flawed actors in a poor play. Though they professed a desire to modernize and liberalize Paraguay, they could not overcome personal rivalries and their shared belief that only the Liberals had the right to rule the country. (Naturally, the Colorados, ousted in 1904, similarly believed that only they had the right to rule Paraguay.) The annual "state of the union" messages of the Liberal presidents in this period are instructive. There are calls for education, urbanization, and respect for democracy. But government decisions gave little priority to social programs that might have redistributed wealth or introduced agararian reform. The democratic ideal of the Liberals remained an ideal only, seldom practiced and usually honored more in the breach than in the observance. Rightly or wrongly, the Liberal period has been criticized as a time of decadence, an era when Paraguayans lost pride and confidence in their nation.

Yet, by planting some seeds of republican (if not democratic) substance, Liberal rule was not entirely negative. The aftermath of the 1922 civil war—the period from 1924 to 1936—produced what were arguably the best governments Paraguay ever had, characterized by the rule of law, civilian control of the military, and competent, honest management of state finances. Although some prosperity had returned to Paraguay during the early 1900s, the country benefited further from the general economic recovery that buoyed the region during the 1920s. Modest advances were made in infrastructural investment. Asunción gained a small working class and a small middle class, and exports revived.

With the arrival of a small group of European teachers and artists, Asunción had acquired the minimal accouterments of a provincial capital city. Urban literary circles witnessed a reawakening that had begun during the last years of the nineteenth century, led by men who combined literary talent with an interest in liberal politics. The first of these writer-politicians was Juan Silvano Godoy (b. 1840), a successful businessman and cosmopolitan collector of art and books who founded the Godoy Museum in Asunción. Cecilio Báez (b. 1862), a lawyer and teacher who bitterly condemned Francisco Solano López in several books, influenced public opinion with a barrage of polemical newspaper articles on the benefits of democratic government and the pernicious influence of the Catholic church.

Manuel Domínguez (b. 1867), a talented poet and orator, was also much taken by the familiar themes of Paraguay's glorious past and the proud national spirit of its people; by the time he died, he was widely recognized as Paraguay's expert on the Chaco boundary question. Manuel Gondra (b. 1871) was a literary critic, educator, diplomat, and often minister and twice president of the Republic. Other famous names of the period include Fulgencio Moreno (b. 1872), politician, diplomat, expert on conflicting Bolivian and Paraguayan claims to the Chaco, and historical journalist; Juan E. O'Leary (b. 1882), who wrote about the Triple Alliance War, fiercely defending the reputation of El Mariscal López; Arsenio López Decoud; and Ignacio Pane. Less politically minded men of letters were poets Alejandro Guanes and Eloy Fariña Núñez.[3]

Eligio Ayala and Eusebio Ayala were prolific writers who each served twice as president of the Republic. After participating in the 1904 revolution, Eligio Ayala (b. 1879) became a prominent author and public servant with a reputation for incorruptibility. He wrote extensively on Paraguay, art, and literature. A cosmopolitan world traveler, Eligio Ayala spent many years living and traveling in Europe and is reputed to have met with Vladimir Lenin in Switzerland during World War I. Eusebio Ayala (b. 1874) was a successful banker who studied law and the theories of Charles Darwin, lectured, and wrote essays on education and history. He later became an expert on political economy and international law and traveled often to Europe and the United States.[4]

Accompanying the blossoming of Paraguayan letters at the turn of the century was an upsurge in education. El Colegio de San José, founded in 1904, became the preferred primary and secondary school for the elite. An evening school of commerce was created in 1906, and El Colegio Internacional opened in 1920. The national university already had been established in 1889. In the 1920s and 1930s, its rector was former president Dr. Cecilio Báez, a Liberal party instigator of the 1904 revolution. With frequent time off for government service, Báez served as rector until 1940. A dignified and erudite individual, he did as much as anyone in the Liberal leadership to establish educational standards at the university, expand its library, and attract competent instructors. But progress was slow and subject to the vagaries of national political life. In contrast to the turbulent decades of the late nineteenth and early twentieth centuries and the subsequent disorder of post-1932 Paraguay, the mid- to late 1920s and early 1930s appear as an oasis in Paraguayan history.

THE FALL OF THE LIBERAL PARTY

By most accounts, the government of José P. Guggiari (1928–1932), which followed the relatively popular administration of Eligio Ayala

(1924–1928), was a failure.[5] Whereas Ayala had had at least some success in moderating the factional divisions within the Liberal party, Guggiari was more skilled at confrontation than diplomacy. Both Guggiari and Ayala were "Gondristas," followers of former president Manuel Gondra, the chief Liberal rival of ex-president Eduardo Schaerer.

Guggiari's government was itself split between followers of Eligio Ayala and followers of Luis A. Riart, a party stalwart, frequent cabinet member, and, briefly, provisional president in 1924. Ayala and Riart each had a large number of supporters in the Chamber of Deputies who bolstered their presidential ambitions for the 1932 election. A third, smaller segment followed the line of Schaerer. And a fourth dissident wing, led by Modesto Guggiari (no relation to José Guggiari), moved fitfully between the two principal camps. A 1928 effort to unite the party failed and the subsequent death of former president Eligio Ayala late in 1930 removed a possible source of moderation.

The Liberals entered the 1930s deeply fragmented and with a poor public image. Guggiari's inability to mediate among squabbling party factions seemed related to the Liberals' inability to agree on a strategy to counter Bolivian encroachments in the Chaco. Criticism of the government's incompetence was widely disseminated in the national press. Social discontent, already on the rise, only intensified after the worldwide economic downturn began in October 1929. The tragic confrontation between the government and the student movement on October 23, 1931, in which a number of students were shot to death, symbolized the desperation of the Guggiari administration. After this incident, Guggiari transferred executive power to his vice-president, Emiliano González Navero, who surprised Guggiari by appointing Luis A. Riart, the principal antagonist of the Ayala-Guggiari forces, to the key position of minister of war.

In late January 1932, Guggiari returned to the presidency as the result of a power play by his faction and immediately ousted Riart and his followers. Riart was defeated in the maneuvering for the 1932 Liberal presidential nomination, and Eusebio Ayala was nominated and subsequently elected (1932–1936) to succeed Guggiari. But the Riart–Eusebio Ayala rivalry was only beginning. From his newly created post as minister of the economy after August 1933, Riart used his considerable influence within the party to undermine the Ayala presidency, and he continued this strategy as minister of foreign relations one year later.[6]

With hindsight, it is clear that war with Bolivia was inevitable by the early 1930s, so much so that only President Guggiari and his cabinet seemed not to notice. Political instability in Paraguay had encouraged Bolivia to extend a string of semi-clandestine forts throughout the Chaco. Bolivia's leaders hoped to annex the territory up to the Paraguay River

Two boys play on an ancient tank, a relic of the Chaco War (1932–1935), left in downtown Asunción as a memorial to the war.

as compensation for Chile's annexation of Bolivia's coastline during the 1879–1883 War of the Pacific. In addition, oil had been discovered in the Bolivian Chaco, and many assumed that a gigantic pool of oil underlay the entire region.[7] Moreover, the Bolivian army seemed more than a match for Paraguay because it was trained, equipped, and commanded by German military officers.

A rising tide of nationalist indignation engulfed the Liberals when armed confrontation broke out in the Chaco. In 1928, national attention focused on the newly constructed Fortín Vanguardia on the upper Paraguay River, one of a series of forts that Bolivia had built in the Chaco. Despite a mounting chorus of criticism from all quarters, the government apparently was not prepared to use more than words against Bolivia.

In December 1928, a young major in the Paraguayan army named Rafael Franco finally acted by attacking, seizing, and burning Fortín Vanguardia to the ground. This only made matters worse for Guggiari, who felt compelled to sue for peace to avoid a war for which he believed Paraguay was unprepared. The government agreed to the humiliating condition that Paraguay would rebuild Fortín Vanguardia for Bolivia.

Meanwhile, Major Franco, who overnight had become a national hero, was dismissed from the army and sent into exile.

As a result, the Liga Nacional Independiente (National Independent League), a new group of nationalist intellectuals led by Juan Stefanich (who would become minister of foreign affairs in 1936), seized the political initiative and agitated for war. Nationalist sentiments under the banners of the New Paraguay movement attracted much support from university students, many of whom regarded the Liberals as little better than traitors. Already at an all-time low, Liberal popularity struck bottom on October 23, 1931, when troops fired on a student mob trying to storm the presidential palace, killing 10. Liberal party control of the electoral apparatus and the army guaranteed that the Liberals could cling to power for nearly a decade more, but this event finished them politically. Many students were reserve army officers. During the 1932–1935 Chaco War with Bolivia, these students would join the army and plan their revenge for the massacre and for what they saw as the government's treasonous inability to defend the nation.

The Chaco War itself has been discussed at length in the literature.[8] On paper, the Paraguayans were no match for the better armed, trained, and financed Bolivians, who also could put more troops in the field. When war was formally declared in July 1932, it was widely assumed that Bolivia would score a quick victory, thereby legitimizing its claims to the vast Chaco region. But the Bolivian soldiers, many of whom were highland Indians from the cool *altiplano*, were unprepared for the tropical climatic conditions of the Chaco. Their leadership was uneven, but more importantly they had little motivation to fight and die to gain the Chaco for Bolivia.

On the other hand, the mobilized Paraguayan peasantry proved to be a fierce and relentless defender of the national patrimony. The professionalization of the Paraguayan Army in the preceding twenty years had yielded a competent, modern officer corps. The Paraguayan high command also had the advantage of knowing the terrain better than the Bolivians. Both sides suffered more from disease than bullets; extended supply lines likewise were a problem for both sides, but a more serious one for the Bolivians. Within a year, the Paraguayans, led by Colonel (later general and marshal) Félix Estigarribia, had retaken most of the lost territory.

In what proved to be a serious political miscalculation, President Eusebio Ayala suddenly proposed a truce in December 1933, at the very moment when a Paraguayan victory seemed near. The Truce of Campo Via (after the battle of the same name) was widely derided in Asunción and within the armed forces. Worse, the Bolivians used the pause in the fighting to regroup. Fighting resumed before long and the bloody war continued for another eighteen months. Once again, the Liberals were seen as incompetent; President Ayala never recovered from the mistake.[9] The nationalist forces that had begun to form in the 1920s around the National Independent League, the university students, the incipient labor movement, intellectuals, and, most of all, army officers began to demand immediate changes toward a "New Paraguay." Although Paraguay ultimately won the war, by the time it was over the Liberals were thoroughly discredited.

THE FEBRUARY REVOLUTION

After a final truce was declared in July 1935, Ayala and the Liberals attempted to reconstruct Paraguay along prewar lines, but this proved to be impossible. The government was maladroit. For example, the Liberal majority in Congress voted down pensions for disabled veterans. Nothing the Liberal government could do would appease the appetite for change. Although the Liberals had led the country to a smashing victory, the end of the conflict in the Chaco sounded the death knell of the party and signaled the beginning of more than fifty years of military rule. On February 17, 1936, the Liberal era ended when the army overthrew the government of Eusebio Ayala. From that date on, the military has dominated politics in Paraguay.

As has happened so often in Paraguay's history, a strongman emerged to galvanize national discontent. The Liberals had exiled, recalled, and reexiled Rafael Franco, the hero of the attack against Bolivia's Fortín Vanguardia. When the troops seized the presidential palace in February 1936, a call went out to Franco, then in exile in Argentina, to form a new government and put an end, once and for all, to the Liberal "betrayal" of the nation.[10]

Franco was a brilliant military leader but a political neophyte. His cabinet—a curious, mutually antagonistic mixture of fascists, socialists, and Nazi sympathizers—reflected Franco's attempt to reconcile the revolution's conflicting political motivations by including representatives from each of its diverse competing factions. Authoritarian in complexion, the Franco government established press censorship, abolished political party activity, and exiled former political activists and government officials. It showed little respect for civil liberties, but not less than had been traditionally shown under the Liberals or the Colorados.

The intellectual roots of the February Revolution were diffuse and highly eclectic. One source was Juan Stefanich and his Liga Nacional Independiente, which espoused a need for a "New Paraguay" but was vague on particulars. Organizations such as the powerful Asociación Nacional de Ex-Combatientes (National Veterans Association) agitated for social and economic reforms. Various diverse elements in society coalesced on November 15, 1936, to form the Union Nacional Revolucionaria (National Revolutionary Union), which would serve as the principal political movement of the short-lived February Revolution.

Unlike those of his predecessors, Franco's regime did introduce meaningful change. The new government created ministries of public health, agriculture, and labor and expropriated over 200,000 hectares of land, which it distributed to 10,000 landless peasant families. The government established an eight-hour day; promulgated the country's first labor code, which guaranteed workers the rights to strike and to bargain collectively; and founded the Paraguayan Workers Confederation (Confederación Nacional de Trabajadores, or CNT).

Symbolically, Franco's most important decision was to rehabilitate the reputation of Franciso Solano López, whom many Paraguayans despised as a mad dictator who had brought ruin and destruction to the country. An expedition disinterred his remains at Cerro Corá, brought them to Asunción, and deposited them in the Pantheon of Heroes, along with the remains of El Mariscal's son and those of his father, Carlos Antonio López. But this symbolism could not substitute for national unity or a coherent political program. The personal and ideological rivalries within the cabinet weakened the government. Constant agitation for further reform outpaced the availability of resources.

The Chaco War had brought the February Revolution to power; ironically, the Chaco War also brought it down. In an effort to reach a final peace agreement, Franco ordered the withdrawal of Paraguayan troops from strategic positions they had held near the Bolivian Andes since hostilities ended. The president and his foreign minister, Juan Stefanich, understood the need to get on with national reconstruction—without the liability of an unresolved international border dispute. The army, however, did not have the same opinion. Conservative army officers who had viewed Franco's social experiments with alarm rallied behind Colonel Ramún Paredes and overthrew the Franco regime on August 13, 1937.

Dr. Félix Paiva, the dean of the National University of Asunción's law school and vice-president of the Republic in the early 1920s, became interim president. His appointment signaled that the Liberal party, once again in power, still wanted to return to the status quo prior to the Chaco War. Paiva's first official act, for example, was to restore the constitution of 1870, which proved to be a futile gesture. As agitation continued for social and economic change, the Liberals signed a permanent peace treaty with Bolivia on July 21, 1938, at Buenos Aires. The treaty was widely believed to be a less than fair recognition of Paraguay's successes in the war. To improve their image, the Liberals nominated war hero Félix Estigarribia, the "General of Victory," for the presidency in a one-man race in 1939. Estigarribia had collaborated with the Liberal government after the end of the war, had served in a temporary ambassadorship as minister in Washington, D.C., and had headed the delegation to the Buenos Aires peace conference.[11]

Once in office in August 1939, with an old-line Liberal cabinet and a Liberal majority in Congress, Estigarribia discovered that none of Paraguay's other political factions would collaborate with his government. The Colorados had been on a political strike since 1931; the Franco forces were adamantly against the Liberal cabinet; and nationalist army officers, who had banded together in 1938 to organize the Frente de Guerra (War Front), a secret authoritarian military fraternity, were conspiring against the Liberal regime.

Estigarribia decided to use his considerable national prestige to free himself of the traditional Liberals. Two days after the cabinet resigned, on February 18, 1940, the chief executive issued a proclamation that granted him dictatorial powers. At the same time, he dismissed the Congress and appointed a cabinet of "New Liberals" drawn from the younger generation of that party's leadership.[12] The 1940 constitution, which replaced the 1870 document, reflected many of the social and political ideals of the February Revolution. It implicitly rejected the laissez-faire doctrines of the 1870 constitution and gave new authority to the state to regulate and direct national affairs. The new constitution created a unicameral legislature and a Council of State made up of notables from Paraguay's major institutions. Power was concentrated in the office of the president. The 1940 constitution, the president reasoned, was necessary to control the "anarchy dangerous to the national existence" that had emerged as a result of the Chaco War.[13] Many thought that the new constitution would have achieved its goals of social harmony and economic progress under Estigarribia. However, the president never received the opportunity to restructure his country. He died in a plane crash on September 7, 1940, under mysterious circumstances.

The authoritarian nationalists in the armed forces moved quickly and imposed General Higinio Morínigo on the stunned Liberal cabinet as provisional president. A veteran of the Chaco War, Morínigo had served as minister of the interior in the interim government of Félix Paiva and had been Estigarribia's minister of war since April 1940.[14] Strong pressure from nationalist military officers had forced these appointments. The traditional Liberals probably hoped that Morínigo would serve solely as a figurehead while they regained their old positions in the power structure, but this was not to be. Within months, Morínigo had forced all the Liberals out of the government, banned the party, and exiled the leadership. He quickly placed loyal supporters in the key military posts around the country. Always sensitive to possible unrest within the armed forces, Morínigo maneuvered with care. He played on nationalist themes, appointed military officers to key cabinet positions, and identified himself as the national leader best prepared to lead the country through the Second World War.

At first, Morínigo turned to the Febreristas[15] and the Tiempistas[16] for civilian administrative talent to run the government. The Tiempistas advocated a form of Catholic socialism that was modeled loosely on the corporatist Estado Novo of Portugal under Antonio de Oliveira Salazar and that had strong support within the officer corps. The Febreristas used their positions in the government to attempt to overthrow Morínigo. After a Febrerista coup attempt in April 1941, Morínigo expelled them from the government and the Tiempistas became his chief civilian advisors. The key leaders of the movement—Carlos Andrada and Luis Argaña—held major cabinet positions throughout the World War II years.

The armed forces–Tiempista coalition created a "regime of earnest and idealistic authoritarians."[17] Both elements were united in their opposition to liberal, progressive, or leftist ideas and to the Liberal party. They favored enlightened dictatorship and wanted "good government" led by nonpartisan national leaders. Morínigo, who called his administration "the Paraguayan Nationalist Revolution," tolerated no civilian opposition. In December 1940, Morínigo ordered the arrests of Liberal leaders. While they languished in detention camps in the north of the country, the Liberal party was declared illegal. In January 1941, Morínigo forcefully repressed a nationwide general strike and dissolved the national labor confederation, and when the Colorados protested the government's restrictions on political life in mid-1941, that party's leaders were also arrested.

The Morínigo government was openly sympathetic to the Nazi regime in Germany during the World War II years. Large numbers of German settlers and large amounts of German investment and trade made the German presence in Paraguay significant. Many in the army's high command openly admired the German armed forces and were convinced that Hitler and the Axis would crush the Allies. The presence in Paraguay of a Vichy French military mission—the only foreign military mission in Paraguay when the United States entered the war in December 1941—reinforced the notion of collaboration with Germany. And the authoritarian orientation of the Axis governments coincided with the political philosophy of the Tiempista–armed forces leadership that dominated the Morínigo administration.

However, the realities of international politics forced some changes by early 1942. With the entry of the United States into the war, Axis penetration of South America ended. Paraguay's leaders (along with those of neighboring Brazil, for example) decided that a show of allegiance to the Allied cause would pay off handsomely. U.S. economic aid to Paraguay began shortly thereafter and continued throughout the war years.

Morínigo was sufficiently confident of his position that he had himself nominated for the presidency in 1943. After a one-candidate election, he was inaugurated in August 1943 for a five-year term. In the same year he paid an official visit to the United States and was received by President Franklin Roosevelt at the White House. While assuring Roosevelt that Paraguay would remain solidly with the United States, Morínigo retained his Axis connections by "simply ignoring all international commitments to restrict Axis activities in his country."[18] As the tide began to turn against the Axis in late 1943 and early 1944, Morínigo imposed the first restrictions on Axis activities in Paraguay. He declared war on the Axis in February 1945 to assure Paraguay's position as a founding member of the United Nations and its eligibility for war-indemnity claims against the defeated Axis powers. Nonetheless, the Paraguayan Nazi party did not disband until 1946.

The U.S. diplomatic position in Paraguay also began to shift toward the end of the war. A new U.S. ambassador arrived in August 1944, with instructions to pressure Morínigo to restore democracy and to hold national elections.[19] In late 1944, fearful of losing the economic aid of the United States, which had become key to his development program, Morínigo allowed the political opposition to hold public meetings. The Paraguayan president found himself in a bind. The U.S. Embassy clearly meant business—democracy was the key goal of the immediate postwar period and the United States was willing to use economic aid as the tool to accomplish it. But the authoritarian nationalists within the regime were unalterably opposed to any form of political liberalization. Finally, in January 1946, Morínigo faced reality and told the military high command that he could no longer resist U.S. pressures. The president announced a three-point democratization program for that year, pledged to restore the freedom of the press, and promised early elections for a new legislature.[20]

POST–WORLD WAR II PARAGUAY

In June 1946, Morínigo confronted discontent from right-wing military elements by firing nationalist officers and exiling them. He restored press freedom and civil liberties to the country's political parties and scheduled congressional elections for 1947. Without his traditional right-wing power base, Morínigo, always the consummate politician, looked for a new constellation of forces to support his regime. In July

1946 he formed a coalition government composed of Febreristas and Colorados, offering them three cabinet posts each. But Morínigo's hope of forming a new power base was destroyed in late July when all the parties banded together in a public rally in Asunción and denounced the dictator.

The free-for-all that erupted in 1946–1947 was a replay of the previous decades of Paraguayan political history. It unleashed another, even more terrible civil war, an ordeal from which Paraguay took decades to recover. While all the parties and factions used their "dedication" to establishing democracy as a smokescreen to hide their intention to seize power, the Liberals smuggled arms into the country, the Communists proposed to hang Morínigo from a lamppost, and the Colorados organized an armed militia to harass their opponents in the streets. And all parties worked to secure support and favor within the armed forces.

Early in 1947, the two government parties (the Febreristas and the Colorados) collided. The Febreristas precipitated the crisis by demanding a majority of cabinet posts and guarantees that neither party in the coalition would accept Morínigo as a presidential candidate in 1948. In response, Morínigo and the Colorados looked to each other for support. On January 12, 1947, this new coalition arrested the Febrerista ministers. For the first time since 1904, Paraguay had a Colorado party government.

Federico Chaves and J. Natalicio González, who led the two major Colorado factions, became the principal Colorado cabinet spokesmen. The Colorados quickly consolidated their control of the country by banning political meetings and seizing opposition newspapers. Febrerista, Liberal, and Communist leaders feared for their lives and left for exile or went into hiding. Within weeks the civil bureaucracy had been purged and only Colorado supporters held office.

On March 7, 1947, the Febreristas attacked the Asunción police station in an attempt to overthrow the government. The attack failed, but the event precipitated a series of military rebellions that attracted support from Febrerista, Liberal, and Communist militants. Before long, a full-scale civil war had broken out. Centered in Concepción, the rebellion quickly won control of the north of the country. Purges in the armed forces had angered officers in all three branches, and a majority of officers joined the revolt. The Colorados turned to their peasant supporters to resist the combined forces of the opposition.

After five months of bloody conflict, the rebel forces attacked Asunción. The only troops the Colorados had to defend the capital were the barefoot peasant reserves[21] and an artillery regiment led by Alfredo Stroessner, an army officer who had remained loyal to the Colorado party. Aided by poor rebel leadership and the timely arrival of weapons from Juan Perón's Argentina, the combined force of the peasant militias and Stroessner's regular troops routed the rebels. In the Colorado tyranny that followed, many lost their property and their lives, simply disappeared, or were forced into exile.

The end of the 1947 civil war renewed factional competition within the Colorado party. Morínigo was no longer necessary; the Colorados discarded him in 1948. An interim government under J. Manuel Frutos, with an all-Colorado cabinet, ruled until August 15, when J. Natalicio González was inaugurated. An authoritarian by ideology and temperament, González had taken the Colorado party nomination away from Chaves, the leader of the Democrático faction, who favored collaboration with other political forces. The months of the interim government were marked by coup attempts and competition within the armed forces. Caught in the cross fire of Colorado factionalism and military conniving, González was removed from office in January 1949.[22] War Minister Raimundo Rolón assumed the presidency for a month, only to be ousted by the combined forces of the primary Colorado groups and a majority of the armed forces, with the active participation of Alfredo Stroessner.

The new Colorado president was Felipe Molas López, who governed from February to September 1949. As a reward for his support of the Molas López faction, Stroessner was promoted to brigadier general. Molas López, however, fell victim to Colorado party intrigue and military plotting. He was overthrown and replaced by the Democrático leader Federico Chaves. Again, Stroessner managed to be on the right side of the fight, and he was given command of all of the nation's artillery forces. In addition, he was named commander of the First Military Region (which includes Asunción and all key bases around the city) and commander-in-chief of the army.

The Chaves presidency was relatively uneventful. As the Colorado party consolidated power in the government, Stroessner did the same within the armed forces. Chaves proved adept as a political leader and unified the party as well as could be expected given the background of civil war, attempted coups, and factionalism. He was reelected when he ran unopposed in 1952. But Chaves faced opposition from Epifanio Méndez Fleitas, formerly the chief of police of Asunción and president of the Central Bank in the second Chaves government. Méndez Fleitas was at the center of a conspiracy to remove Chaves and replace him with a new generation of Colorado party leaders. He and Stroessner conspired during 1953 but Méndez Fleitas was found out and fired in January 1954, and his friends were purged from the government and the party.

Chaves knew of Stroessner's role in the conspiracy but did not believe he could confront the powerful army commander. Instead, he tried to build a parallel military structure using the national police. In

May 1954, feeling ready to take on Stroessner, Chaves ordered the arrest of a Stroessner protégé. This provoked the coup that unseated Chaves. Claiming his honor had been sullied, Stroessner demanded the president's resignation and ordered the army to occupy the presidential palace. Although the police resisted in a battle that raged for hours,[23] in the end Chaves resigned. Tomás Romero Pereira, one of the party's grand old men, served as provisional president from May to August 1954.

Although the Colorado party was divided, the leadership did not want a military man as president, particularly Stroessner. Some supported Méndez Fleitas, but the Democráticos rejected his candidacy because he had turned on their leader, Federico Chaves. No other faction of the party was able to impose a candidate. Finally, reluctantly, the party acknowledged Stroessner as the only acceptable candidate. He won the election and took the oath of office on August 15, 1954.

THE STROESSNER YEARS

Stroessner's career had been meteoric. As a junior officer, he had received decorations in the Chaco War for bravery and superior performance of duty. After the Chaco War, he avoided politics, devoting himself to advanced study that included a stint in Brazil for special artillery training. On his return to Paraguay, he quickly became embroiled in the intrigue of the Morínigo regime. In 1943, as a reward for supporting the government against an attempted coup, Morínigo appointed Stroessner, who was then only thirty years old, to the Superior War College. Stroessner excelled at the college. After completing the course of study, he was promoted to lieutenant colonel and then colonel and given the command of an important regiment. The following year, the young colonel was assigned to the army general staff.

When civil war broke out in 1947, Stroessner was one of relatively few officers who remained loyal to Morínigo. In the most decisive battle of the war, Stroessner's troops played a crucial part in breaking the advance of the united opposition forces on Asunción. Identified as a Colorado, Stroessner easily transferred his loyalty from Morínigo to the series of Colorado party presidents that governed Paraguay from 1948 to 1954, when he emerged as the strongman of the regime and, ultimately, its leader.

When the new chief executive appointed a conventional Colorado cabinet following his inauguration, the party assumed that Stroessner would serve only one term in office, after which political power would revert to the party. Just as the Liberals had underestimated Morínigo, the Colorado party elders underestimated Stroessner. The general manipulated the armed forces and the party with consummate skill. Soon after beginning his term, he got the party to declare an amnesty that allowed the followers of J. Natalicio González to return from exile. González himself became the Paraguayan Ambassador to Mexico. By allowing the Guión Rojo[24] to return, Stroessner prevented them from organizing an armed resistance on Paraguay's borders and presented himself as the arbiter between Colorados who followed Chaves and those who followed González.

The new leader of the Guionistas was Edgar Ynsfrán. The followers of Méndez Fleitas and those of Federico Chaves probably thought they could recruit the Guionistas and thereby take control of the party and, ultimately, the government. Méndez Fleitas used his considerable influence to have Ynsfrán appointed to a job in police intelligence. Ynsfrán's responsibility was to keep Stroessner and his supporters under surveillance for Méndez Fleitas, who was organizing a coup for December 1955.

Ynsfrán, an astute political operative, quickly understood that Stroessner would probably win any confrontation and switched sides. Characteristically, Stroessner then made the first move. On the night of December 20, 1955, Stroessner personally deposed disloyal military commanders, surrounded the presidential palace with loyal troops, and ordered dozens of Méndez Fleitas's supporters arrested. The plotter lost his job as president of the Central Bank. Over the next few months, Stroessner removed all Méndez Fleitas supporters from the army and the party. In May 1956, Méndez Fleitas himself was arrested and allowed to go into exile in Buenos Aires, from where he continued to plot unsuccessfully for decades to overthrow Stroessner.

The late 1950s were touch-and-go years for the Stroessner regime. The Paraguayan economy was at the point of collapse during the decade following the 1947 civil war (see Chapter 4) and urgent austerity measures were required. These measures were brutally imposed by Stroessner's new minister of the interior, Edgar Ynsfrán. Discontent within the business community and the organized labor movement was ignored or violently repressed. Another problem was the appearance of guerrilla groups that harassed and attempted to overthrow the regime. Made up of Febrerista and Liberal exiles, these groups moved back and forth across the Argentinian border with relative freedom.

By the end of the decade, everyone in Paraguay seemed to be discontented. The business community complained about economic policy. External critics asserted that the country was little more than a police state as Ynsfrán's secret police constantly harassed the families of exiles within Paraguay. The president's problems heightened when the followers of Federico Chaves openly criticized the government's policies, implying that a true party regime would follow a different course of action. The stage was set for a Colorado party revolt.

On April 1, 1959, Stroessner announced to the annual session of the Congress that his government would cancel the state of siege, which had been in effect since 1947. Press censorship was to end, as was government intervention in the labor unions. Political prisoners would be released and elections were to be held for a constitutional assembly in which all political parties could participate. In the following weeks, opposition leaders returned from exile. However, antigovernment sentiment escalated as violence broke out in Asunción. When the police arrested three members of Congress, the Chaves wing of the Colorado party argued that the government had violated congressional immunity. The anti-Stroessner majority in Congress demanded the release of the arrested officials as well as the dismissal of Ynsfrán and the chief of police. After hurried consultations with the military high command, Stroessner reimposed the state of siege and dissolved Congress.

From the summer of 1959 through the middle of the 1960s, Paraguay turned inward and became a classic example of a police state. Guerrillas were actively pursued and killed in an orgy of reprisals and counter-reprisals. Freedom of expression ceased to exist. Stroessner retained a firm grip on power, attracting support from the army and from the peasant base of the Colorado party. With the elimination of the party's traditional *caudillos* (strongmen), all of whom were either dead or in exile, Stroessner began to identify himself as the Colorado leader par excellence.

By the mid-1960s, his austerity program had begun to win support from influential Paraguayan economic groups. In 1962, the first split in the opposition appeared. A small group of Liberals decided to seek an accommodation with the regime. They were given legal status by the government and were allowed to use the Liberal party name. The Liberals were also allowed to run for seats in the Congress at the next general election. In 1964, the Febreristas returned from exile and accepted legal status. Finally, the traditional Liberal party gave in and was legalized in 1967; it became known as the Radical Liberal party. The Communists and the followers of Méndez Fleitas—the Movimiento Popular Colorado (MOPOCO)—remained the only groups beyond redemption.

By the end of the 1960s, Stroessner sought international respectability. The economy had recovered, the country was at peace, the guerrilla threat had been eliminated, and political exiles had returned to accept the prevailing political order. But the issue of Stroessner's 1968 reelection campaign was the principal topic of conversation in Paraguay. He already had served two terms, as provided by the 1940 constitution (not counting 1954–1958, when he served four years of Chaves's second term), but was now seeking reelection for an unconstitutional third term. Stroessner dealt with this problem by calling a constitutional convention in 1967, which resulted in the promulgation of a new Magna Carta that legitimated his candidacy.

The 1967 constitution, which was amended once in 1977 to allow Stroessner's reelection to successive presidential terms, reestablished a two-house national legislature. According to this document, two-thirds of the seats in both houses are automatically allotted to the majority party, which has always been the Colorado party; the remaining one-third are divided among the participating opposition parties in proportion to their received vote. Throughout the Stroessner years, the Congress served as a rubber stamp for presidential initiatives (see Chapter 6). With the promulgation of the 1967 constitution and his subsequent election in 1968, Stroessner settled in as one of the hemisphere's senior statesmen. Future presidential and congressional elections were carefully scheduled according to the constitution.

The outcome of these elections, however, was predictable. Stroessner repeatedly was reelected as chief executive by huge margins, and loyalists in the Colorado party were approved for election to the two houses of Congress. The cabinet rarely changed; during the period of 1985–1987 the average age of cabinet members was sixty-five. Many ministers appointed in the 1950s served for decades, a reflection less of their competence than of their devotion to the Stroessner cause. One casualty of the 1968 election was Edgar Ynsfrán, the powerful minister of the interior. Ynsfrán was discontented with Stroessner's decision to seek another term, which eliminated his own chances to become president. As a result, Stroessner found a pretext to dismiss Ynsfrán and his collaborators in the government.[25]

In the presidential election of February 1973, Stroessner was reelected to his fifth term of office.[26] Predictably, the general went on to carry almost 90 percent of the popular vote in the February 1978 presidential election, winning his sixth term. And in September 1982, a congress of the Colorado party met and nominated the president again for the February 1983 elections, which he carried with the usual lopsided majority.

Beginning in the early 1970s, some voices of dissent were heard with recurring frequency in Paraguay. The Roman Catholic church, one of the more docile churches in Latin America in the 1950s, by the late 1960s had changed its tune. Partly as a result of the historic meeting of the bishops of Latin America in Medellín, Colombia, in 1968, the Catholic church took up the causes of the poor, the marginal, and the political prisoners in Paraguayan society. Amnesty International and other groups joined in the continual public criticism of the Stroessner regime over its well-known violations of human rights, but to no avail. Success finally came in 1977, when the administration of U.S. President Jimmy Carter joined the public pressure to bring about a change in Paraguayan domestic policy.[27]

The Stroessner regime, throughout the 1970s, was accused of implementing a policy of genocide against Paraguay's indigenous Indian population. Professor Miguel Chase Sardi and his colleagues, who had established the Marandu Project for Indian relief at the Catholic University in Asunción, were arrested and tortured and the project was closed in December 1975. In May 1976, six Roman Catholic priests who had denounced the genocide of the Indians were deported and six Protestant missionaries doing Indian relief work were arrested. Professional associations worldwide publicly condemned the Stroessner regime for its brutal Indian policy, but the government response was that some unfortunate, unrelated individual incidents had occurred and nothing more. The Paraguayan Roman Catholic church refused to accept the government's interpretation and spoke out strongly on behalf of the indigenous population.[28]

In February 1979, the political opposition announced the formation of the National Accord.[29] The accord included the newly formed breakaway from the Radical Liberal party, the Authentic Radical Liberal party (PLRA), the Revolutionary Febrerista party (PRF), the Christian Democratic party (PDC), and part of the Movimiento Popular Colorado (MOPOCO). The accord renounced the use of violence and outlined fourteen demands in its program, including the installation of a democratic, republican form of government. The United States was instrumental in aiding the organization of the multiparty accord, reflecting the activism of the Carter administration in seeking to further the causes of democracy and human rights in Latin America. In response to pressure applied by the Roman Catholic church and by Ambassador Robert White and the U.S. Embassy, the Paraguayan government released hundreds of political prisoners.

The 1970s were most notable for economic development projects and foreign policy, discussed elsewhere in this book (see Chapters 4 and 7). Internally, little, if anything, changed in Paraguay. Key Colorado party functionaries continued in office; the major military commanders retained their positions of preeminence in the regime. Trade in contraband flourished and benefited the regime by providing an alternative source of income for senior military officers and government officials. The opposition parties remained hopelessly divided. Organized labor was a minor irritant from time to time, as were the small intellectual community and the national press, both concentrated in Asunción. But throughout the decade of the 1970s and into the early 1980s, President Stroessner dominated events in Paraguay. With the twin support of the party and the military, he remained unchallengeable—and unchallenged. But increasingly Stroessner's strength reflected the absence of alternatives, as Paraguayans wearied of the gerontocracy that was running the country's ossified political structure.

NOTES

1. Paul H. Lewis, *Socialism, Liberalism, and Dictatorship in Paraguay*, New York: Praeger, 1982, p. 35.

2. Paul H. Lewis, *Paraguay Under Stroessner*, Chapel Hill: University of North Carolina Press, 1980, p. 21.

3. George Pendle, *Paraguay: A Riverside Nation*, London: Royal Institute of International Affairs, Oxford University Press, 1967, pp. 27–31.

4. Ibid.

5. Even a sympathetic observer, Liberal activist Efraím Cardozo, characterized Guggiari as "ni mediocre, ni muy brillante [not mediocre, not really brilliant]" (Cardozo, *23 de Octubre: Una pagina de historia contemporanea del Paraguay*, Buenos Aires: Editorial Guayra, 1956, p. 15).

6. Riart probably would have prevented Eusebio Ayala's renomination had the Liberal government not been overthrown on February 17, 1936. But Riart would have at least one more laugh. He became Félix Estigarribia's vice-president in 1939 when the new chief executive formed a basically Riartista cabinet. In the end, however, the Riartistas lost out with the promulgation of the new constitution in early 1940.

7. The unproved but persistent Paraguayan assumption was that the Bolivians pursued the Chaco War against them at the behest of Standard Oil Company, a belief that became one of the two main anti-U.S. issues in Paraguayan history. The other was the 1855 *Water Witch* incident.

8. David H. Zook, Jr., *The Conduct of the Chaco War*, New Haven, Conn.: Bookman Associates, 1960; and Pablo Max Ynsfrán (ed.), *The Epic of the Chaco: Marshal Estigarribia's Memoirs of the Chaco War 1932–1935*, New York: Greenwood Press, 1969 (original printing, Austin: University of Texas Press, 1950).

9. David H. Zook argued that "the truce had in fact been opportune for both belligerents: Paraguay because she was physically incapable of completely annihilating the enemy; Bolivia because she was unable any longer to resist Paraguay without pausing to form a new army" (Zook, *Conduct of the Chaco War*, p. 173).

10. The overthrow of the Ayala government was almost entirely a military event. And, as Paul H. Lewis stated, "The revolt of February 17, 1936, might not have taken place at all had it not been for the vague, widespread, anti-Liberal sentiments. . . ." Lewis quotes in full the "Proclamation of the Liberating Army," issued by the military officers responsible for the coup on February 17, 1936 (Lewis, *The Politics of Exile: Paraguay's Febrerista Party*, Chapel Hill: University of North Carolina Press, 1968, p. 41).

11. Organized under U.S. auspices, the conference had been deadlocked for more than three years over the final Chaco demarcation line, until Estigarribia himself, solely on his own authority, announced that he would sign the treaty.

12. The Estigarribia proclamation admitted that after six months of effort to reconstruct postwar Paraguay he and his government had failed. "Hatred divides Paraguayans. Respect for the Magna Carta, law, and authority has been lost," Estigarribia stated (Harris Gaylord Warren, *Paraguay: An Informal History*, Norman: University of Oklahoma Press, 1949, p. 325).

13. Lewis, *Socialism, Liberalism, and Dictatorship*, p. 41.

14. Morínigo first gained national recognition by leading the expedition to Cerro Corá to retrieve the remains of Francisco Solano López.

15. The Febreristas were named for the February Revolution of 1936, the army coup (which was later supported by diverse sectors of the population) that had overthrown the Liberal government of Eusebio Ayala.

16. The Tiempistas were named for *El Tiempo*, a newspaper they had begun in the late 1930s, and were drawn from "a small group of devoutly Catholic, Jesuit-trained professors from the business and law faculties of the national university" (Michael Grow, *The Good Neighbor Policy and Authoritarianism in Paraguay*, Lawrence: Regents Press of Kansas, 1981, p. 50).

17. Ibid., p. 62.

18. Ibid., p. 99.

19. In a classic understatement, Ambassador Willard L. Beaulac recalled: "When I let drop the word, during one of our conversations early in 1946, that my government would probably feel better about its cooperation with Paraguay if some steps were taken to lay the political basis for the establishment of democratic institutions, Morínigo readily fell into line . . . " (Beaulac, *Career Ambassador*, New York: Macmillan, 1951, p. 212).

20. In July 1946, revolutionists overthrew Bolivia's right-wing government and hanged Colonel Gualberto Villaroel, the chief executive, from a lamppost. These actions doubtless encouraged Morínigo to continue to opt for more democracy in Paraguay (Lewis, *Paraguay Under Stroessner*, pp. 25–26).

21. These units were known as *py nandí*, "the barefoot ones," in Guaraní.

22. In the tradition of earlier Liberal politicians, González was a prolific writer. One of his best-known works is *Proceso y formación de la cultura Paraguaya*, first published in 1948. For the major speeches of his presidency, see J. Natalicio González, *Como se construye una nación*, Asunción: Editorial Guaranía, 1949.

23. The independent power of the police was broken by the 1954 coup. Since that time, all police chiefs have been military officers who owed their first allegiance to the army. J. Eugenio Jacquet's preparations to organize a militia outside military auspices during the period 1987–1989 was one element that precipitated the February 1989 coup.

24. Guión Rojo (Red Banner) was the name given to González's storm troopers during the intraparty struggles of the 1940s.

25. Ynsfrán retired from public office and public life and stayed inactive politically until 1985, when he organized the Movimiento Independiente Colorado (MIC). During 1988–1989, he actively conspired to overthrow Stroessner and helped plan the February 1989 coup.

26. The Paraguayan Congress approved a constitutional amendment in July 1976 to allow Stroessner to stand for reelection in 1978, a decision ratified by a constitutional convention that convened in March 1977.

27. When U.S. Ambassador Robert White arrived in Paraguay in 1977, Stroessner had over 1,000 political opponents behind bars; when White left, all but 20 had been released.

28. Richard Arens, *Genocide in Paraguay*, Philadelphia: Temple University Press, 1976. See Chapter 5 for the dissenting view of Maybury-Lewis and Howe, who believed that the government had, in fact, pursued no conscious policy of destroying the Indians.

29. For a useful analysis of the National Accord, see Roberto Luis Céspedes, "Actores sociales subalternos y Acuerdo Nacional," *Acción* (Asunción), 73, October 1985, pp. 14–20.

4

The Paraguayan Economy

MODERN ECONOMIC HISTORY, 1954–1989

Paraguay has passed through roughly five economic periods since 1954, when Stroessner seized power: (1) stabilization (1956–1959); (2) a prolonged period of negligible growth (1960–1972); (3) the Itaipú boom (1973–1981); (4) stagnation (1982–1986); and (5) a modest recovery (1987–1989), during which agriculture emerged as the leading economic sector. The stagnation period undermined Stroessner's popularity among key players within the public and private sectors and set the stage for the growing dissent and the internal Colorado party disputes that finally unseated him (see Chapter 6). In 1989, President Andrés Rodríguez seemed to be taking measures that would improve Paraguay's fiscal situation and balance of payments. He abolished the multiple exchange rate system, eliminated the system of minimum surrender prices for export crops,[1] raised public utility and transport rates, and began to reform the tax structure.

The twenty years of political chaos and social upheaval that dated from the Chaco War (1932–1935) and led to the 1947 civil war (see Chapter 3) had severely weakened Paraguay's economy. During 1947–1955, Paraguay was chronically wracked by currency depreciation, shortages of all kinds, capital flight, and low rates of investment. Paraguay's inflation rate was the highest in South America, averaging over 100 percent per year.[2]

One of Stroessner's achievements was to stabilize economic conditions in Paraguay. From the mid-1950s until the early 1970s Paraguay had low inflation and little external debt. The exchange rate for the guaraní, Paraguay's monetary unit, remained stable from 1959 until the early 1980s at 126 guaraní = US$1. Yet by the end of the 1980s, this idyllic interlude was over (Table 4.1). In January 1989, the exchange rate had topped 1,100 guaraní = US$1, the official inflation rate was about 25 percent annually (the unofficial rate was 35 percent), and external debt was close to $2.5 billion. After imposing a strenuous political order

TABLE 4.1 Exchange Rate, 1984–1988

	1984	1985	1986	1987	1988
Official (unit per $US)	354.0	503.0	633.0	696.0	742.0
Real effective exchange rate (1980 = 100)	83.5	72.3	72.7	58.3	60.6
Free fluctuating market rate (Dec. 1988)					1,025.0

Source: Interamerican Development Bank figures.

on the country in 1954, Alfredo Stroessner forced Paraguay's business and financial sectors to accept the strong medicine of an International Monetary Fund (IMF) adjustment program. As a result, inflation fell, Paraguay's currency stabilized, and investor confidence was restored. Stroessner also acted to tame the labor movement by crushing a 1958 strike.[3]

During the construction of Itaipú, the world's largest hydroelectric plant, Paraguay experienced a string of boom years that gave it the fastest growing economy in Latin America. The boom was related partly to Itaipú construction and partly to sharp increases in prices for Paraguay's main export goods (soybeans and cotton). During 1974–1981, Paraguay's gross domestic product (GDP) grew faster than that of any country on the South American continent, averaging increases of 8.5 percent per year (4.7 percent per capita per year) and climbing 11 percent annually from 1977 to 1980 (see Table 4.4). Moreover, agricultural output grew 7.8 percent annually from 1975 to 1980, and exports soared.[4]

But the Itaipú boom years abruptly gave way to a severe recession that lingered for most of the 1980s. This economic slowdown was characterized by persistent inflation and unemployment, mounting external debt, and slow growth. The flood of foreign capital into Paraguay that accompanied the Itaipú boom also had diverted the economy from its traditional outward, export-based orientation and had masked serious underlying structural weaknesses.[5] Because capital inflows related to Itaipú construction had produced inflationary pressures, an overvalued currency discouraged exports and investment and caused heavy losses in foreign exchange reserves. Simultaneously, Paraguay's regressive, obsolete, and largely unenforced tax system produced little revenue, severely limiting the government's ability to invest in needed infrastructure improvements. The music stopped in 1981, when the principal construction work at Itaipú was finished. Trade in contraband—always a fact of life in Paraguay—became much more pronounced in the 1970s and 1980s. At the same time, large amounts of Itaipú boom money (as much as 80 percent of the total, according to some estimates) left the country.

Despite its evident economic problems, Paraguay finished the 1980s in comparatively better shape than its Latin neighbors. Although the 1988 current-account deficit was estimated in excess of $250 million,[6] Paraguay's external imbalances are moderated by contraband trade, which produces its own foreign exchange independent of Central Bank resources. Smugglers pay cash, so Paraguay's imports to date have been largely unaffected by balance of payments problems. In addition, Paraguay's debt situation is not as dire as that of Brazil or Argentina because the private sector (which has little debt) does not depend on the government for access to foreign exchange. Brazil, which needs Paraguay's continued cooperation on Itaipú, renegotiated over $435 million of debt with Paraguay in 1989.[7]

Inflation, which may have reached an annual rate of 35 percent briefly during January 1989, is still low compared with the hyperinflation that has threatened Argentina, Bolivia, and Brazil. Per capita income growth was faster in Paraguay (1.3 percent) than in the rest of Latin America (0.3 percent average) during 1987.[8] In the same year, Paraguay's debt-to-exports ratio (185 percent) was lower than those of its Latin neighbors (382 percent average) and its rate of export growth was higher (39.2 percent vs. an average of 14.2 percent).[9]

With competent leadership, Paraguay's economic prospects are good. As the $5.8 billion Yacyretá Dam project between Paraguay and Argentina slowly nears its mid-1990s completion date, Paraguay is poised to become the world's largest exporter of electrical power. Endowed with fertile soil and a favorable climate, Paraguay has great potential as an exporter of agricultural products. Currently, Paraguay's main export crops are soybeans and cotton. Given the proper investment climate and marketing opportunities, exports could also include vegetables, wood and wood products, shoes and leather goods, and cotton textiles. Much of Paraguay's future as an exporter will depend on the extent of its access to Brazilian and Argentine markets. For good or ill, Paraguay's future is linked, as it always has been, to the political and economic futures of its two giant neighbors.

HISTORICAL OVERVIEW

Landlocked and devoid of precious metals, strategic importance, and population, Paraguay stagnated for centuries as a colonial backwater with an economy based on subsistence agriculture (see Chapter 2). Because the Guaraní Indians were too poor to pay tribute, the early conquistadores had to accept lower standards of living than their European counterparts in Peru or Mexico. The most important product Paraguay furnished the Spanish Crown was soldiers for the colonial service. Close contact between Europeans and Indians produced a markedly homogeneous population and rapidly socialized succeeding generations of Paraguayan mestizos into Spanish culture. Thus Paraguay avoided the racial divisions prevalent elsewhere in Spanish America, such as in neighboring Bolivia and Peru.

The growth of Buenos Aires as the region's port city during the seventeenth and eighteenth centuries gave Paraguay its first export market.[10] Paraguayan *yerba maté*, tobacco, and hides were highly valued by the more cosmopolitan city dwellers downstream. Settlers and Jesuit colonies competed in producing for this trade, which continued after independence. Until the 1970s, Argentina remained Paraguay's most important export market and source of capital.

After independence in 1811, Dr. José Gaspar Rodríguez de Francia imposed a system of state control over the economy (see Chapter 2). Under Francia, the state became an autonomous entity that was independent of class ties.[11] The state quickly became Paraguay's largest landlord, owning up to 60 percent of all land. Francia's government financed itself through taxes and expropriations of wealthy individuals and the church, taxes on exports, land leases to peasants and others, and profits from state enterprises (such as cattle breeding, shipping, an ironworks, etc.). Until 1865, the Paraguayan state was reasonably progressive. During the 1850s, Paraguay built one of South America's first railroads, established a national system of primary schools, and equipped a large standing army. Throughout this period, the general standard of living in Paraguay was quite low.

The disastrous outcome of the 1864–1870 Triple Alliance War brought fundamental changes in Paraguay's economy. Lack of income and huge debts forced the government to sell vast tracts of state lands to foreigners, mainly Argentines. Entire regions of the country came under foreign ownership. The Paraguayan state welcomed foreign investment and took a pronounced laissez-faire, liberal stance. Both traditional parties, the Colorados and the Liberals, espoused this liberal ideology. By 1935, 19 companies owned over half of Paraguay. Because foreigners had gained control of important segments of local industry and agriculture, Paraguay's economy ceased to be dominated by a despotic state but fell under the sway of foreign economic interests.

The state's orientation changed once more when the military seized power in 1936 after the Chaco War (1932–1935). The state became more nationalist and interventionist, passing labor and land reform legislation and insisting on its exclusive role in leading economic policy. This new stance was confirmed by the successive governments of Félix Estigarribia and Higinio Morínigo (1940–1948) and by the constitution of 1940. Wartime prosperity buoyed Paraguay's economy, but another national disaster—the 1947 civil war—then wrecked it. Revolving-door governments brought chaos and spiraling inflation and discouraged a potentially beneficial flow of immigration from war-torn Europe. The cost of living in Asunción was around 20 times higher in 1955 than it had been in 1946.[12] Inflation in Paraguay was the worst in Latin America.[13]

THE ECONOMY UNDER STROESSNER

Paraguay made impressive economic strides under Stroessner, primarily because of the political stability of his regime. After the devastation of the 1947 civil war and the revolving-door governments that followed it, the economy probably would have improved under any Paraguayan administration capable of imposing order. Nonetheless, order and prosperity proved popular. Economic growth and stability were major underpinnings of the Stroessner regime and its primary sources of legitimacy. By 1956, Stroessner was able to halt the populist financial manipulations and easy credit policies of Central Bank President Epifanio Méndez Fleitas, and he then succeeded in imposing a stabilization package on the country with the support of the International Monetary Fund. Monetary expansion was slowed, credit to local businessmen tightened, and the currency was devalued.[14]

These measures, though not without political risk, paid off by gaining investor confidence. In addition, the government created a number of new public bodies to micromanage the economy, which swelled the ranks of government employees and increased the size of the public sector. With trains, shipping, meat, alcoholic beverages, and telecommunications already under government control, Stroessner acquired an even firmer grip on the main levers of Paraguay's economy.[15]

Support from abroad, especially from the United States and Brazil, was crucial to Paraguay's economic successes (see Chapter 7). In the early 1960s, the amount of aid and economic grants received from the United States at times approached the size of Paraguay's annual state expenditures. The United States helped Paraguay secure vital development funds from multilateral lending institutions such as the World Bank, the IMF, and the Interamerican Development Bank (IDB).[16]

During the 1950s and 1960s, Paraguay's economy was still largely agricultural. Even as late as 1984 nearly half the labor force was employed in agriculture (Table 4.2). Agriculture accounted for almost 40 percent of GDP in 1960, around 32 percent in 1970, and just over 27 percent in 1987 (Table 4.3). During this period (1950–1970), livestock, wood, tobacco, and quebracho extract (a substance from the bark of hardwood trees in the Chaco that is used in tanning hides) were Paraguay's main exports (Table 4.4). The country's largest export markets before 1970

TABLE 4.2   Labor Force[a] (percentages by sector, 1984)

Agriculture	48.0
Mining	0.9
Manufacturing and construction	12.8
Transportation	2.6
Trade	9.4
Services	21.5
Others	4.8

[a]Economically active population = 1,212,400.

Source: Interamerican Development Bank figures.

TABLE 4.3   Sectoral Composition of Gross Domestic Product (percentages)

	1960	1970	1975	1980	1984	1987
Agriculture	38.8	32.1	36.9	29.5	28.7	27.3
Mining	0.1	0.1	0.2	0.4	0.4	0.5
Industry	17.3	16.7	15.6	16.5	16.1	16.2
Construction	2.4	2.8	3.8	6.1	6.2	5.9
Electricity, gas, water	0.8	1.1	1.4	2.3	2.4	2.5
Transport and communication	4.0	3.9	4.0	4.2	4.1	4.4
Commerce and finance	18.4	24.4	22.9	25.8	25.5	26.6
Government	4.4	5.3	3.4	3.4	4.2	4.2
Miscellaneous services	13.8	13.6	12.0	11.8	12.4	12.4
Total	100.0	100.0	100.0	100.0	100.0	100.0

Source: Werner Baer and Melissa Birch, "Expansion of the Economic Frontier: Paraguayan Growth in the 1970s," *World Development,* 12:8, 1984, p. 785; Interamerican Development Bank figures.

TABLE 4.4   Commodity Composition of Paraguayan Exports (percentages)

	1960	1970	1975	1981	1987
Wood products	14.9	19.7	15.8	12.3	7.8
Livestock	35.2	26.7	19.5	2.3	9.9
Tobacco	5.9	9.0	6.8	2.2	2.8
Cotton	1.1	6.3	11.4	43.7	28.6
Soybeans	—	—	9.9	16.1	34.7
Sugar	0.3	—	3.8	—	0.7
Vegetable oils	5.7	10.9	6.0	7.6	2.7
Essential oils	3.7	3.2	5.5	2.2	1.6
Quebracho extract	10.9	3.1	1.4	1.9	1.5
Other	7.4	21.1	19.9	11.7	9.7
Total	100.0	100.0	100.0	100.0	100.0

Source: Compiled from Paraguayan government figures (*Boletín Estadístico,* November 1988) and from Werner Baer and Melissa Birch, "Expansion of the Economic Frontier: Paraguayan Growth in the 1970s," *World Development,* 12:8, 1984, p. 787.

TABLE 4.5   Estimated Exports and Imports Including Contraband, 1960–1987 (in millions of U.S. dollars, FOB)

	Exports	Imports	Implied Trade Deficit
1960	36.5	43.4	6.9
1970	70.6	75.6	5.0
1971	76.6	89.0	12.4
1972	109.7	103.3	−6.4[a]
1973	170.7	162.8	−7.9[a]
1974	206.9	273.5	66.6
1975	234.7	285.2	50.5
1976	243.9	331.4	87.5
1977	387.2	493.0	105.8
1978	432.3	662.9	230.6
1979	597.3	997.7	400.4
1980	715.2	1094.4	379.2
1981	663.5	1058.4	394.9
1982	635.2	759.8	124.6
1983	562.9	710.0	147.1
1984	538.2	740.2	202.0
1985	620.2	727.3	107.1
1986	537.4	735.5	198.1
1987	800.0	934.7	134.7

[a]Surplus.

Source: M. A. Romano and J. Dinsmoor, Informe Socioeconómico: Paraguay, Washington, D.C.: Interamerican Development Bank, March 1989, apéndice estadístico, cuadro 9, cuadro 10.

were Argentina, the United States, and the European Economic Community (EEC) (see Figure 7.1 and Tables 7.1 and 7.2). Major imports included foodstuffs, machinery, transportation, equipment, fuel, and lubricants. The industrial sector was weak, concentrated on processing agricultural raw materials. Argentina, the United States, and Great Britain were Paraguay's principal import suppliers and investors.[17] Stroessner's conservative policies kept inflation low at 2 percent annually throughout the 1960s, while annual GDP growth averaged 4.2 percent. Trade volume increased by a factor of 20 from 1960 to 1987 but imports increased even faster than exports, which led to widening, persistent annual trade deficits in the early 1980s (Table 4.5).[18]

Stroessner's government played a large role in Paraguay's economy as a regulator and promoter of investment and exports. Economic controls covered prices, wages, banking, and insurance. Certain farm products (mainly sugar and meat) received price supports, subsidies, and marketing quotas. The state was directly involved in banking; public utilities and telecommunications; air, sea, and rail transportation; and cattle ranching.

Its stake in industry included ship repair, furniture, quarries, sawmills, meatpacking, and alcoholic beverage marketing, not to mention cement and steel plants.

Despite the state's role as a regulator, 1986 government revenue was less than 8 percent of GDP, the lowest figure for South America and one of the lowest in the developing world. Direct taxes as a proportion of GDP were only 2.1 percent in 1986, the lowest in South America aside from Bolivia.[19] There are several reasons for this bizarre fiscal situation. Except for an ungraduated and seldom collected corporate profits tax, Paraguay does not tax personal income. Also, the country's schedule of import and export duties became obsolete many years ago. But the main reason for persistent fiscal shortfalls in Paraguay is that a highly politicized state has not been able to summon the will or authority to tax its main economic actors. One result of the government's weak revenue base is to make Paraguay dependent on borrowed money or foreign aid for infrastructure improvements.

While Stroessner was in power, the state dealt with Paraguay's inability to finance investment domestically by opening the country to foreign investors, at the price of increasingly denationalizing the economy. Government policy encouraged foreign capital with liberal tax benefits and measures such as Law 550, which provided investment incentives in export industries and in less-developed parts of the country. Brazilians were the biggest investors in Paraguay, followed by West Germans, Americans, Argentines, Japanese, French, and Italians.

Differences in income and cultural levels are not as extreme in Paraguay as elsewhere in Latin America, but Itaipú money made many fortunes. During the Stroessner years conspicuous consumption became noticeable. A small, tightly knit group, the elite owed their positions mainly to their ties with the chief executive and the ruling party. The middle class presently contains professionals, middle ranking officials, and a few who have achieved modest prosperity as corporate officers. About 80 percent of the population of Asunción is lower class.

THE BOOM OF THE 1970s:
COMMODITIES AND ITAIPÚ

Cooperation with Brazil began to overshadow U.S. involvement during the 1970s. Brazilian President Juscelino Kubitschek signed a 1956 treaty with Stroessner that by the late 1960s had led to the construction of the Friendship Bridge over the Paraná River, a paved road to the Brazilian coast, and duty-free port facilities under Paraguayan control at the Brazilian port of Paranaguá (see Chapter 7).

Overflow gates at Itaipú.

These arrangements gave Paraguay incalculable advantages, not least of which was access to the Brazilian economy. But these advantages were soon overshadowed by the immense Itaipú project, which involved construction of the world's largest hydroelectric power plant. Completed in the 1980s at a cost of about $20 billion, Itaipú has an installed generating capacity of 12.6 million kilowatts, far in excess of Paraguay's needs. Paraguay sells most of its 50-percent share of the electricity to Brazil for around $200 million a year. Itaipú employed thousands of Paraguayan *campesinos* who had never before held paying jobs and fundamentally altered Paraguay's age-old status as a lethargic backwater.

Paraguayans received contracts of around $2 billion in Itaipú-related construction. Construction replaced agriculture as Paraguay's most vibrant economic sector, increasing its share of GDP by around 30 percent annually from 1977 to 1980, largely at the expense of agriculture (Table 4.6). With billions of dollars in foreign funds flowing into the country after 1973, Paraguay was poised for a few economic "miracle" years.

Aside from the general euphoria and confidence of the period, concurrent booms in agricultural land and commodity prices contributed to growth and economic activity. The 1960s and 1970s were a period of "rural-rural" migration of Paraguayan *campesinos* to the relatively undeveloped eastern border area. Government-sponsored infrastructure

TABLE 4.6 The Itaipú Boom—Real Sectoral and Gross Domestic Product Growth Rates (percentages)

	GDP	Agriculture	Industry	Construction	Commerce
1960–1969	4.2	—	—	—	—
1970	4.8	2.2	8.0	7.2	4.0
1971	5.4	6.5	1.7	14.3	6.2
1972	6.4	6.2	11.0	2.6	3.1
1973	7.2	6.4	8.4	16.5	8.5
1974	8.2	9.8	7.4	14.1	8.8
1975	6.3	8.2	−1.8	21.2	4.4
1976	7.0	3.7	5.5	18.1	10.1
1977	12.8	11.1	20.1	31.1	12.0
1978	10.9	5.9	13.7	32.0	12.8
1979	10.7	6.7	10.5	30.0	11.6
1980	11.4	9.2	12.6	26.0	10.5
1981	8.5	6.7	8.0	16.7	8.4
1982	−2.5	—	—	—	—

Source: Data from Banco Central del Paraguay, Cuentas Nacionales, as reported in Werner Baer and Melissa Birch, "Expansion of the Economic Frontier: Paraguayan Growth in the 1970s," World Development, 12:8, 1984, p. 790.

investments during the 1960s helped open land for development, while the government's rural welfare office sponsored a program to aid campesinos who wanted to move to the unexploited lands in the east.

In addition to the internal migration of Paraguayan campesinos from the core regions of minifundio (small-holding) settlement near Asunción, hundreds of thousands of Brazilian[20] and Japanese immigrants moved to Paraguay's eastern border region. These capitalist farmers were lured by low Paraguayan land prices[21] and skyrocketing profits for Paraguay's main agricultural commodities: soybeans and cotton (Figure 4.1). Large-scale investments in modern farming methods and equipment quickly quadrupled the cultivation area of these crops, leading to four- and fivefold production increases.[22] Legal and contraband trade between Paraguay and Brazil flourished.

THE BUST OF THE 1980s

After 1981, things began to fall apart as construction at Itaipú neared completion and international prices for Paraguay's commodity exports fell. The end of the Itaipú boom coincided with interlocking crises in balance of payments, fiscal policy, monetary policy, and international debt. Poor weather conditions in 1983 and 1986, world economic recession, Paraguay's rising debt service obligations, and unstable political and economic conditions in Argentina and Brazil combined to hurt Paraguayan economic performance.

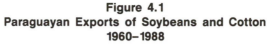

Figure 4.1
Paraguayan Exports of Soybeans and Cotton
1960–1988

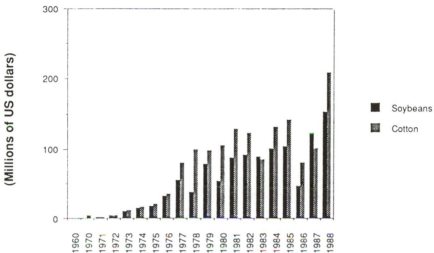

Note: Paraguay experienced a tremendous boom in cotton and soybean production during the 1970s and 1980s as thousands of Brazilians, lured by low land prices in Paraguay, invested heavily in producing these crops and selling their output to eager overseas markets. *Source:* Banco Central del Paraguay, Departamiento de Estudios Económicos, *Boletín Estadístico*, November 1988, p. 40.

Per capita GDP fell an average of 2.5 percent annually from 1982 to 1986.[23] Exports suffered as inflation overvalued the guaraní. By granting preferential exchange rates to the government, the Central Bank began to suffer large foreign exchange losses, and accumulated reserves shrank. In addition, these disguised subsidies were creating future inflationary pressures because the government was spending beyond its means. As a result, inflation rose steadily in Paraguay after 1970 (Table 4.7). Government spending began to increase in 1982 precisely when the economy suffered a sharp downturn and Itaipú money had dried up. This deterioration in the fiscal balance forced austerity measures in government budgets and services in 1983, not to mention dramatic cuts in infrastructure investments. The huge project at Itaipú also had imposed less quantifiable moral costs by encouraging corruption and undermining ethics, by outpacing the government's administrative capacity, and by creating false expectations for rapid economic growth based on future plans to build hydroelectic dams at Corpus and Yacyretá.

TABLE 4.7   Percentage Increase in Cost of Living (average of estimated annual averages)

1965–1969	2.2
1970–1974	10.5
1975–1979	11.9
1980–1984	14.9
1985–1988	20.5

Source: Compiled from Paraguayan government figures, International Development Bank figures, and Werner Baer and Melissa Birch, "Expansion of the Economic Frontier: Paraguayan Growth in the 1970s," *World Development,* 12:8, 1984, p. 791.

FOREIGN DEBT

Another looming problem during the 1980s was Paraguay's burgeoning foreign debt, which exceeded $2.5 billion in 1989. Paraguay managed to reach an agreement with Brazil in April 1989 (although it did not contain extremely favorable terms) on rescheduling the country's $436 million debt to Brazil. The terms of this agreement feature a twenty-year moratorium on principal payments, floating interest rates, a renegotiated interest payment schedule, and the possibility of swapping Paraguayan debt for Brazilian bonds at attractive rates should Paraguay have any spare cash.

Paraguay's net external debt remained a constant 15 percent of GDP until the early 1980s. Although it quadrupled from $200 million in 1972 to almost $850 million in 1980, the debt did not grow faster than GDP. This changed after 1982, as debt spiraled to over 50 percent of GDP by 1988 while debt service reached 78.7 percent of export earnings.[24] Expanded public sector borrowing—mostly in the form of "soft" loans, which have low or deferred interest rates, from other countries (notably Brazil) and from multilateral institutions (such as the World Bank)—was largely responsible for these increases. Part of the debt problem is due to the regime's sponsorship of costly and inefficient public sector projects that provide new sources of patronage in a period of economic stagnation.

About one-quarter of Paraguay's total external debt is concentrated in state-sponsored cement plants and a steel mill (Table 4.8), which most observers have dismissed as boondoggles. In essence, Industria Nacional de Cemento (INC, or National Cement Industry) and Acero del Paraguay (ACEPAR, or Paraguay Steel) invested hundreds of millions of dollars of borrowed funds in projects that are worth only a fraction of their total cost and that have a production capability many times larger than any currently existing local market.

TABLE 4.8   Real Production and External Debt, 1984–1988

	1984	1985	1986	1987	1988
Real production					
GDP (millions, 1988 $US)	5,461	5,678	5,680	5,925	6,290
External debt (millions of US dollars)					
Disbursed debt	1,460.9	1,791.4	2,040.2	2,447.2	2,569.6
Debt paid (long-term)	137.5	162.1	223.4	226.6	279.3
Interest payments as					
percentage of exports	10.1	8.3	18.5	9.2	9.2
External debt as					
percentage of GDP	49.1	64.0	65.6	59.7[a]	n.a.
Total debt service	143.0	175.0	214.0	292.5	n.a.
External debt attributed					
to ACEPAR and INC[b]	362	396	492	n.a.	n.a.
ACEPAR	180	224	271	n.a.	n.a.
INC	182	172	221	n.a.	n.a.
Debt service					
of ACEPAR and INC	24	27	80	n.a.	n.a.

[a]Estimates.

[b]ACEPAR = Acero del Paraguay; INC = Industria Nacional de Cementos.

Source: Interamerican Development Bank figures.

INC's first plant, capable of producing 200,000 tons a year, was completed in 1977. Capacity was quadrupled with the construction of two more plants and simultaneous modifications to the original one. The main justification for expanding capacity was to supply cement to Itaipú. But construction of the two additional plants only began in 1982, after demand for cement at Itaipú had fallen off. Even though the smaller Yacyretá hydroelectric project on the border with Argentina will use Paraguayan cement, the original plant as modified would have been able to meet demand. In any case, Paraguay agreed during the negotiations with Argentina that INC cement would not be used at Yacyretá. Paraguay currently has enormous overcapacity. The new plants cost $295–$335 million;[25] in contrast, the old plant was updated under private contract for $15 million.

Another Paraguayan pork barrel is ACEPAR. The workings of ACEPAR, which is a joint venture with a Brazilian firm but is run solely by Paraguayan Army generals, are still largely hidden from the public. Located on the Paraguay River in Villa Hayes north of Asunción, the plant uses imported Bolivian iron ore and has an annual capacity of 150,000 tons. Preexisting wire extrusion plants, under German ownership, were already adequate for the local market. In 1988, demand for ACEPAR products was less than 30,000 tons. The steel mill cost $293 million and has an external debt of $330 million. Even if we assume the debt could be paid off from revenues at full production (experts doubt this), low demand has forced INC and ACEPAR plant managers to restrict production to less than one-quarter of capacity. In 1988, ACEPAR and INC showed losses because sales did not cover operating expenses. In other words, the firms lost money simply by operating. The steel mill also poses an environmental problem: It uses charcoal in place of coking coal (Paraguay has no exploitable coal deposits and little iron ore). The charcoal will come from Paraguay's shrinking eastern forest reserves. During 1981–1985, Paraguay had the third highest deforestation rate in the world, behind Ivory Coast and Nigeria.[26]

INC and ACEPAR illustrate clearly a tendency that became pronounced during Stroessner's terms in office: the feudalization of Paraguay's economy. Economic enterprises, including smuggling operations, began to take on aspects of feudal baronies. These fiefdoms were founded by the grace of Stroessner's benevolent patronage and bestowed on men who henceforth owed their continued financial well-being and their political allegiance to Stroessner. Gifts of state-owned land became one of Stroessner's favorite methods of rewarding loyal subalterns. The dictator dispensed and disposed of these concessions as he wished.

CONTRABAND AND SMUGGLING

Like everything about Paraguay, the country's economy possesses some unusual features. Probably the most notable of these is the contraband trade, which for several years has likely exceeded registered (that is, legal) trade, in both exports and imports. The favorite items in this illicit trade are soybeans, coffee, and stolen automobiles (all from Brazil); scotch whiskey, cigars and cigarettes, and perfume; consumer electronics and household appliances; and drugs, especially cocaine bound for the United States and Europe and marijuana bound for Brazil.

Paraguay's proximity to South America's two largest economies makes it an ideal base for smugglers. Both Brazil and Argentina have pursued import-substituting industrialization and anti–free market policies in recent decades and both have erected high tariff barriers to keep out competing products from the rest of the world. Because Paraguay is only an hour or two by plane from either São Paulo or Buenos Aires, its cut-rate prices make it a tempting stop for bargain hunting consumers. Paraguay's enterprising businessmen can arrange delivery for a fee that includes the necessary bribes to Brazilian or Argentinian officials. Motorists going to Brazil from Ciudad del Este (formerly Puerto Presidente Stroessner) can drive over the Paraná River on the Friendship Bridge without any customs inspection whatever.

A young street vendor in Puerto Presidente Stroessner hawking "genuine" French perfume.

Low Paraguayan taxes on agricultural goods has tempted Brazilian farmers to ship their harvests (especially soybeans and coffee) to Paraguay to evade the higher Brazilian levies. Produce enters Paraguay across the Friendship Bridge or else comes through the long *frontera seca* (dry, or "riverless," frontier) along the Brazilian border. There are no customs or border controls at Paraguayan and Brazilian towns such as Pedro Juan Caballero and Ponta Pará, which share the same main street, so driving a truck across the border is an easy matter. Drivers must stop at a military checkpoint a few kilometers into Paraguay, but a small bribe to the commanding officer is the only formality required.

Official connivance in Paraguay obviously has encouraged smuggling. Stroessner's frequent use of the phrase "el contrabando es el precio de paz" (contraband is the price of peace) signaled official approval of the traffic, which became a normal part of economic life. Under the Stroessner regime, the country was divided among smugglers to diminish the potential for violent competition and to ensure that a share of the spoils went to military officers or Colorado party officials.[27]

Cocaine smuggling in 1988–1989 was confined to and controlled by the highest echelons of Paraguayan society. Coca is not grown in Paraguay, and no processing plant has yet been found on Paraguayan soil, although precursor chemicals and equipment have been seized. Apparently Bolivian cocaine smugglers fly the drug to Paraguay via the unpatrolled Chaco. With the connivance of high-ranking Paraguayans, drug cargos are transferred to Asunción and then flown to Europe or North America via Lineas Aereas Paraguayas (LAP), the Paraguayan national airline.[28] For several decades, Paraguay has been a major producer of marijuana (3,000–4,000 tons a year) for markets in Brazil and Argentina. Marijuana plantations along the Brazilian border came under aerial attack during 1988–1989 through a U.S.-financed herbicide spraying effort.

One sign of how much Paraguay may change under President Andrés Rodríguez will be whether his government takes measures to reduce smuggling. Rodríguez will find himself under pressure to do so, especially from Brazil. The trade in stolen Brazilian automobiles and trucks is particularly notorious. Most of the vehicles being driven in Asunción were probably stolen from Brazilian motorists. Theft on that scale implies a huge loss to Brazilian insurance companies and private individuals. Roadside assassinations by car thieves who double as drug runners was becoming a serious threat on Brazilian roads leading to Paraguay in 1988–1989. The Brazilian government forced the March 1988 recall of Justo Eres Almada from his post as consul in the Paraguayan free port of Paranaguá after Almada was accused of running a large-scale smuggling enterprise using stolen Brazilian trucks.[29]

RURAL PARAGUAY

Paraguay has long been one of the most rural areas on the South American continent, and although it it still a rural society, it has recently become less so (Table 4.9). The government's efforts to resettle landless peasants in the undeveloped eastern border region helped Paraguay avoid the rampant urbanization that is prevalent elsewhere in South America.[30] Almost 60 percent of Paraguayans lived outside of cities in 1988, an amount not significantly different from the 1950s and 1960s figures. But urbanization is not negligible. In 1988, almost 23 percent

TABLE 4.9 Urban/Rural Population Distribution in Paraguay, 1962–1982 (percentages)

	1962	1972	1982
Urban	30	33	43
Rural	70	67	57

Source: Adapted from Domingo M. Rivarola, "Los movimientos sociales en el Paraguay," in Domingo M. Rivarola (ed.), Los movimientos sociales en el Paraguay, Asunción: Centro Paraguayo de Estudios Sociológicos, 1986, p. 21.

of all Paraguayans lived in Asunción (population 900,000). The population of Paraguay's capital city grew 11.5 percent from 1983 to 1986, and that of its suburbs grew 19.6 percent. These figures imply that Asunción is replacing Buenos Aires as the destination of Paraguayan economic migrants. Urbanization will likely increase during the 1990s, especially if political and economic conditions improve under Rodríguez and his successors and if Paraguayans now living in Brazil and Argentina decide to come home.[31]

With a 1988 per capita gross domestic product of around $1,600, Paraguay ranks as a middle-income South American nation, ahead of Peru, Ecuador, and Bolivia but behind Chile, Uruguay, and Argentina.[32] Paraguay has so far avoided the massive rural-urban migrations that have swamped other cities in the hemisphere, bringing them with "zones of misery." Still, poverty in Paraguay seems to be associated with rurality. The biggest problem facing rural Paraguayans is landlessness, but this is a recent development. Since the arrival of the Spaniards Paraguay has always had more land than it could use. This began to change in the 1970s with the advent of large-scale capitalist farming for export combined with Stroessner's habit of rewarding his cronies by giving away or allowing them to buy state-owned land.

By the 1990s, Paraguay no longer had excess land. Many landless peasants are squatting on land they do not own. The lack of surplus land will deprive the state of a useful safety valve during times of economic decline. In the past, discouraged urban workers always had the option to return to farming. According to the 1981 agricultural census, 1 percent of Paraguay's 275,000 farms (average size: 7,299 hectares) accounted for 79 percent of all land under cultivation; but another 35 percent of all farms cultivated only 1 percent of the land.[33] The face-off between subsistence agriculture and capitalist farming, unless the situation is alleviated, will continue to increase the number of urban migrants or may produce a revolt in the countryside. Soybean and cotton exports continue to increase rapidly, and agriculture has regained its position as the leading economic sector (Table 4.10). Although 1987 was

TABLE 4.10   Gross Domestic Product by Sector (percentage growth rates)

	1984	1985	1986	1987	1988
Total GDP	3.1	4.0	0.0	4.3	6.2
Agriculture	5.9	4.6	−6.1	7.0	11.3
Manufacturing	4.5	5.0	−1.4	3.5	5.3
Construction	−2.4	−1.0	1.0	2.0	2.6
Commerce	1.8	4.7	3.3	3.5	4.2

Source: Interamerican Development Bank figures.

a good year for soybean and cotton exports, 1988 soybean exports were 25 percent higher and cotton exports more than doubled (see Figure 4.1).

Paraguay remains one of the least industrialized nations in South America. Agriculture, cattle ranching, and lumbering have long been the basis of the economy. Although agriculture employed almost half (46 percent) of the labor force in 1987, it produced only about one-quarter of GDP (Table 4.3). Manufacturing in Paraguay mainly processes agricultural raw materials. Otherwise, industry consists of small factories and handicraft workshops.

Economic development has not reached the rural Paraguayan population. Health and sanitation needs are particularly acute: As late as 1980, indoor water supplies and sewerage services were available to only 18.4 percent and 6.5 percent of the population, respectively.[34] On the other hand, Paraguay has thus far avoided the widespread misery that has afflicted some of its Latin neighbors. Because Paraguay is aided by a benign climate and a high number of independent food producers, the country's health indicators are relatively good. But despite some improvements in education (literacy is officially 92 percent) and life expectancy (66 years in 1988, up from 56 years in 1960), per capita income in 1986 was the lowest in South America aside from Bolivia.[35] Government spending on education in Paraguay as a percentage of GDP (1.2 percent in 1985) is one of the lowest in Latin America. Per capita health spending, on the other hand, compares well with other South American countries and is on about the same level as health spending in Chile.[36]

POST-STROESSNER PROSPECTS

After the February 1989 coup, President Rodríguez acted decisively to redress some of the more glaring anomalies in Paraguay's economic picture. He abolished the two-tier exchange rate (which had penalized exporters and investors), renegotiated Paraguay's external debt with Brazil, and made new ministerial appointments.[37] Rodríguez also ex-

A mostly rural society, Paraguay avoided the problems associated with rapid urbanization for a long time. The increasing number of young boys who rush into restaurants to eat customers' leftovers is an index of the growing problem of urban poverty.

panded credit to the public sector by a whopping 70 percent and granted large salary increases to military personnel and to doctors and nurses at Asunción's public hospital (Hospital de Clínicas).[38]

Remarkably, inflation was holding steady at 1.5 percent a month until several months after the coup. The inflationary pressures created by the two-tier exchange rate of the 1980s[39] finally emerged in May 1989, immediately after the presidential elections, when President Rodríguez announced large hikes in power, water, telephone, and public transportation tariffs. Rodríguez also announced a modest general pay increase at that time, yet he had already granted larger increases to the military, teachers, and police. Still, hyperinflation and currency instability in Argentina and Brazil, the sources of many Paraguayan imports, were working in Paraguay's favor in 1989 by keeping import prices down.[40]

By reforming currency exchange, abolishing minimum surrender prices for agricultural exports, studying privatization of inefficient state-owned industries (such as INC), and removing import restrictions, the new government has begun to reorient the economy toward the outside world. Naturally, this policy was welcomed by exporters but greeted with dismay by some local manufacturers, who feared competition from cheaper imported goods. The extent of Paraguay's outward economic orientation in coming years may be determined more by decisions made in Buenos Aires and Brasilia than by those made in Asunción.

Public deficits, inflation, debt obligations, and low levels of public expenditures will continue to be problem areas for Paraguayan policy makers in coming years. Adopting a single free-market exchange rate for the guaraní (thus eliminating the privileged rate for public sector transactions) was a bold step, but one of its effects was to increase pressure on the public purse. Already cut to the bone, public spending cannot fall further without serious political and economic implications. A thoroughgoing tax reform and vastly increased direct taxes are urgently needed in Paraguay; so far the regime has dithered. By increasing credits to the private sector and expanding the money supply during the first half of 1989, the government was trying to spark an economic upturn and improve its public relations. But these measures are inflationary over the medium term. A further question mark is the future of the contraband trade. Smuggling is already a deeply ingrained habit in Paraguay. If it proves resistant to change, it will tend to rob the government of income from import and export duties. This is another reason that direct taxation will remain a priority.

NOTES

1. This system was known as *aforos*.

2. Compared with annual inflation rates in Latin American countries during 1987, 1988, 1989, and 1990, which averaged 116 percent, 218 percent, 350 percent, and 672 percent (first quarter 1990), Paraguay's "runaway" inflation figure of 100 percent annually between 1947 and 1954 seems tame indeed (Alfred L. Malabre, Jr., "The Outlook—Problems Abroad Dwarf U.S. Troubles," *Wall Street Journal*, June 4, 1990, p. 1).

3. Daniel Seyler, "Growth and Structure of the Economy," in Sandra W. Meditz and Dennis M. Hanratty (eds.), *Paraguay: A Country Study*, Washington, D.C.: U.S. Government Printing Office, 1990.

4. Werner Baer and Melissa Birch, "The International Economic Relations of a Small Country: The Case of Paraguay," *Economic and Cultural Change*, 35:3, April 1987; and "Expansion of the Economic Frontier: Paraguayan Growth in the 1970s," *World Development*, 12:8, 1984, pp. 783–798; Werner Baer and Luis Breuer, "From Inward to Outward Growth: Paraguay in the 1980s," *Journal of Inter-American Studies and World Affairs*, 28:3, Fall 1986, pp. 125–139; and M. A. Romano and J. Dinsmoor, *Informe socioeconómico: Paraguay*, Washington, D.C.: Interamerican Development Bank (GN-1646), March 1989.

5. Baer and Breuer, "From Inward to Outward Growth."

6. "Foreign Economic Trends and Their Implications for the United States" (Paraguay, FET 88-114), U.S. Department of Commerce, November 1988, p. 2.

7. *Hoy* (Asunción), April 25, 1989, p. 12. The deal included an eight-year grace period on interest payments, a twenty-year moratorium on principal payments, a floating interest rate defined at LIBOR (London inter-bank offer rate) plus 13/16 of 1 percent, and the possibility of trading Paraguayan debt for Brazilian bonds at a concessionary rate. The terms of this deal have been criticized within Paraguay as being anything but concessionary and considerably worse than those that Brazil itself is hoping to secure from its own international creditors. For instance, LIBOR plus 13/16 of 1 percent is essentially a market interest rate, and the debt-bond swap will only be possible if Paraguay somehow raises a large amount of cash, an unlikely prospect.

8. Romano and Dinsmoor, *Informe socioeconómico*, p. III-5.

9. *El Diario* (Asunción), May 9, 1988.

10. Paraguay had no direct access to European markets. Spanish law at that time prohibited any direct trade between Paraguay and Spain (See Chapter 2).

11. Guido Rodríguez Alcalá, *Ideología autoritaria*, Asunción: R. P. Ediciones, 1987.

12. Baer and Birch, "International Economic Relations," p. 602.

13. See note 2, this chapter.

14. Paul H. Lewis, *Paraguay Under Stroessner*, Chapel Hill: University of North Carolina Press, 1980, pp. 151–154.

15. Ibid.

16. Ginny Bouvier, *Decline of a Dictator: Paraguay at a Crossroads*, Washington, D.C.: Washington Office on Latin America, 1988, pp. 7–8.

17. Argentine capital was concentrated in tannin, agriculture, electricity, and streetcars; Americans mainly invested in cattle, petroleum exploration, and tannin; and the British concentrated on the railroad, banking, and meatpacking (Baer and Birch, "International Economic Relations," p. 602).

18. Ibid.

19. Romano and Dinsmoor, *Informe socioeconómico*, apéndice estadístico, cuadro 7.

20. According to a survey conducted by the Brazilian Embassy in Asunción, about 450,000 Brazilians, the vast majority of whom were of German descent, were living in these regions in 1986.

21. Land in Paraguay during the late 1970s and early 1980s was sometimes sold for one-tenth the price of comparable land on the other side of the Brazilian border.

22. Seyler, "Growth and Structure of the Economy."

23. M. A. Romano, "Paraguay: Situación económica reciente," Washington, D.C.: Interamerican Development Bank, May 17, 1989 (mimeo).

24. "Foreign Economic Trends" (Paraguay, FET 88-114), U.S. Department of Commerce, p. 9.

25. Romano and Dinsmoor, *Informe socioeconómico*, pp. IV-23, IV-24.

26. Ibid., apéndice estadístico, cuadro 28.

27. Gregorio Selser, "Paraguay: Octavo mandato presidencial de Alfredo Stroessner," unpublished manuscript presented at the Latin American Studies Association Conference, New Orleans, La., March 1988, p. 10.

28. For example, on August 14, 1987, customs officials seized 114 kilograms (251 pounds) of cocaine that had been hidden in a Paraguayan Airlines (LAP) shipment of coconut soap; on May 12, 1988, officials at the Miami airport discovered 34 kilograms (75 pounds) of cocaine in a suitcase left unclaimed on LAP's baggage carousel (see Chapter 7).

29. Almada was behind bars in Paraguay at the time of this writing.

30. The Instituto de Bienestar Rural helped resettle 41,000 peasant families to the sparsely populated eastern border region during the 1960s and 1970s. This figure may represent a total of 225,000 Paraguayans. Two other elements were also at work in maintaining Paraguay's rural character: (1) up to 1 million Paraguayans have emigrated, mainly to Argentina and mainly for economic reasons; and (2) new road construction opened up previously inaccessible forest areas in eastern Paraguay during the 1970s, attracting new settlers and expatriate Paraguayans fleeing the Argentine economic downturn (Fran Gillespie, "Comprehending the Slow Pace of Urbanization in Paraguay Between 1950 and 1972," *Economic Development and Cultural Change*, 31:2, January 1983, pp. 355–375).

31. Romano and Dinsmoor, *Informe socioeconómico*, Annex 2, "Aspectos demográphicos generales."

32. See Romano and Dinsmoor, p. IV-36.

33. Seyler, "Growth and Structure of the Economy."

34. Aníbal Miranda, *Desarrollo y pobreza en Paraguay*, Rosslyn, Va., and Asunción: Inter-American Foundation and Comité de Iglesias para Ayudas de Emergencia, 1982, p. 156.

35. World Bank, *World Development Report: 1988*, New York: Oxford University Press, 1988.

36. Romano and Dinsmoor, *Informe socioeconómico*, pp. IV-36 (cuadro IV-7), IV-46 (cuadro IV-13).

37. Shortly after the coup, Rodríguez named Antonio Zuccolillo (brother of newspaper publisher Aldo Zuccolillo) as industry and commerce minister and Enzo Debernardi as finance minister.

38. Interview with World Bank official, May 8, 1989.

39. The preferential exchange rate system was essentially a subsidy paid to the government by the Central Bank, which in turn posted large losses in its foreign exchange transactions. The inflationary pressures arose because the government could not support current expenditures from current income and eventually had to raise prices for government services when it moved to abolish preferential exchange rates.

40. Romano, "Paraguay: Situación económica reciente."

5

Culture and Society

Stroessner's personal control over the political system is helped by Paraguay's very backwardness. Here is a rural nation with no really large city, no complex industrial economy, and no highly organized system of interest groups. The vast majority of the population is illiterate, ignorant, passive, and obedient. Public opinion, insofar as that is politically relevant, is limited to a small segment of the population. In order to rule an ambitious person has only to win over a core of loyal followers in that small segment, uproot those who . . . oppose him, and buy off the remainder.
—Paul H. Lewis, *Paraguay Under Stroessner*

CULTURE

Bilingualism

Little can be understood about Paraguayan culture without reference to the Guaraní language. Paraguay is a bilingual country, but, although nearly all Paraguayans can speak Guaraní, about half cannot speak Spanish. Article 5 of the 1967 constitution recognizes both Guaraní and Spanish as national languages. Spanish is the official language used exclusively in conducting government business; it is also the dominant language in commerce and in schools. But Guaraní is the national language par excellence, the language one learns by virtue of being born in Paraguay,[1] the "main, distinctive feature of the nation itself."[2] A non-Guaraní speaker is not considered a true Paraguayan.[3]

Paraguayans enjoy the distinction of being the only national group in the Western Hemisphere that speaks an aboriginal language (Guaraní) more widely than a European one. They are also the only group in the Western Hemisphere that accords an aboriginal language such a high degree of importance.[4] All Paraguayan presidents have been able to speak Guaraní, and many have used the language to gain political advantage while campaigning.

TABLE 5.1 Paraguayans Speaking Guaraní and/or Spanish (percent of population over age five)

Languages	Urban	Rural	Total
Only Guaraní	14	60	40
Guaraní and Spanish	71	31	49
Only Spanish	13	2	6
Others[a]	2	7	5

[a]About 122,000 people primarily spoke "other" languages in 1982. Most of these speakers were Mennonites (who speak a German dialect called Plattdeutsch) and Japanese and German agricultural colonists; a few were Korean and Chinese city dwellers.

Source: 1982 census figures provided by Graziella Corvalán.

TABLE 5.2 Predominant Home Language (percent)

	Asunción	Other urban	Rural (average)
Guaraní	9	33	75
Spanish	41	22	2
Spanish and Guaraní	49	42	22

Source: Adapted from Bartomeu Melià, Una nación, dos culturas, Asunción: R.P. Ediciones, 1988, p. 46.

Despite its widespread use, Guaraní has no standardized grammar or orthography.[5] Vocabulary used by Guaraní speakers varies and includes many words of Spanish origin. In addition, Paraguayan attitudes about Guaraní are contradictory. Whereas the ability to speak Guaraní carries no special social status (because everyone speaks it), knowledge of Spanish does confer status. Because it was the language of the conquistadores, the value of Spanish as a means of communication was never questioned. In addition, ability to speak Spanish is a mark of education. Nonetheless, monolingual Spanish speakers are relatively rare and have no standing in Paraguayan society.[6] As shown in Table 5.1, Paraguay also had about 122,000 speakers of other languages in 1982.[7] Most of these were Mennonites (who speak a German dialect called Plattdeutsch), along with Japanese and German agricultural colonists and a sprinkling of Korean and Chinese city dwellers.

Guaraní is spoken almost exclusively in some parts of rural Paraguay. About 90 percent of Paraguayans speak Guaraní with some degree of proficiency, about 6 percent speak only Spanish, and around half are bilingual.[8] An estimated 71 percent of Asunción residents speak both languages. Although the largest group of bilingual speakers is aged 15–45,[9] fully 70 percent of three- and four-year-olds speak only Guaraní: This indicates that Guaraní continues to predominate as the language most Paraguayans speak at home (see Table 5.2).

The fact that many Paraguayan children come to school as monolingual speakers of Guaraní has implications for education and literacy in Paraguay. Spanish was the only language permitted in the schools until the 1960s, when teachers were first allowed to use some Guaraní in the lower grades on an informal basis. Naturally, many children had difficulty following their lessons because the teacher was speaking to them in a foreign language. In the late 1980s, the education system began experimenting with bilingual education in the early grades.

Because Spanish is known far less widely and far more superficially than Guaraní, one may doubt the accuracy of the government's claim of a national Spanish literacy rate of 92 percent. One reason for this claim is that the government counts as literate any person who has attended primary school, however briefly. Many of these people may be able to write their name but not much else. School dropouts are a vexing problem in Paraguay: Fewer than half of elementary pupils complete their studies (see Table 5.3, below). Another piece of evidence that the official literacy figure is too high is the circulation figures for Asunción newspapers. The four Asunción dailies (the only daily newspapers in Paraguay) have a total daily circulation of about 250,000—a suspiciously low figure for a country with a population of 4 million and a supposed literacy rate of over 90 percent. In fact, according to census figures, the illiteracy rate in Paraguay for people over ten years old was 21 percent in 1982. In rural areas, the illiteracy rate for people over twenty years old was 29 percent for men and 38 percent for women.[10]

Spanish may carry more status than Guaraní in Paraguay, but Spanish usage probably is not as widespread as the figures indicate. In rural areas one encounters an almost entirely Guaraní-speaking culture. Spanish is spoken but often without much facility. People who can read Spanish aloud often have very little idea of what they are reading.[11] Most Spanish-speaking Paraguayans have to translate their thoughts from Guaraní. Even Paraguay's most accomplished literary figure, Augusto Roa Bastos, someone whose knowledge of Spanish is beyond reproach, describes his writing method as a process of translating from Guaraní into Spanish. Some professional linguists have concluded (1) that most Paraguayans (although they might not like to admit it) probably are incapable of thinking in Spanish,[12] and (2) that Paraguayans are not really bilingual but Guaraní-speakers who, for historical reasons, use Spanish widely in administration, education, and commerce. But few Paraguayans learn to write Guaraní, and although some newspapers include one or two pages of Guaraní, Paraguay has no national Guaraní press. Paraguay also lacks a widely published or vigorous Guaraní literature.[13]

Paraguay's historical development is responsible for the predominance but questionable status of Guaraní. Owing to the shortage of European women and to the willingness of the Guaraní Indians to ally themselves with the Spanish newcomers, the conquistadores took many wives and concubines from among the local women. Guaraní naturally was the language used in these households. Mestizo Paraguayans grew up speaking Guaraní; European-born men used Guaraní so habitually that they sometimes had trouble remembering how to speak Spanish. The predominance of Guaraní was such that colonial administrators had problems communicating with the colonists. Even clerics usually gave their sermons in Guaraní, by popular preference. The Jesuits took a keen interest in Guaraní as a mode of instruction and as an academic pursuit, producing Guaraní dictionaries and grammars and publishing books in Guaraní. Widespread racial mixing combined with limited immigration to inhibit the development of a Spanish-speaking social elite, such as those that appeared in Peru and Mexico. Instead of a rigidly stratified society, Paraguay was forced in the direction of social egalitarianism (see Chapter 2).[14]

The fortunes of Guaraní as a recognized linguistic medium have waxed and waned over the years. The leaders of Paraguay's independence movement banished Guaraní from the classroom, an action that had little effect on the population at large because Paraguay had so few schools. Public education deteriorated under José Gaspar Rodríguez de Francia (1814–1840) and did not revive until the reign of Carlos Antonio López (1841–1862). But even under López, education meant education in Spanish; the use of Guaraní in the schools was severely punished. Later, during the Triple Alliance War, Francisco Solano López discovered that Guaraní could be used with great effect as a symbol and rallying point for Paraguayan nationalism.[15]

The standing of Guaraní plummeted again after the Triple Alliance War (1864–1870), when Paraguay was occupied by Brazilians and Argentines. Guaraní became a source of embarrassment for an elite much impressed by the cultural achievements of Buenos Aires. A motion by a delegate to the 1870 constitutional congress to allow the use of Guaraní in the proceedings was greeted with hilarity and scorn by an overwhelming majority. As Argentine cultural hegemony grew and Paraguay mimicked Argentina's civil code, school system, and courts, the status of Guaraní shrank. None of this meant that Guaraní speakers declined in number. In fact, Spanish usage was largely confined to Asunción, where well-to-do Paraguayans had influence over the education system and could discourage their sons and daughters from learning Guaraní.[16]

This situation lasted until the Chaco War (1932–1935), when the Paraguayan high command banned the use of Spanish on the battlefield for security reasons. With Paraguayan nationalism once again a precious commodity, Guaraní was thrust into the forefront of the national consciousness. In 1933, enthusiastic theatergoers mobbed an opening night performance of a Guaraní play, and police were called to restore order. Present-day Paraguayans feel more comfortable using Guaraní to express their most intimate emotions, one reason that Guaraní poetry has caught on more than the use of Guaraní in other literary forms.

Paraguayans have mixed emotions about Guaraní. While some have derided it as "merely Indian," others have exaggerated its influence, trying to show that place names in foreign countries as far away as the Caribbean derive from Guaraní. The latter tendency may be a psychological reaction of people who want to feel proud of their language. For instance, expounding on many technical subjects in Guaraní is not possible at present because the language lacks the necessary specialized vocabulary. Yet many Paraguayans will insist that Guaraní expresses the most abstract of thoughts; their pride in Guaraní as a "great" language makes them reluctant to admit its limitations.[17] Clearly, most Paraguayans are quite "language conscious" and can be moved to rage or hilarity by the mere mention of the Guaraní language in a particular context. The delegates to the 1870 constitutional convention laughed uproariously at the suggestion that Guaraní be permitted in the discussions; they then voted overwhelmingly to disallow future motions about Guaraní. During the 1960s, a writer's request that a class of youngsters in a rural school speak in Guaraní occasioned a similar outburst.[18] Yet in some rural parts of Paraguay, a person who addresses monolingual Guaraní-speakers in Spanish risks being ridiculed. In general, despite everything, Paraguayans are very proud of their language; they will likely continue attempting to find ways to expand its use as a cultural medium.

Education

Paraguay has made significant progress in building schools and increasing enrollments during the post–World War II period (Table 5.3), but many problems remain. The registration figures for the primary grades show slow but steady progress (an increase of 30 percent from 1975 to 1988), although they have lagged behind the jump in secondary school enrollments, which increased 83 percent during the same period. Illiteracy has become a rural phenomenon. About 86 percent of eligible children register for primary school, a higher rate than in Bolivia, Brazil, or Colombia, but these figures are somewhat misleading because attendance rates in Paraguayan schools are poor and the dropout rate is high. The education system in Paraguay is also hampered by the tendency for pupils to repeat grades and by poorly staffed, poorly equipped buildings.

TABLE 5.3   Schools and School Enrollments in Paraguay

	1954	1975	1986
Primary pupils	254,000	452,500	580,000
Percentage of children enrolled	—	79.1	85.1
Secondary pupils	14,500	81,800	148,500
Percentage of children enrolled	—	—	24.0
University students		17,200	29,154
Primary schools	1,781	—	4,101
High schools	94	—	757

Sources: Interview with Marcos Martínez Mendieta, Paraguayan ambassador to the United States (November 21, 1988); M. A. Romano and J. Dinsmoor, "Informe socioeconómico: Paraguay," Washington, D.C.: Interamerican Development Bank (GN-1646), March 1989, p. IV-43.

Although the proportion of children attending school has risen in recent years, the dropout rate continues to be quite high. A 1980 survey showed that 62 percent of children nationwide (75 percent of rural children, 33 percent of urban children) fail to complete their elementary education.[19] The prevalence of monolingual Guaraní speakers of school age, especially in rural areas, contributes to the problems of the education system as whole. But socioeconomic causes such as the demand for agricultural labor, health problems, frequent changes of domicile, and lack of permanent domicile are probably more important. This implies that conditions outside the educational system as such may be impeding the effects of attempted improvements within the system. Given that conditions in the countryside are significantly worse than in the towns, the trend toward urbanization may go a long way toward improving educational levels generally.[20]

The trouble remains that relatively few Paraguayans complete the primary grades. As shown in Table 5.3, barely 1 first-grader out of 4 eventually enters secondary school. Moreover, around 10 percent of primary school students in any given year repeat a grade.[21] Although the number of schools seems adequate and well distributed, many rural primary schools offer only a few grades of instruction and many are seriously understaffed. Lack of qualified personnel and materials means that pupils will probably learn more slowly than they might otherwise.

Paraguay is an extremely young country, so demographic realities make educational issues even more pressing. In 1980, fully 44 percent of Paraguayans were under the age of fourteen; 70 percent were younger than twenty-six years old.[22] A resulting problem is that Paraguay has too few secondary schools. Fewer than 12 percent of secondary school–age students in rural areas attended school in 1986.[23] The ultimate limiting factor in education is money. In 1985, Paraguay spent less on education as a percentage of GDP (1.2 percent) than practically any country in South America. Even poorer Bolivia spent twice as much on education in terms of GDP (2.4 percent) as Paraguay.[24] As a result, Paraguayan teachers are very poorly paid, a condition that encourages the most talented of them to seek work in other sectors. Here again, the educational problem depends on solving the fiscal crisis, which will require a major tax reform (See Chapter 4).

The subject of university education has fewer complications. The country has two universities: one public, with 70 percent of the students (Universidad Nacional de Asunción, or UNA), the other private and religiously based, with 30 percent of the students (Universidad Católica de Asunción). Enrollments probably have fallen slightly in recent years, but this has some positive aspects because teaching quality and entrance requirements probably suffered during the 1970s and early 1980s when enrollments swelled. Even now, full professors are rare. In addition, students seem to concentrate in areas (law, social sciences, philosophy, and economics) that require no laboratories or special equipment but only verbal transmission of information. These favored subjects are not necessarily those that conform best with the actual economic needs of the country.[25]

Colonial education in Paraguay was mostly religious and confined mostly to the upper classes, who alone had the means to hire tutors or to send their children to study abroad. Francia's government did little to encourage education. Although Asunción had a few private schools, Francia closed the nation's only secondary school (the San Carlos Seminary) in 1822. By the mid-1880s, only around 14 percent of the population could read and write. Some progress was made on the national and university levels under the Liberals. By 1929 Paraguay had seven teacher-training schools, three high schools, a few technical schools, and an expanded curriculum in UNA that included sciences and medicine. However, education was probably poorly suited to the practical needs of illiterate peasant families, while upper-class education was probably not practical enough.[26]

Like those in many countries of the world, Paraguayan textbooks and teachers stress patriotic topics under the rubric of "Guaraní heritage," sometimes presenting folklore as fact. For instance, pupils memorize poems that extoll the great beauty of Paraguay's forests, skies, and streams. Much emphasis is placed on the superiority of the Guaraní language, race, and culture. Although instruction is in Spanish, pupils learn that Guaraní is superior to Latin and other European languages; that the Guaraní once had conquered all of South America and the Caribbean; that the Guaraní were not really Indians but were taller and had lighter complexions, higher brows, and lighter eyes than surrounding peoples; and that the Guaraní possessed highly developed music, art, and political organization and were not cannibals. The Paraguayan national character is held to be superior because of the fierceness, bravery, and amorousness of the men and the beauty and fearlessness of the women.[27]

Food, Drink, Arts, Crafts, and Music

Paraguay has a wide variety of unique culinary and artistic traditions. Anyone traveling by bus in Paraguay will see vendors approach the windows carrying baskets filled with homemade *chipas* (a hard cornbread made with cheese) and *sopa paraguaya*, which is a soft, tasty baked pudding (but not a dessert) made with cornmeal, eggs, and onions. Local soups include *bori bori* (meat and vegetables with corn and cheese), *soyo* (meat and vegetables), and *albóndigas* (meatball soup). *Palmitos* (palm hearts) have become a local favorite in recent years among urban dwellers, as have the large river fish *surubí* and *dorado*.

The national pastime is sipping *tereré*, an iced tea of yerba leaves that one drinks through a metal tube with a filter at the end (called a *bombilla*) from a hollowed out, often beautifully carved cow's horn (called a *guampa*). During the cold days of Paraguay's brief winter or early in the morning, the preferred drink is *maté*, which is yerba tea served hot, usually in a ceramic cup. Cane juice (*mosto*) is highly regarded by Paraguayans, as are *caña*, its distilled, alcoholic form, and *chicha*, a fermented beverage made from pineapple or maize.

The most typical Paraguayan meal is *asado* (barbecue), which is served at a *parrillada* (literally, "grill") restaurant where one may order a variety of grilled meats that are served with boiled manioc roots (*mandioca*). Almost every *parrillada* has a band (typically two guitars and a Paraguayan harp, differently constructed and tuned than a European harp) that performs the country's distinctive songs and ballads.

The larger *parrillada* restaurants may feature several bands and dancers who perform the bottle dance. During this spectacular performance, several dancers may appear on stage while one dancer in the middle dances with a bottle on her head. After a short while, a helper comes out and places a second bottle on top of the first. Sometimes the bottles are designed so that the neck of the one below fits into a groove in the bottom of the one above. The performance continues until the dancer has seven, eight, or even as many as fourteen bottles on her head. The helper adds (and removes) the bottles by climbing a tall ladder.

Local handicrafts include the renowned *ñanduti* lace (from Itagua city); fine, handmade *aho poi* cloth (from Yataity city); and pottery.

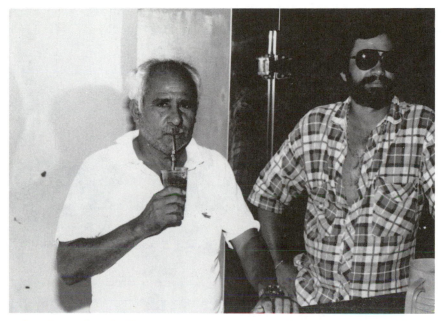

A favorite pastime in Paraguay: sipping *tereré* (a cold brew of yerba maté) from a *guampa*, or cow's horn cup.

Pottery today is mainly a decorative art. Paraguay's potters, all of whom are women, practice a unique but not very well known craft, concentrating on the human form in fanciful, sometimes erotic shapes, whether they are producing jars or figurines. Until recent decades many Paraguayan homes (even in Asunción) lacked running water. Families typically bought water from vendors on the street, storing it in their clay *cantero*, or water jar.

SOCIETY

The Roman Catholic Church

Until rather recently, the Roman Catholic church has had little influence in Paraguay's national and political affairs. Although the church in Paraguay is weaker than in some neighboring countries, at least 90 percent of Paraguayans are Roman Catholics. Rome created the first diocese in Paraguay in 1547, but because only twenty of the first forty bishops successfully reached their destination, the Paraguayan church often had no leader. The primary exceptions to the general weakness of the Paraguayan church were the Jesuits and the missions they organized

A typical Paraguayan band at a *parrillada* (barbecue) restaurant in Pedro Juan Caballero. The harp has a resonating chamber like a guitar and is tuned differently from a European harp.

during 1609–1767 (see Chapter 2). But the Jesuit organized and administered *reducciones* of southeastern Paraguay were independent of the formal church structure and separated from Asunción by weeks of arduous travel; the church hierarchy and the Paraguayan elite in Asunción welcomed the 1767 decree that expelled the Jesuits from Spain and its colonies.

During the nineteenth century, after José Gaspar Rodríguez de Francia confiscated church lands and closed the covents and the seminary of San Carlos, the country remained formally Roman Catholic but had few priests and little formal religious education.[28] Bishop Juan Sinforiano Borgarín, appointed in 1894 at age thirty-one, had the task of rebuilding the church in the wake of the Triple Alliance War, the antireligious heritage of Francia, and the indifference of the López dynasty. Borgarín became the first archbishop of Asunción in 1930. He was succeeded as archbishop in 1949 by Aníbal Mena Porta, who retired in December 1969. Monsignor Ismael Rolón Silvero led the Paraguayan church 1970 to 1989, a period that included a surge in church-supported social activism. In May 1989, Monsignor Felipe Santiago Benítez assumed the post of archbishop when Rolón retired.

A cautious institution during the first decades of the Stroessner regime, the Paraguayan church later responded strongly to the revolutionary changes wrought by the Vatican II conference in the early 1960s and by the meeting of the Latin American Catholic bishops in Medellín, Colombia, in 1968. Vatican II modernized the social message of the church; the Medellín conference stated a "preferential option for the poor" in its work. Since the late 1960s, the Catholic University in Asunción has played a critical role in providing training and research for reform-oriented Catholics in Paraguay. The Stroessner government often criticized the church for its militancy, accusing it of politicizing the university, the teaching faculty, and student organizations.

During 1968–1969, the church joined with the Christian Democratic party and the Christian labor unions to work in the countryside in the first efforts to protect the rights of rural workers. Church activists organized a series of Christian Agrarian Leagues (LACs) and worked diligently to mobilize the passive rural population. The LACs operated literacy programs, welfare services, and small cooperatives. Predictably, the Colorado party and the government responded with repression, both in 1969 and in 1975–1976. The LAC movement was finally destroyed after the arrest and deportation of many LAC leaders, despite vigorous protests from the Paraguayan Episcopal Conference (CEP), which represents the church leadership.

As relations between state and church deteriorated in the 1970s, the church fought back. On two separate occasions, the church excommunicated Minister of the Interior Sabino Montanaro and Chief of Police Francisco Brítez. Starting in 1971, Archbishop Rolón refused to sit on the Council of State, an advisory body to the government. Increased church involvement in human rights and social justice issues paralleled the change in policy by the U.S. government under President Jimmy Carter, particularly regarding the assertive role that the U.S. Embassy in Paraguay undertook in human rights. The increased involvement of the church also accompanied the rollback of repressive military regimes in South America that made Stroessner's Paraguay an anomaly.

In 1986, the Roman Catholic church was instrumental in initiating the National Dialogue, a series of discussions among social and political sectors on a wide range of issues including political participation, social justice, and the need for political pluralism in Paraguay. The government bitterly attacked the church, calling the discussions a "divisive" activity, but the dialogue played a key role in mobilizing the opposition and public opinion in the last years of Stroessner's government.

The historic visit of Pope John Paul II to Paraguay in May 1988 was another milestone in establishing the church as a serious and respected advocate of social justice and political liberty. Government efforts to manipulate the papal visit to reflect positively on the regime failed. When Stroessner attempted to cancel a planned meeting between the pope and the political opposition, the pope threatened to cancel the visit. Throughout his brief visit the pope called for stronger efforts by the regime to protect the human rights of all Paraguayans, to foster social peace, and to promote civic participation. In addition to his veiled calls for democratic reform, the pope strongly defended the right of Catholics to speak out against social injustice.[29] During the last months of the Stroessner regime, the church continued to promote the National Dialogue and to criticize the government for its policies of repression in the countryside and its lack of concern for social justice throughout the country.

On February 3, 1989 (the day of the coup against Stroessner; see Chapter 6), General Andrés Rodríguez publicly stated his aim to repair relations between the Paraguayan state and the church. Rodríguez then demonstrated his desire to mend fences on the evening of February 5, 1989, when he attended a memorial mass at the Asunción cathedral for those killed and injured in the coup. After the service, Rodríguez publicly greeted the archbishop of Paraguay, Monsignor Ismael Rolón Silvero. A photo of Rodríguez and Rolón sharing a warm embrace was given wide coverage by the Asunción press, which viewed the event as a sign of reconciliation. Given its institutional network and its positive record of defending human rights and democracy, the church is well positioned to help further the goals of political democracy and social justice in Paraguay in coming years.

The Status of Women

Though it is changing, Paraguay is still a conservative, male-dominated society. Paraguayan women were among the last in the Western world to vote in elections, a right they gained as recently as 1963.[30] Although changes to the civil code in recent years have given women protection in the division of marital property in the event of separation, divorce is still not a legal option in Paraguay. Yet broken marriages are common (women headed 18 percent of all households in 1982).[31] The women's movement as such is still embryonic. Paraguayan society frowns on women who demand things for themselves, branding them as "egoists" who have lost their femininity. This is not to say that Paraguayan women are marching in the streets demanding equal treatment or equal opportunity. Even politically active women are likely to fulfill their traditional roles within their families.[32]

Public health statistics for women are troubling. High maternal mortality rates (469 per 100,000 live births in 1980)[33] imply that women are not receiving the pre- or postnatal care that they need. Although abortion is a significant social issue in other Latin American countries (such as Brazil, where it is legal), it is still illegal in Paraguay. In general, although many women have jobs outside the home, they tend to earn less money than men. One reason is that women tend not to hold well-paying salaried positions as often as men; rather, they are apt to be independently employed in small businesses or as maids or laundresses. Men outnumber women in the labor market (four to one), where women have only a 20 percent participation rate.[34] Working women earned less than the minimum wage on average in 1986, and salaries for women in the private sector totaled less than half of male salaries.[35]

Women in Paraguay play important roles within the family and within the economy but have almost no power to influence public decision making on the local or national level. In other words, their political power is next to nil. Although a few women have seats in the Congress, women almost never hold positions of civil authority; a female mayor or judge is an extreme rarity in Paraguay. On the other hand, the economic role of women in Paraguay is very important, especially in the countryside. The economic contribution of Paraguayan women has always been crucial to society; the 1864–1870 holocaust of the Triple Alliance War (see Chapter 2), after which very few men were left alive, furnishes only one example.

Rural women in Paraguay perform all domestic work and most of the field work as well. They cook, collect firewood, tend the hearth, and raise the children. If a woman accompanies her husband on a trip, she carries their goods in a great basket on her head or back. Women also spin, weave, and dye cloth and carry water. With the exception of clearing land, plowing, and planting manioc, women do all the agricultural work as well, performing such tasks as planting, weeding (whether with hoe or machete), harvesting, and gathering wild fruits. Little wonder, perhaps, that feminist spokeswomen in Paraguay claim that peasant women are "raised to be servants."[36]

The arrival of the Spaniards in 1537 and their "alliance" with the Guaraní tribes (see Chapter 2) were disasters of the first magnitude for women. Overnight, women were transformed into concubines, field hands, and procreators—a chattel that could be bought, sold, traded, or even wagered in a game of cards. Women were valued only for the economic work and sexual services they could perform. Although some Spaniards doubtless felt genuine love for their multiple consorts, in general they did not exactly regard these Indian women as fully human. Often they thought nothing of cohabiting with sisters or with a mother and her daughters, which the Guaraní considered even more incestuous than the Spaniards did. Sometimes the *encomendero* would not permit a woman to nurse her own child because he required her services as a wet nurse. The colonial system killed more Indians than it produced mestizos; the Guaraní population took centuries to regain the level it had attained before the conquest.

Desperate in their new situation, as Paraguay "was being converted into a concentration camp of physically violated, . . . prostituted women," these Indian women resorted to suicide and murdering their children. As exploitation increased and the initial "friendship" between the races waned, the Spaniards resorted to kidnapping women from Indian villages. The frequent Indian revolts against Spanish authority (there were at least 23 rebellions between 1537 and 1660) were the direct result of these raids.[37]

Little changed regarding the condition of women for centuries after the conquest. The first female feminist thinkers and writers appeared in Paraguay after 1900, as part of the general cultural enlightenment that accompanied the first Liberal governments. During the 1980s, feminist circles in Asunción rediscovered the frankly feminist doctoral dissertation of Serafina Dávalos, Paraguay's first female lawyer. Entitled "Humanism," the 1907 dissertation analyzed the position of women in the lower, middle, and upper classes and proposed radical changes in the law to allow a massive incorporation of women into civil society.

The Chaco War offered women an opportunity for organizing independent groups, as much to help nurse the wounded as to help organize public administration. Because most of the leaders of these groups were mothers, daughters, or wives of Liberal party politicians, many were exiled and their groups disbanded after the February Revolution of 1936. But this "feminist boom" continued under Febrerista auspices as María Casati, an Italian woman with anarcho-syndicalist tendencies, organized the Feminine Union of Paraguay and founded a newsletter.[38]

By the late 1940s, Colorado and Liberal politicians were promising women absolute legal equality before the law, although not much was actually being done. By 1951, the League for Women's Rights (La Liga pro Derechos de la Mujer) was formed to struggle for equal rights. A 1954 law finally established a framework of legal rights for unmarried women and widows, but changed little about the status of married women.[39] Organizing for women's rights stagnated under Stroessner, as did all organizing activity not directly controlled by the Colorado party. Current and future opportunities for women will improve to the degree that Paraguay liberalizes in the post-Stroessner era. Nonetheless, in their struggle to break free of the roles that many societies have traditionally assigned to women, Paraguayan feminists identify their biggest enemy as the Roman Catholic church.

An upsurge in women's organizing activities, especially in Asunción, accompanied the general increase in social unrest that followed the abrupt end of the Itaipú boom. Groups of female writers and intellectuals began to study the social condition of women in Paraguay. Female journalists played a key role, publicizing the activities of various women's groups. By 1986, the women writers and intellectuals had helped prepare society for the beginnings of a public discussion of women's issues. One women's group that appeared at this time—Women for Democracy (Mujeres por la democracia)—became an important actor in the struggle against Stroessner. The group was largely organized by middle- and upper-class wives of politicians who were interested in politics and were tired of being *"pastelitos"*[40]—tired of having to cook for and organize the social functions of their husbands. Not overtly feminist, Mujeres por la democracia nonetheless helped advance the cause of all women in Paraguay by demonstrating the success of a women's group that was willing to struggle for social goals. A variety of women's groups have since emerged (many of them in Asunción), from associations of female lawyers to the Association of Rural Women (Coordinación de las mujeres campesinas). Nonetheless, no large, fully constituted, nationwide movement of women exists today in Paraguay.[41]

Paraguay's Indian Minority

Paraguayans speak Guaraní, an Indian language, and are descended from Indians and Europeans. However, they do not consider themselves Indians, nor should they, as their culture is thoroughly Hispanicized. Following Maybury-Lewis and Howe's definition, Paraguay's Indian community is made up of those descendants of the indigenous inhabitants of Paraguay who consider themselves distinct from the prevailing Paraguayan culture, who themselves are considered Indians by Paraguayans, and who speak an indigenous language different from the Guaraní of Paraguayan *campesinos*.[42]

Paraguay's Indian communities can be divided into 17 ethnic groups and 5 language families. Estimates of Indian population vary from 50,000 to 150,000 people; although they comprise only 1–3 percent of the population the Indians account for 10 percent of the very poorest part of Paraguayan society. All of these ethnic groups tend to live entirely on one side or the other of the Paraguay River. About two-thirds of Paraguay's Indians (13 of 17 ethnic groups) live in the Chaco. Of the 4 groups that live on the east bank of the Paraguay River, the 3 largest speak languages related to Guaraní, while the fourth, the Aché, speaks an unrelated language.[43]

When the Spanish arrived in Paraguay in 1537, they found the country around Asunción inhabited by the Guaraní. A naturally friendly race of gentle and generous disposition, the Guaraní inhabited a far-flung area stretching from the Guyana Highlands in Brazil to the Uruguay River. Frequently at war, the Guaraní welcomed the Spaniards as friends and allies. In return for a military alliance, the Guaraní gave the Spaniards the status of chiefs and access to Guaraní women as wives and concubines (see Chapter 2). Marital relations among the Guaraní were loose; polygamy and concubinage were widespread, but divorce could be initiated by women as well as men. Guaraní chiefs often had 20 or 30 concubines, whom they shared freely with visitors. Like the area's other tribes, the Guaraní were occasional cannibals who ate their most valiant enemies, hoping thereby to gain the enemies' bravery and power. Yet the Guaraní looked to the Spaniards for protection from the much fiercer tribes surrounding them.[44]

In contrast to the hospitable attitude of the Guaraní, the Chaco tribes carried an implacable hostility toward the Europeans and their Indian allies. These fierce people were formidable enemies. Travelers reported that Guaykurú warriors (known today as the Toba, Toba-Lengua, or Emok) could lasso and mount wild horses in full gallop and catch deer bare-handed. In fact, Paraguayan towns remained open to Indian attack until well into the nineteenth century.[45] Under Spanish rule, this chronic insecurity further impoverished an already poor colony, because men had to serve in the colonial militia at their own expense.

If the inaccessible thorn forest of the Chaco remained a veritable "Palestine for the savages"[46] for centuries, Paraguay proper also afforded ample opportunities for seminomadic tribes of hunters and gatherers or for slash-and-burn agriculturalists. Much of the country well to the east of Asunción was sparsely inhabited forest where surviving Indian groups could pursue their traditional lifestyles and avoid repression or assimilation by the mestizo majority. However, some changes began to appear during the nineteenth century. By wiping out half of Paraguay's population, the Triple Alliance War postponed economic development in eastern Paraguay for decades. Yet the government land sales, pursued with vigor after war's end, led to land commercialization that ultimately proved disastrous for the Indians.

The situation in the Chaco remained largely unchanged until the 1930s. Ranching, *quebracho* production, and missionary activities steadily increased along the periphery of the Chaco. A major event was the arrival of several waves of Mennonite[47] settlers from Canada and Europe starting in 1926. The Mennonites established their capital near the exact center of the Paraguayan Chaco, at Filadelfia, and soon began hiring Indians as farm laborers. The settlers only started to have a serious effect on Indian life when their agricultural colonies began to prosper in the 1950s. In general, the Chaco's impenetrability, the river barrier, and Indian hostility toward the outside world kept the traditional Indian areas unmolested until the Chaco War (1932–1935) turned these lands into battlegrounds. Some Indians participated in the fighting as soldiers or scouts; many were forced to flee. More permanent changes came after World War II, with the construction of the Trans-Chaco highway and a bridge over the Paraguay River at Asunción, both completed by 1980. In particular, in 1960 the Mennonites began to offer employment, medical and educational benefits, and a land settlement scheme to Indians. As a result, at least 10,000 Indians have settled in the Mennonite area.[48]

The most serious challenge to Indians between the Paraguay and Paraná rivers came during the 1960s and 1970s. In 1963, the government began a policy of encouraging *campesinos* to settle in the eastern forest regions near the Brazilian border, forcing Paraguayans and Indians into contact, mostly with tragic results. Paraguayan and Brazilian settlers poured into this once neglected, sparsely populated area, dispossessing the Indians and forcing them to move elsewhere. The start of construction at Itaipú gave a big push to development pressures in eastern Paraguay, increased land values, brought in thousands of new people, encouraged further deforestation, and generally increased pressure on the eastern Indian communities.

Paraguay's Indians face many problems, but chief among them are landlessness and persecution due to prejudice. As was common throughout the Americas, native Indians seldom retained title to the land they had inhabited for millennia. Although the new settlers coveted Indian lands, the entire concept of private land ownership was alien to the Indians. Not surprisingly, therefore, not many Indians are landowners. Landlessness damages Indian culture and society by robbing it of security and cohesion; destroys its traditional spiritual connection with the land; and makes Indians destitute, dependent on handouts, prone to illnesses because of inadequate diet, etc. With the general development of the country, hunting and slash-and-burn agriculture are disappearing from Paraguay as viable lifestyles. Instead, Indians are increasingly dependent for their survival on money wages at low-paying, tenuous jobs.

Despite their own Indian heritage, many Paraguayans regard Indians as dirty subhumans not far removed from animals.[49] This attitude, when combined with increased population pressures in eastern forest areas, produced a genocidal situation for the Aché tribe.[50] Killing and enslavement of Aché by Paraguayans had been common practice for centuries prior to the great population movements of the 1960s and 1970s. With contacts between the forest-dwelling, hunting-and-gathering Aché and settlers becoming more common, Paraguayans and Brazilians mounted Aché "hunts." The government established a reservation for the Aché, but there the situation grew worse, if possible. At the reservation, the

Aché were exposed to the depradations of a drunken manager who embezzled supplies, sexually abused Aché women, beat people, sold children into slavery, exploited Aché labor, suppressed their culture, and failed to provide elementary medical care. Many surviving Aché died in epidemics in 1972. The last recorded raid occurred in 1974, mainly because few if any Aché remained in the forest. The bulk of the 1,000 or so surviving Aché now live with missionaries.[51]

Indeed, missionaries maintain ambiguous relations with Paraguay's Indian groups, influencing them in far-reaching and fundamental ways. By trying to convert Indians to Christianity, thereby radically altering Indian culture and beliefs, missionaries may introduce fundamental changes to Indian society, subvert group identity, rob Indians of self-confidence, and undermine Indian self-respect. On the other hand, Indians can hardly consider going back entirely to their old ways and beliefs. In addition, few people besides missionaries are willing to offer aid to Indians. Missionaries may offer Indians the only protection they have in an otherwise hostile world, but in so doing, the missionaries increase Indians' dependence on them.[52]

One of the few examples of successful Indian adaptation to the prevailing cultural and political realities in Paraguay are the Mac'á. Their traditional area of settlement—directly across the river from Asunción— gave them some prominence and recognition in the capital. But their greatest boon was their patron and protector, General Juan Belaieff, a white Russian who fought in the Chaco War. Belaieff had used Mac'á as scouts during the war and launched a personal crusade on their behalf at war's end. His public relations efforts from 1938 to 1943 brought a Mac'á theatrical tour as far as Buenos Aires, but his most important accomplishment was getting 355 acres of land where the Mac'á lived deeded in their name. This group of about 1,000 survives today from the tourist trade. Mac'á hawking gaudy handicrafts are ubiquitous in downtown areas of Asunción. They also lead tours of their home village. Far from destroying village life, this arrangement helps preserve it. The Mac'á lands are separated from the city by the river and are surrounded by a roadless swamp, which helps preserve their isolation. In addition, though they value the income-producing aspects of commercializing their village life, the Mac'á carefully manage the movements of their guests within the village. To the rear of the garish tourist areas a vibrant culture and village life continues.[53]

Labor in Paraguay

Labor movements in Paraguay have always been marginal players in national events,[54] mainly because of their small size: Paraguay has

Mac'á Indians selling trinkets in Asunción.

experienced little industrialization during the twentieth century and is one of the least industrialized countries in South America. Nor has labor, concentrated in a few towns, ever forcefully defended the interests of the rural poor and disadvantaged. Peasant movements rarely have organized themselves as structured units to defend the rights of agricultural workers; rather they have been movements of social protest. In addition, the repressive Paraguayan state almost always has discouraged the growth of labor movements by inhibiting and controlling efforts to organize rural and urban workers.

The earliest efforts to organize urban workers took place during the first decades of the twentieth century. Leadership was provided by anarcho-syndicalists who organized the first craft unions and mutual benefit societies in Asunción. In 1917, small groups of artisans (dominated by shoemakers, bakers, and printers) founded the Regional Workers Central of Paraguay (CORP). The political environment of the 1920s encouraged labor mobilization. Strikes were frequent, and the first recorded collective bargaining between labor and management took place. The Paraguayan Communist party (PCP) used the incipient labor groups to create the National Workers Confederation (CNT) in 1930, which purported to represent all existing labor organizations. A nationwide strike was called in 1931 but the government used the occasion to imprison the CNT leadership and to dissolve the country's labor organizations.

When hostilities ceased in the Chaco in 1935, labor reemerged as a component of a widespread social movement for radical change. Labor activists who had fought in the war against Bolivia participated in the National Association of Ex-Combatants, organized in 1935. Many had been active before the war in the Liga Nacional Independiente, which was organized in 1928 by Juan Stefanich and other intellectuals.

The February Revolution of 1936 introduced changes in the status accorded to labor. The Febreristas purported to speak for the workers— but from a distinctly authoritarian perspective. Colonel Rafael Franco's Decree-Law 152 of March 10, 1936, assigned control of labor-industrial relations to the Interior Ministry for one year. In June 1936, a Department of Labor was created and proceeded to define workers' rights and interests. But the attitude of the government was puzzling. Though it recognized the "rights" of organized labor, it expected labor to support fully all government measures in the economic and social fields. Labor demurred. A number of strikes and labor walkouts occurred during the short-lived Franco regime. When the army overthrew Franco in August 1937, relations between the government and labor already were tense.

The tumultuous years of the Paiva and Estigarribia governments did little to improve the status of organized labor. The Liberal governments were suspicious of labor and of the strong role Febreristas played in labor organizations. Estigarribia's new constitution, implemented in August 1940, gave the state wide powers to intervene in economic and social affairs. It soon became obvious that organized labor would be given a corporatist, paternalistic role in the New Paraguay. Estigarribia's death and Morínigo's succession in the same year ended even the faint hope of labor-government cooperation. The labor confederation was closed by the new government, its leaders were exiled or jailed, and a new and compliant Workers Council of Paraguay was created to represent the interests of workers.

Labor became a pawn in the political game that followed World War II. All of the parties purported to have a labor wing. Labor leaders were actively involved in the violence that accompanied the 1947 civil war, but they generally sided with the rebels against the Morínigo-Colorado alliance. When the rebellion was crushed, all party labor groups were outlawed with the exception of the Republican Workers Organization (ORO), which was controlled by the Colorado party. The ORO called a workers' congress in 1951, under government auspices, and renamed itself the Paraguayan Confederation of Workers (CPT).

Stroessner was frankly and openly anti-union and used the CPT to coopt, disrupt, and paralyze the labor movement. Only about 2 percent of the total economically active population is unionized in Paraguay, and the vast majority of this group are members of the CPT. Public sector workers have been excluded from the union movement; the CPT claims to represent over 90 percent of the industrial workers in the country. Following a general strike by the CPT in 1958, its leadership went into exile and organized the Paraguayan Confederation of Workers in Exile (CPTE), which has been recognized by the International Labor Organization (ILO).

The Ministry of Justice and Labor, the Colorado party, and the police for decades have manipulated the labor movement. New unions must have the approval of the ministry; only loyal Colorado party members are allowed to occupy union leadership positions; and the police have been vigilant in seeking out dissidents in the labor movement and discouraging criticism of the regime's economic policy.

In 1985, after the outbreak of a strike wave that it could not control, the regime allowed the Inter-Union Movement of Workers (MIT) to organize as a formal alternative to the CPT. The MIT coalition includes the Bank Workers Confederation, the Paraguayan Journalists Association, the Construction Workers Union, the Trade and Commerce Workers Union, the Graphic Workers Association, the Paraguayan Theater Center, the Union of Social Workers, and the Union of Collective Transportation Workers. However, in 1987 the U.S. Congress suspended Paraguay's status as a beneficiary under the Generalized Systems of Preferences (GSP) program, when Paraguay was found not to be in compliance with the GSP requirements regarding internationally recognized workers' rights.

The situation of the workers in the countryside is even more marginal than that in the urban centers. The government crushed the attempts by the Roman Catholic church to organize agrarian leagues in the countryside during the 1970s. During the 1980s, four national, autonomous peasant organizations were formed: the Paraguayan Peasant Movement (MCP) in 1980; the National Coordinating Committee for Small Farmers (CONAPA) in 1985 (CONAPA comprised regional organizations that had emerged in the late 1970s with support from Protestant and Roman Catholic church groups); the National Peasant Union in 1984; and the National Peasant Organization (ONAC) in 1986, which emerged with support from the Christian Democrats.

The work of the rural peasant organizations has focused on the desparate need for more equitable land distribution and land title legalization in Paraguay. Large tracts of land have been sold to agro-industrial interests, both domestic and foreign; Brazilians in particular have bought large portions of northeastern Paraguay. A series of land occupations by land-hungry peasants has swept Paraguay since the mid-

1980s and continues under the Rodríguez regime. Typically the land seizures are condemned as illegal by the government, and a good deal of violence and confusion usually results from government and landowners' efforts to evict the squatters. Paraguayan churches have been staunch supporters of efforts to encourage land reform, to reserve rural Paraguay for Paraguayans, and to provide minimal standards of law and order in the rural sector.

The February 1989 coup freed private sector workers to form and join unions of their choice without prior authorization (public sector workers are still subject to laws that prohibit them from organizing). Unlike the Stroessner regime, which frequently withheld legal recognition, often arbitrarily, for political reasons, the Rodríguez Labor Ministry soon began to recognize labor unions that met the legal requirements. By the beginning of 1990, the some 200 unions had achieved recognition.

By the beginning of 1990, most Paraguayan trade unions had broken free of government and Colorado party control. A second labor central (in addition to the government-controlled CPT), the National Workers Central (CNT), was formed in July 1989, and a third, the Unified Workers Central (CUT), emerged in August 1989. Legally recognized in October 1989, CUT began to dominate the labor scene after the CPT fell prone to internal divisions. At that time, the MIT (not a labor organizing central per se), had about 30 member unions.

Under the new regime, workers are free to hold meetings, stage protests, and organize, but some problems remain. The right to strike is still problematic in Paraguay because legal recognition of a strike can take literally years to obtain, as it involves a complex process of factfinding, arbitration, and adjudication. None of the walkouts staged in 1989 was declared legal. Also, the government harassed selected labor leaders, such as Efigenio Lisboa, a Ciudad del Este trade unionist who was arrested twice in 1989 and spent much of the year behind bars. In October 1989 police arrested three CUT activists for leading a march on the National Palace and used water hoses to break up demonstrations by workers protesting the arrests.

In addition, in December 1989, Paraguayan troops shot and killed two striking Itaipú dam workers and wounded several others who were trying illegally to block an access road. In the aftermath of the violence, which shocked labor, management, and society as a whole, government negotiators insisted that all parties to the dispute sit down to negotiate a settlement, putting an end to the strike.

Public Health

The biggest problems affecting Paraguay's public health are the poverty of the rural part of its population, the country's shortage of trained medical staff, and publicly supplied drinking water and sewerage service. However, the relative compactness of the country's population of only 4 million, concentrated as it is in a small portion of the national territory (within a few dozen kilometers to the south and east of Asunción), tends to reduce health sector costs and increase efficiency. Budget problems (see Chapters 4 and 5) and skimpy sources of government finance (that is, low rates of taxation) contribute to health care inadequacy in Paraguay. Still, the availability of international aid grants has offset some of these disadvantages in the recent past. Paraguay spends less on health care as a proportion of GDP than Chile, Ecuador, Peru, and Uruguay, but health sector spending per capita is not nearly so low. Paraguay's public health status is by no means the worst on the continent. For instance, Paraguay's infant mortality rate of 49 per 1,000 live births compares favorably with infant mortality in Brazil (68 per 1,000 live births), Colombia (61), and Peru (90). Consequently, Paraguay's public health occupies a middle position with respect to its South American neighbors.[55]

Poor environmental conditions cause much of Paraguay's infant mortality. During the 1980s, the four leading causes of infant mortality in Paraguay were diarrhea, pneumonia, malnutrition, and infections, in that order. All four are diseases conditioned by a newborn's home environment. Another indication that environmental causes (among them, malnutrition) are to blame is that the majority of infant deaths occur during the last year or two of infancy (defined as ages zero through four, inclusive). Asunción's lower rate of infant mortality (37 per 1,000 live births compared with 49 countrywide) implies that health care, nutrition, and sanitary conditions are all better in the capital, and reflects the lack so far of a pronounced trend toward urban migration in Paraguay. Malnutrition as a cause of death among infants increased in importance during the 1980s, moving from fourth place to third. Although clearly more needs to be done—malnutrition affects about one-fifth of the infant population—it accounts for only 1.7 deaths per 100,000 inhabitants in the general population, and its importance for Paraguay should not be exaggerated. Like other deficiency diseases (such as anemia and goiter), malnutrition seems largely confined to the rural and indigenous sectors of the population. An additional problem that requires immediate attention is that roughly one-third of the children in Paraguay have not been vaccinated against polio or measles.[56]

According to 1984 government figures (the latest statistics available), the public health status of Paraguay's adult population is beginning to approximate that of the developed world. For instance, life expectancy regardless of sex is about 68 years at birth. The death rate is 6.6 per 1,000 inhabitants. The leading causes of death among adult Paraguayans are the familiar triumvirate of heart disease, strokes, and cancer, followed by two "underdeveloped world" diseases, diarrhea and pneumonia.

Most Paraguayans have no access to publicly supplied drinking water or sewerage services. As of 1980, piped water and piped sewerage services reached only about 18 and 7 percent of the total population, respectively.[57] CORPOSANA, Paraguay's publicly owned water and sewer provider, is active only in towns with more than 4,000 people. Yet it reaches only 38.5 percent of its client population with piped water and only 28.3 percent with sewerage service. Although tuberculosis, another indicator of poor living conditions, slipped from seventh to tenth place as a cause of death among the general population between 1981 and 1984, malnutrition advanced from tenth to ninth place.[58]

As mentioned already, Paraguay suffers from a lack of state funding for health care—a great problem because nearly all health care in Paraguay (97 percent) is publicly provided. Low salaries, a result of low spending, probably are the main reason why Paraguay has so few doctors and nurses. In 1980 (no 1984 statistics are available), the country had only 5.1 doctors and 2.4 nurses for every 10,000 people. This works out to one doctor for slightly fewer than 2,000 people (1:1,961) and one nurse for slightly more than 4,000 (1:4,167). Indeed, the scarcity of personnel is starting to slow the entire system down by causing some health outlets to close. Some evidence exists that insufficient funding for recurrent expenditure (as opposed to investment) also has led to a drop in utilization of public health care facilities in recent years.[59]

Foreign aid, which normally is earmarked only for capital investment, has played an important role in Paraguay's most recent health care picture but has distorted spending patterns. For example, the ratio of current versus capital spending in 1975 was almost 23 to one; by 1981 the ratio had dropped to one to one, and it increased slightly in 1983 to 1.7 to one. Almost all of the increase in capital investment was supplied by foreign aid. The figures denote a serious lack of balance between recurrent expenditures and investment in Paraguay's public health sector, a solution that ultimately depends on a long overdue fiscal reform to make available more funds for recurrent spending needs. Nonetheless, the government's 486 diverse health establishments (167 added between 1973 and 1983) provide health care for an estimated 75 percent of the population.[60] Providing the remaining 25 percent with adequate health care is a challenge that remains to be met.

NOTES

1. Joan Rubin, *National Bilingualism in Paraguay*, The Hague: Mouton, 1968.

2. José Pedro Rona, "The Social and Cultural Status of Guaraní in Paraguay," in William Bright (ed.), *Sociolinguistics*, The Hague: Mouton, 1966, pp. 277–298. A Spanish version of this article is contained in Graziella Corvalán and German de Granada (eds.), *Sociedad y lengua: Bilingüismo en el Paraguay* (Vol. 1), Asunción: Centro Paraguayo de Éstudios Sociológicos, 1983, pp. 233–267.

3. Ibid.

4. Haiti is the only other obvious example of bilingualism in Latin America, but it differs from Paraguay in that far fewer Haitians who speak Creole can also speak French (15 percent in Haiti compared with 50 percent in Paraguay). Another difference is that Creole, unlike Guaraní, is not an aboriginal language. Although countries like Peru count numerous speakers of Quechua and Aymara, Peru's urban elites shun these languages, speaking Spanish exclusively as a badge of social status. But Paraguayans of all social classes speak Guaraní (Rubin, *National Bilingualism*).

5. Rona, "Social and Cultural Status of Guaraní."

6. Ibid., pp. 286, 293.

7. 1982 census figures supplied by Graziella Corvalán during interview, February 13, 1989.

8. Some authors feel that these data exaggerate the number of people who speak Spanish (Rona, "Social and Cultural Status of Guaraní," pp. 283–285).

9. About 59 percent of those aged 15–45 were bilingual in 1962 (Bartomeu Melià, "Hacia una 'tercera lengua' en el Paraguay," in Graziella Corvalán and German de Granada (eds.), *Sociedad y lengua: Bilingüismo en el Paraguay*, Asunción: Centro Paraguayo de Estudios Sociológicos, 1983, p. 127).

10. María Victoria Heikel, "Ser mujer en Paraguay: Estadísticas de la discriminación, según datos censales de 1982," in Encuentro nacional de mujeres, *Por nuestra igualdad ante la ley*, Asunción: R. P. Ediciones, 1987, p. 31.

11. Lorenzo Livieres Banks and Juan Santiago Dávalos, "Las lenguas de Paraguay," in Graziella Corvalán and German de Granada (eds.), *Sociedad y lengua: Bilingüismo en el Paraguay*, Asunción: Centro Paraguayo de Estudios Sociológicos, 1983, p. 74.

12. William Bright (ed.), *Sociolinguistics*, The Hague: Mouton, 1966, p. 285.

13. Rona, "Social and Cultural Status of Guaraní," pp. 285–286.

14. Rubin, "National Bilingualism," pp. 24–25.

15. Ibid., p. 27. During the nineteenth century, merely using Guaraní at school within earshot of the teacher was grounds for corporal punishment. A student could be disciplined with four or five lashes for this offense.

16. Ibid., pp. 27–28.

17. Rona, "Social and Cultural Status of Guaraní," pp. 287–288.

18. Rubin, "National Bilingualism," pp. 27–28, 80.

19. Aníbal Miranda, *Desarrollo y pobreza en Paraguay*, Rosslyn, Va.: Inter-American Foundation, 1982, p. 144.

20. Ibid.

21. M. A. Romano and J. Dinsmoor, *Informe socioeconómico: Paraguay*, Washington, D.C.: Interamerican Development Bank (GN-1646), March 1989, p. IV-44, Table IV-12.

22. Miranda, *Desarrollo y pobreza,* pp. 128, 143–144.

23. Romano and Dinsmoor, *Informe socioeconómico.*

24. Ibid., p. IV-43.

25. Ibid.

26. Elman R. Service and Helen S. Service, *Tobatí: Paraguayan Town,* Chicago: University of Chicago Press, 1954, pp. 227–228.

27. Ibid., pp. 231–233.

28. Jerry W. Cooney, "The Destruction of the Religious Orders in Paraguay, 1810–24." *The Americas,* 36:2, October 1979, pp. 177–198.

29. Roberto Suro, "Pope Lectures Paraguay Leader on Human Rights," *New York Times,* May 17, 1988, p. A11.

30. *La liga Paraguaya de los derechos de la mujer* formed in 1961 and waged a successful two-year campaign for women's suffrage under the slogan "El extrañero vota, la paraguaya no" ("Foreigners vote in Paraguay but not Paraguayan women") (Line Bareiro and Esther Prieto, "La condición legal de la mujer en el Paraguay: Parte general," in Encuentro nacional de las mujeres, *Por nuestro igualdad ante la ley,* Asunción: R. P. Ediciones, 1987, p. 79).

31. Heikel, "Ser mujer en Paraguay," p. 43.

32. Interview with Line Bareiro, February 13, 1989.

33. World Bank, *World Development Report: 1988,* New York: Oxford University Press, 1988, p. 286, Table 33.

34. Heikel, "Ser mujer en Paraguay," p. 36.

35. Graziella Corvalán, Mirtha M. Rivarola, and Olga M. Zarza, "Discriminación de la mujer en la actualidad en el Paraguay," in Encuentro Nacional de las Mujeres, *Por nuestra igualdad ante la ley,* Asunción: R. P. Ediciones, 1987, pp. 22–23.

36. Interview with Line Bareiro, February 13, 1989.

37. Bartomeu Melià, "Para una historia de la mujer Paraguaya," in *Una nación, dos culturas,* Asunción: R. P. Ediciones, 1988, pp. 79–88.

38. Graziella Corvalán, "La acción colectiva de las mujeres urbanas en el Paraguay," in Domingo M. Rivarola (ed.), *Los movimientos sociales en el Paraguay,* Asunción: Centro Paraguayo de Estudios Sociológicos, 1986, pp. 107–108. Casati's newsletter was called "Por la mujer y para la mujer que trabaja y piensa."

39. Interview with Line Bareiro, February 13, 1989.

40. A *pastelito* is a little pastry or sweet.

41. Interview with Line Bareiro, February 13, 1989.

42. David Maybury-Lewis and James Howe, *The Indian Peoples of Paraguay and Their Prospects,* Peterborough, N.H.: Cultural Survival, 1980, p. 7.

43. Ibid.

44. For more on the early history of Paraguay's Indian peoples, see Harris Gaylord Warren, *Paraguay: An Informal History,* Norman: University of Oklahoma Press, 1949; Philip Caraman, *The Lost Paradise,* London: Sidgwick & Jackson, 1975; George Pendle, *Paraguay: A Riverside Nation,* London: Royal Institute of International Affairs, Oxford University Press, 1967; Charles A. Washburn, *The History of Paraguay* (in 2 vols.), New York: AMS Press, 1973 (original printing, Boston: Lee and Shepard, 1871).

45. John Hoyt Williams, *The Rise and Fall of the Paraguayan Republic, 1800–1870*, Austin: Institute of Latin American Studies, University of Texas Press, 1979, pp. 3–7.

46. John Hoyt Williams, "Paraguayan Isolation Under Dr. Francia: A Reevaluation," *Hispanic American Historical Review*, 52:1, February 1972, p. 102. Williams quotes Martín Dobrizhoffer, S.J.: "Such is the aspect of the Province of the Chaco—the Spaniards consider it the theater of their misery, and to the Indians, it is their Elyseum, their Palestine" (Dobrizhoffer, *Historia de los Abipones*, 2 vols., Resistencia, Argentina, 1967–1968, I: 221).

47. The Mennonites are members of a Protestant religious order founded in Europe in 1526.

48. Maybury-Lewis and Howe, *Indian Peoples of Paraguay and Their Prospects*.

49. Ibid., pp. 106–107.

50. Richard Arens, *Genocide in Paraguay*, Philadelphia: Temple University Press, 1976. Maybury-Lewis and Howe dispute Arens's contention that persecution of Paraguayan Indians was government policy during this period.

51. Maybury-Lewis and Howe, *Indian Peoples of Paraguay and Their Prospects*, pp. 26, 34–50.

52. Ibid.

53. Ibid., pp. 50–51.

54. As general references to this topic, see Riordan Roett and Amparo Menéndez-Carrión, "Paraguay," in Gerald Michael Greenfield and Sheldon Maram (eds.), *Latin American Labor Organizations*, Westport, Conn.: Greenwood Press, 1987, pp. 595–606, and *Country Reports on Human Rights Practices for 1989*, U.S. Department of State, February 1990, pp. 703–707.

55. Despite these optimistic 1984 figures, the government has no reliable up-to-date statistics that show how the economic crisis of the 1980s may have affected Paraguay's health status. See M.A. Romano and J. Dinsmoor, *Informe socioeconómico: Paraguay*, Washington, D.C.: Interamerican Development Bank (GN-1646), March 1989, pp. II-17–19 and IV-35–40.

56. Ibid.

57. See Miranda, *Desarrollo y Pobreza en Paraguay*, p. 156.

58. Romano and Dinsmoor, *Informe socioeconómico*, pp. II-17–19 and IV-35–40.

59. Ibid.

60. Paraguay's health care service comprises four distinct levels of increasing size, specialization, and locale. For instance, rural dispensaries, serve communities of fewer than 2,000 inhabitants, who may be widely dispersed; hospitals with more than 50 beds and all specialty services are found exclusively in the larger towns or in the capital.

6

Politics and Government

The course the armed forces under my command have taken today is directed toward realizing a democracy based on equal opportunity for all political parties. . . . For human rights to be a tangible reality and not a mere wish, democracy must be real, not just a facade. . . . It must have a strong and independent judicial branch. . . . Within this democracy the right to express opinions and the right to meet peacefully must be respected so that each and every Paraguayan can have the same opportunities, with special privileges for no one.

—General Andrés Rodríguez, February 3, 1989

Tobatí: Paraguayan Town, by Elman and Helen Service, appeared in 1954 (see epigraph, Chapter 3), the same year that General Alfredo Stroessner overthrew the government of Federico Chaves and was elected president of the republic. Forty years after the Services left Paraguay, another general, Andrés Rodríguez, overthrew Stroessner and was elected to serve out his term as president.

Enough has changed in Paraguay since 1948–1949, when the Services conducted their research, to make their book quite out-of-date. But an astonishing number of other things have not changed. True, the middle class is bigger today, the country is more urbanized, literacy is up, and public opinion is more important than it was forty years ago. But Paraguayan society is still largely depoliticized. Politicians still have to worry about being overthrown by a coup. Parties are still composed of "factions of would-be officeholders."[1] Most important, the army still occupies a position of supreme power in Paraguay.

Stroessner managed to stabilize the inherent volatility of Paraguay's politics and held power for thirty-five years, nearly a full decade longer than José Gaspar Rodríguez de Francia's term. This was a remarkable feat in a country where most presidents did not complete their first term. Stroessner survived and prospered by suppressing factionalism, strengthening the bonds between the army, the Colorado party, and the government bureaucracy (the so-called triad), intensifying the Colorado

113

party's commitment to himself, and dominating the political process in the countryside.

Ironically, the man who came to symbolize the total stagnation and unchangeability of Paraguayan politics—Alfredo Stroessner—also presided over a period of great change. By the late 1960s, Paraguay began to feel the stiff breezes of modernization. These "winds of change" were spawned by the economic boom of the post–World War II years, by the Cold War, and by development pressures in neighboring Brazil and Argentina. Stability itself induced economic growth. But Stroessner was careful to take personal credit for events, such as the construction of Itaipú, that were largely not his own doing. How Stroessner's government came about, how it worked, and why it ended form a large part of the discussion in this chapter.

The February 3, 1989, coup that overthrew Stroessner was directed by one of his closest associates, General Andrés Rodríguez, who immediately announced that he would lead the country toward democracy. In itself, the coup represented no basic change at all in Paraguay's political heart: One general overthrew another general in a bloody coup that the voters were then permitted to ratify. In some countries, generals who become president resign their military commissions before taking office. Not so in Paraguay, where, it seems, a general can "order" his citizens to be free. Whatever his intentions, Rodríguez will not be able to rule as long or as dictatorially as Stroessner did: Paraguay's internal conditions and external relations will not permit it. Whether Paraguay is headed toward genuine democracy is addressed in the final part of this chapter.

PERSONALIST POLITICS AND *CAUDILLISMO*

Politics and political parties in Paraguay are based on patron-client relationships that give rise to *caudillismo* and political factionalism.[2] The political system has its roots in the aftermath of the Triple Alliance War (1864–1870), a time when Paraguayans faced defeat, foreign economic domination, and economic insecurity. Francia's system—based on state ownership of the land, state control of the economy, and strict limits on the economic activities of foreigners—was breaking down. Land sales to foreign speculators were forcing thousands of peasants into penury or exile. Foreign interests and corrupt politicians controlled most of the country's assets while dubious financial manipulations plunged Paraguay further into debt. Society was prostrate—unable to produce enough jobs, access to land, or settled legal conditions to guarantee survival on a purely impersonal, objective basis. Under these conditions, it was natural

Demonstrators at the February 11, 1989, opposition rally. The signs say, "We want a government that is pro-life, pro-this, pro-that, and anti-nothing," and "Be free—that's an order!"

that people sought economic security through person-to-person relationships.

The services furnished an example of these relationships based on reciprocal obligation and mutual loyalty in describing employment arrangements in the Paraguayan countryside. Because secure, paid employment in Paraguay is rare, people regard jobs less as a source of financial gain than as a way of establishing personal relationships that may be handy in the future. Within these largely precapitalist social relations, ". . . a *patrón* hires a person as though he were asking a personal favor, and the *peón* responds as though he were obliged to grant it. The payment of wages is played down, almost as an undercover act."[3] The favors that the other may be able to render in times of need have greater meaning to each person than money. The individualistic, capitalist work-ethic of the developed world is shunned as antisocial.

Where patron-client relationships are widespread, certain well-placed individuals inevitably acquire large and loyal followings, which they can use to their political advantage. Politicians control access to jobs and money and can grant such access as favors. Thus, the most normal route to social and economic advancement (sometimes the only practical route) is not through individual efforts but through politics and favoritism.

POLITICAL PARTIES

An important political fact of life in Paraguay is that nearly all Paraguayans are either Liberals or Colorados. Paraguay's Colorado and Liberal parties are among the oldest continuously functioning political organizations in the world; as such, they are well adapted to the society in which they function.[4] Nonideological, nationally organized, and mass-based, the two parties were founded slightly over one hundred years ago by politicians who drew their inspiration from the Masonic order. Both the Colorado and Liberal parties have extensive organizations in the countryside. Traditionally their followings have been approximately equal. The May 1, 1989, elections, though flawed (see "Whither Paraguay?" below), proved that the Colorado and Liberal parties remain the only viable political vehicles in Paraguay. The elections also revealed how forty years of repression weakened Liberal organization, financial resources, and popular support.[5]

Paraguayans generally become Liberals or Colorados at birth. Allegiance is lifelong; changing political affiliations is rare and is regarded as akin to treason. People have been conditioned to respond more to the party colors (red for Colorados, blue for Liberals) than to the content of their political proposals. Personalism explains why ideology is a relatively minor consideration. What really counts in Paraguayan politics are personalities and their entourage of loyal supporters.

Knowing a person's political affiliation is essential to know how to deal with him and interpret his statements and to know how one's own statements will be interpreted. Paraguayans would suspect a person who declares his political neutrality of trying to hide his true motivations. Because ideology is almost irrelevant, many people believe a person who changes parties could only be doing so for narrow reasons of personal self-interest; a person willing to sacrifice years or generations of time invested in personal relationships therefore seems undependable and untrustworthy.

Factionalism arises because individuals owe their loyalty to particular leaders, not to a party or an ideology in general. As a consequence, political parties lack cohesion: "real" politics is found in factional maneuvering. During the eighteen months prior to the February 1989 coup, the Colorado party fractured into as many as 9 factions, the *militantes* and the *tradicionalistas* being the most prominent. The Liberal party had split into more than 3 separate groups in the decades before the coup. These included the Partido Liberal (PL), the Partido Liberal

Radical (PLR), and the until-recently unrecognized Partido Liberal Radical Auténtico (PLRA), the last being by far the largest.[6] These three Liberal parties also were factionalized internally.

Not only is politics faction prone, factions tend to endure. Formed during the late 1950s by anti-Stroessner Colorados, MOPOCO (Movimiento Popular Colorado) was an unrecognized and harassed dissident Colorado party faction that survived in the shadows for thirty years. Accepted back in Colorado ranks in 1989, MOPOCO is still an organized, independent entity within the party. In addition, factional disputes and hatreds are often more acrimonious than party differences. Factional fighting was partly to blame each time the party in power lost power to the opposition, which happened in 1904, 1936, and 1948.

Another reason for the lack of ideological emphasis within Paraguay's traditional parties is the relatively egalitarian nature of Paraguayan society. Social distinctions between racially homogenized Paraguayans have always been less important than in other Latin American countries (Mexico and Peru, in particular), and politics has never been class-based. Access to wealth and power, not differences in culture or class or caste, are decisive in establishing social status in Paraguay.[7] In the absence of a genuine aristocracy of birth and privilege, the armed forces have served as a power and status elite. Stroessner guaranteed their loyalty to him by granting them ample opportunities for self-enrichment. Yet the poor are not prevented from using politics or joining the army as a means to improve their social standing. On the other hand, because the ruling Colorado party includes all classes, a Colorado government has trouble entertaining class-based demands (such as those of peasants and workers). Typically, the government brands such movements as "destructive of social peace."

Party leaders keep close tabs on local politics. Local party organizations are called *seccionales*. The party's Junta de Gobierno (governing board or national committee) supervises the choice of local candidates for party office by the *seccionales*, and agreement is reached by negotiation. Obtaining uncontested electoral lists is ordinarily a priority. Trips to the countryside by national committee delegates, who supervise the local party elections, give politicians on the national level an opportunity to familiarize themselves with local problems and personalities and give ambitious locals the chance to attract attention to themselves. As in many underdeveloped countries, the government has the country's largest payroll, and access to government jobs is controlled by local Colorado party officials. In a sense, the parties function as large mutual-aid societies and channels for social mobility. Since 1948, the Colorado party has monopolized nearly all the best jobs.[8] Under Stroessner, with only token exceptions, all civil servants, including teachers, judges, soldiers, most employees of state enterprises, and even physicians practicing in government facilities, had to be Colorado party members—Liberals were kept out.

The two parties combined have almost universal appeal and for decades were assumed to have nearly equal support regardless of which party held power. Politicians nurtured the perception that the parties were roughly the same size because of the benefits it produced for the political system. For one thing, it helped cement party allegiances. Without a widespread belief in size equality, the supporters of the party currently out of power might have lost the feeling of true competition. Another benefit of this system was that size equality limited the number of clients among whom patronage had to be distributed: If the Colorados were in power, they only had to worry about "their" half of the population, which is an important consideration in a poor country. The system also furnished a socially acceptable way of depriving large segments of the population of economic rewards.[9]

Party competition tends to divert public attention from Paraguay's lack of progress in solving its social and economic problems and thereby reduces discontent. Instead, the relative advantages of party membership are emphasized. The party in power obviously will have more patronage to dispense, so the opposition bides its time, knowing that it will control access to resources when it gains power. Although the Colorados have continually harassed the Liberals, resorting at times to state terrorism, the Colorado leaders have consciously abstained from trying to destroy the Liberal party.[10] Yet the Colorados have done all they could to permanently weaken the Liberals by engineering and recognizing a docile, "kept" opposition and giving it a monopoly on opposition patronage.

A great many urban intellectuals have become disillusioned with the two main parties and have dropped out of politics altogether or joined the smaller parties, such as the Revolutionary Febrerista party (Partido Revolucionario Febrerista, or PRF), the Christian Democratic party (Partido Democrático Cristiano, or PDC), or the newly formed (1985), Marxist-oriented Democratic and Popular Movement (Movimiento Democrático y Popular, or MDP). By removing most of the barriers to party registration, Rodríguez has stimulated the birth of this clutch of new parties. The continued exercise of a free press could do much to change Paraguay's political demographics in the future. However, as the 1990s begin, still only the Colorados and the Liberals will count.

ORIGINS OF THE STROESSNER REGIME

The foundation for Stroessner's regime was laid during the twenty-two years of crisis and social upheaval that preceded the 1954 coup (see Chapter 3). After 1931, Paraguay experienced (1) the sanguinary, cathartic Chaco War (1932–1935), the second epic struggle in the country's history; (2) the brief but violent Febrerista social revolution, in which the army for the first time overthrew a legally constituted government (1936–1937); (3) the reactionary Morínigo regime that openly sympathized with Nazi Germany (1940–1948); (4) a bloody and traumatic civil war (1947); and (5) a period of coups and counter-coups by cynical Colorado party politicians from 1948 to 1954, when Paraguay had six presidents.

The political situation in Paraguay from 1954 to 1989, the period of Stroessner's rule, was a direct outgrowth of the events that led up to the 1947 civil war. This bitter, eight-month conflict pitted a coalition of Liberals, Febreristas, Communists, and most of the army (four-fifths of the officers joined the rebels) against the Morínigo regime and the Colorado party. Following the rebel defeat in August 1947, the Colorados launched a wave of savage repression that drove one-third of Paraguay's population into exile.[11] Paraguay was ruled under a state of emergency that lasted, with few breaks, for forty years, from January 1947 until April 1987.

By the early 1950s, the two main pillars of Alfredo Stroessner's regime—the Colorado party and the army—were firmly in place. Paraguay at that time was not unlike Spain after its 1936–1939 civil war, when the victors of an exhausted and socially traumatized nation indulged in mass expulsions and executions of the political opposition. Many Paraguayans welcomed Stroessner as a strongman who could impose order.[12]

In a sense, Stroessner's May 4, 1954, coup was no more than a roll of the dice, because its success was by no means assured. Yet with support from sections of the Colorado party and from the military, Stroessner successfully purged the leaders of the Epifanista, Democrático, and Guionista opposition[13] and co-opted their supporters. By 1967, the Colorado party was thoroughly Stronista. With a favorable international climate that produced aid from the International Monetary Fund, Brazil, and the United States and with support from a party and an army loyal only to him, Stroessner consolidated his leadership into what would become the longest dictatorship in the modern history of Latin America.

Stroessner owed much of his success in the 1950s, 1960s, and 1970s to his excellent political judgment and to hard work.[14] Unlike many dictators who surround themselves with sycophants, Stroessner kept open his lines of communication. He personally reviewed all military promotions and was intimately informed on the capabilities, performance, and attitudes of his officers, who depended on him for their positions and their future. But lest his officers feel too secure, he met regularly with noncommissioned officers and enlisted men.

Before illness and advancing age reduced his resiliency after 1985, Stroessner maintained a high visibility. He kept tabs on the internal political situation by visiting virtually every area of the country at least once a year, being present at almost every ribbon-cutting and bricklaying ceremony of note, speaking at selected graduations (including those of the military academy), and in general having his name associated with every new road, building, or piece of equipment constructed or installed in Paraguay. Personal familiarity with officials, soldiers, businessmen, and ordinary citizens was Stroessner's invaluable method of making political judgments, evaluating his intelligence sources, and influencing the course of events.[15]

GOVERNMENT MACHINERY

The extent of change and democratization that will come to Paraguay in the wake of Stroessner's overthrow will depend largely on what changes, if any, are made to the constitution. During the 1989 election campaign, the Colorado party's platform called for sweeping constitutional changes or for scrapping the document altogether, mainly to reduce presidential powers. President Rodríguez has openly discussed his preference for a one-term presidency. Democratization will also depend on the extent to which the constitution is respected. Paraguayans have rarely deferred to constitutional restrictions on political activity.

Adopted after the crushing victory of the Brazilian and Argentine armies in the Triple Alliance War, the 1870 constitution was never more than a scrap of paper, mainly because it ignored the realities of Paraguay's political culture. Although the 1870 constitution fostered a laissez-faire liberal traditon in Paraguayan statecraft, the 1936–1937 Febrerista revolt and Marshal Félix Estigarribia's 1940 constitution reversed this. After 1936, the state was to be activist and interventionist.

Estigarribia's constitution overtly gave the executive most of the power. It was a dictator's constitution, allowing the president to declare a state of emergency at any time. The intention was, naturally, to give the chief executive the means to stifle Paraguay's coup-prone political culture. Yet the 1940 constitution did not change Paraguayan political culture, which remained authoritarian and hence susceptible to any strongman who had the means to impose his own "rules of the game." A system that can maintain order only under the direction of a strongman consequently lacks order when it lacks a strongman. Thus, the 1940 constitution could not have prevented the 1947 civil war or the spate of coups that followed that war, nor did it prevent Stroessner's 1954 coup or Rodríguez's 1989 coup. Stroessner amended the constitution twice, in 1967 and 1977, to ratify his decision to seek more than the mandated maximum of two consecutive terms.

Under the present document of 1967 (a partial rewrite of Marshal Estigarribia's 1940 constitution, amended in 1977), the president is the linchpin of the government, overshadowing by far the judiciary and the legislature. The president must be a native-born Roman Catholic at least forty years of age and is elected to a five-year term by popular vote. A president may serve an unlimited number of terms.

The legislature—which became a bicameral institution in 1967 called the National Congress (or just Congress)—contains an upper house called the Senate and a lower house called the Chamber of Deputies. Senators and deputies are elected by direct vote.[16] Paraguay's electoral law grants the majority party two-thirds of the seats in both the Senate and the Chamber of Deputies, regardless of electoral proportions, while the minority parties are proportionally represented in the remaining one-third of the seats. The opposition parties demanded changes in the electoral law to allow for full proportional representation and to legalize coalitions for the May 1, 1989, elections, but Rodríguez refused.

Under Stroessner the legislature had no autonomous power. Its main duty was to approve bills submitted to it by the president. The 1967 constitution gives the Senate nominal jurisdiction over treaties and national defense and some power in naming Supreme Court justices; the Chamber of Deputies concerns itself with taxation, spending, electoral, and municipal matters. Since 1962, when they made their first appearance, opposition delegates have served a purely decorative function—the Congress has never approved a bill initiated by them. Although an absolute majority vote in both chambers can compel the president to promulgate a bill, the executive can dissolve the legislature at any time by calling a "constitutional crisis" and subsequently may rule by decree for three months, when new elections must be held.[17] Stroessner ruled Paraguay under a state of emergency that suspended individual rights and constitutional guarantees; the state of emergency was automatically renewed every three months with few lapses until the political thaw of 1987, when he allowed it to expire in response to pressure from the United States and other foreign powers. During this period, he never failed to gain permission from the legislators to renew the state of emergency.

The Supreme Court consists of at least five native-born Paraguayans who are each at least thirty-five years of age and educated as doctors of law. Although the court has the power to declare presidential acts unconstitutional, this never occurred during Stroessner's tenure. The judiciary could hardly function as an independent branch of government in this system where the executive controlled all court appointments and nearly all judges were Colorado party members.

OPPOSITION FORCES

Paraguay's opposition parties are financially and organizationally weak, fragmented, riddled with factions, and as prone to *caudillismo* and intrigue as is the Colorado party. With the encouragement of U.S. Ambassador Robert White, Stroessner opponents banded together in 1979 to form the Acuerdo Nacional, an umbrella organization that attempted, without notable success, to coordinate opposition strategy. This group included the PLRA, PRF, PDC, and MOPOCO. Their declared aims include abolishing repressive laws, establishing an independent judiciary, and ending the practice of reserving government and military jobs for Colorado party members. The degree of their commitment to democracy is untested. Opposition politicians often seem as interested in internal squabbles, petty rivalries, and jockeying for political advantage as in opposing the regime. As well, the present electoral law handicaps the organization by forbidding electoral coalitions.

Opposition political groups under Stroessner fell into four categories:

1. "Participationist" parties[18] enjoyed legal status and participated in elections in return for the one-third minority seats in Congress. This group included the Partido Liberal (PL) and the Partido Liberal Radical (PLR). The other opposition groups regarded these parties as "sell-outs" due to their close collaboration with Stroessner.
2. One officially recognized party abstained from elections, the Partido Revolucionario Febrerista (PRF), which stopped participating in 1968.
3. Some nonrecognized parties were tolerated by the regime to some degree and were allowed to hold some internal meetings but could not demonstrate, publish newspapers, or participate in elections. This category included the Partido Liberal Radical Auténtico (PLRA) and the Partido Democrático Cristiano (PDC).
4. Certain parties were illegal and not tolerated. Leaders or members of these parties were subject to immediate arrest, torture, or execution. This group included (at various times) the Partido Communista Paraguayo (PCP) and, until 1983, the Movimiento Popular Colorado (MOPOCO). After 1983, MOPOCO leaders were kept under close police surveillance and were not allowed to hold intraparty meetings.[19]

Stroessner used fraudulent elections to repress those who opposed his rule. The congressional delegations of the "official" opposition parties, the PL and PLR, were known widely as *zocateros* ("scavengers") for their zealous commitment to collecting their parliamentary stipend.[20] Their participation in the system lent a patina of democratic legitimacy to Stroessner's regime. Meanwhile, the Colorado party controlled the electoral apparatus and—not surprisingly—always won.[21] The margin of victory was often particularly huge in rural areas.[22] In 1988, President Stroessner officially received 89 percent of the vote.

Domingo Laíno, who heads the Authentic Radical Liberals (PLRA), the anti-Stroessner faction of the Liberal party, is the best known of the regime's opponents. Laíno is a former professor of economics and was a PLR congressman before the PLRA was formed on the basis of electoral abstention. His speeches in Congress denouncing corruption and human rights abuses earned him Stroessner's wrath. Laíno's fame (or notoriety) is largely due to the regime's attempts to muzzle him. A victim of countless detentions and brutal treatment, Laíno was forced into exile after his book *The Merchant General* was published in 1982.[23] His sojourn abroad gave him an opportunity to make contacts with sympathetic politicians in foreign countries, including members of the U.S. Congress. Subsequently, under pressure from the United States, Argentina, and other foreign observers, Stroessner finally allowed Laíno to return in 1987. Nonetheless, the regime continued its political harassment, arresting him nearly a dozen times in 1988.

Of Laíno's many attempts to reenter the country, probably the best known occurred in June 1986. Despite the presence of former U.S. Ambassador Robert White, several Uruguayan and Argentine congressmen, and three U.S. television crews, police at the Asunción airport forced Laíno back onto the airplane that had brought him to Paraguay. His readmission to the country in April 1987 coincided with Stroessner's decision not to renew the perennial state of emergency. Laíno immediately launched an audacious political campaign, speaking to as many as 150,000 people at mass rallies in the countryside. His charisma and his reputation for personal bravery have helped to focus the opposition and to reduce their internal bickering. Nonetheless, the PLRA is not wholly behind Laíno, with one faction more supportive of the Saguier brothers, Hermes and Tito.

The Febreristas are few in number but their intellectual following gives them greater influence than their numbers would imply. The PFR's president is the youthful Euclides Acevedo, who may be the opposition's "toughest, smartest" political operator, according to one retired U.S. diplomat.[24] An indigenous adaptation of socialist currents, Febrerismo is similar in some ways to Aprismo[25] in Peru. The Febreristas are a diverse and somewhat odd ideological mixture. The party's youth looks to European social democracy for inspiration.

Other regime opponents that Stroessner refused to recognize included the small Christian Democratic party (PDC);[26] the newly organized, youth-oriented, leftist Popular Democratic Movement (MDP); and the minuscule, outlawed Communist party, which operates in exile with a few other semiclandestine groups. The once-dissident Colorado breakaway, MOPOCO, rejoined the Colorado party after the February 1989 coup.

Launched in 1960, the Christian Democratic movement proclaimed itself a political party in 1965. Although it maintains close ties with the church, it is not a church-sponsored party and has a minuscule political following. Its goals include democratization, agrarian reform, and ending government control of the universities and labor unions.

The Colorado Popular Movement (MOPOCO) was set up by dissident Colorados after Stroessner took over the party in the 1950s. They challenged Stroessner and managed to gain control of Congress in 1959, after which, for the most part, they were forced into exile. MOPOCO sponsored a number of unsuccessful guerrilla invasions in the 1960s that were brutally suppressed by Stroessner's interior minister, Edgar Ynsfrán. Most of their leadership was in exile prior to 1983. After their return to Paraguay they were kept under close surveillance, yet they managed to maintain a strong if shadowy presence inside the Colorado party. MOPOCO left the Acuerdo Nacional in February 1989 after it received seats on the Colorado Junta de Gobierno. Some MOPOCO members will sit in the Paraguayan congress after the 1989 election—evidence of a remarkable political comeback.

Last in the pre-Rodríguez political lineup was the Popular Democratic Movement (MDP), a left-leaning group of activist-minded students and young people that emerged only since 1985. Although most of the leadership is of Marxist, Trotskyist, or Fidelista persuasion, they have not called for violent revolution or guerrilla warfare. The group has links with some of the various Paraguayan peasant organizations that have similar political views. MDP rhetoric is anachronistic—reminiscent of 1960s U.S. and European student protest rhetoric—and quite clearly obsolete.

Finally, the Communist party of Paraguay (PCP), founded in 1928 with student and labor support, has been legal for only nine months, during 1946–1947. The party wound up on the losing side of the 1947 civil war and has been outlawed ever since. The Communists probably have an active membership of no more than 4,000, all but a handful of them in exile in various Latin American and European countries. PCP action within Paraguay is minimal.[27] Somewhat unexpectedly, noises from within the Colorado party establishment suggest that legalization of the Communists is a possibility.

Another persistent opposition voice in Paraguay, and in many ways the focal point of the opposition, has been the Catholic church. Rodríguez has said that one of the motives for his coup was to improve relations between the Paraguayan state and the Catholic church. In the late 1960s, the church dropped its traditional political neutrality and began to work for social reform. It also began to criticize Stroessner's reelections, the regime's human rights violations and its treatment of political prisoners, inequitable distribution of wealth, and official corruption.

The church opposed the continued concentration of land holdings and organized Christian Land Leagues and peasant cooperatives to resist tenant evictions. These new groups soon took on lives of their own, and some moved beyond the ability of the church to control them. The regime answered with repression, banning the leagues, closing church publications and newspapers, expelling non-Paraguayan priests, and arresting and sometimes executing activists and peasants.[28] The church retaliated against Stroessner's repression by excommunicating government officials accused of engaging in torture and corruption.[29]

The church's cohesiveness strengthened its position despite repression. After the closing of Paraguay's largest independent daily, *ABC Color*, in March 1984; *Radio Ñandutí* in January 1987; and the Febrerista weekly, *El Pueblo*, in August 1987, the only independent news media in Paraguay were the church-run *Radio Caritas* and the weekly *Sendero*. Stroessner was an uncomfortable host to Pope John Paul II during his May 1988 visit, when the pope called for democracy and respect for human rights.

Paraguay's minimal level of industrialization has limited the political roles of labor and capital. Economic enterprises are small, class consciousness is low, and personal (not professional) relationships between employers and workers prevail. The state has always preempted and circumscribed any independent labor organizing activity. After destroying the last independent labor confederation in 1959, the regime controlled organized labor directly through the government-sponsored Paraguayan Confederation of Workers (CPT). The CPT, which never organized a strike, was expelled from the International Confederation of Free Trade Unions (ICFTU) in 1979.

Labor unrest reappeared vigorously after the economic downturn of the 1980s. A series of strikes and organizing activities among beverage workers, bank employees, journalists and typographers, and doctors and nurses brought an end to the "social peace" that Stroessner had bought with the massive infusion of foreign capital during the construction of Itaipú.[30] In 1985, a new labor group, the MIT (Movimiento Intersindical de Trabajadores), with its core support among the relatively affluent

Bank Workers Federation,[31] emerged as an activist, socially conscious, labor rights clearinghouse and as an effective rival to the CPT. Even with MIT's limited success, due to various forms of unremitting government repression only a tiny portion of Paraguay's workers are unionized. Labor relations continue to be woefully inadequate for anyone but employers. Rural workers (40.4 percent of the labor force is engaged in agriculture) enjoy few of the meager benefits given urban labor.[32]

University students traditionally have been outspoken politically, although Stroessner's 1960 antistudent repression muzzled student protests for nearly thirty years. In the mid-1980s, politically independent students began once more to issue publications, hold seminars on social issues, and demonstrate against the regime. They often have worked with the church but constant police harassment has prevented them from organizing effectively. Paraguay is an extremely youthful country;[33] one challenge facing Paraguay's politicians is how to harness youthful idealism as a constructive force for change. A more concrete problem is the geriatrification of the bureaucracy and the lack of people within it under fifty years of age.

NATURE OF THE STROESSNER REGIME

Stroessner ruled in the manner of a nineteenth-century *caudillo*. He resembled Rafael Trujillo of the Dominican Republic, Papa Doc Duvalier of Haiti, and Anastasio Somoza Debayle of Nicaragua. Unlike Somoza, however, Stroessner did not flaunt a lifestyle of conspicuous consumption. Although the family's assets doubtless were sizeable, Stroessner himself had little visible wealth. Few observers would disagree that the Stroessner regime was unusual,"particularist" in the sense that it was similar to few other Latin American regimes. Unlike many Latin countries, Paraguay did not experience the socioeconomic stages outlined by Thomas Skidmore and Peter Smith: integration into the world economy, import-substituting industrialization, and elite formation.[34] Paraguay's sociopolitical forms are marked by the country's long isolation and backwardness. Until quite recently, the country was linked only tenuously to the world economy and never had any industry to speak of. Francia, Francisco Solano López, and the Triple Alliance War wiped out Paraguay's "pure-blooded" Spanish elite and with it nearly all social differentiation based on race. The state often enjoyed an unrivaled degree of autonomy and typically could ignore or manipulate the elite's preferences. As a result, Paraguayans seemed immune to the forces that motivated political change in the rest of Latin America.

Even after the Itaipú economic boom of the 1970s, Paraguay remained an agricultural economy. The government used the proceeds of Itaipú not to industrialize but to redistribute wealth in the form of sinecures and privileges used to buy political support and legitimacy. The marginal urban middle class might have preferred a more open political system but it largely owed its social position to the government. In other words, there was no force strong enough to upset the politics bred by the traditional clientilistic social relations that predominated in the countryside. The widespread corruption did spawn a new elite group who gained political currency in the *militante* faction of the Colorado party (discussed late in this section) and had a vested interest in maintaining the social and political arrangements that had made them rich. Their interests tended to conflict with those of the older military and Colorado elites and produced the tensions that led to the February 1989 coup.

Imbued with *caudillista*[35] and totalitarian or "semifascist"[36] elements, Stroessner's state was a military dictatorship cloaked in the mantle of a traditional political party. The state was "omnivorous," selectively using corporatism, ritualized politics, and patronism to suppress and attempt to eradicate all political or social forms not subordinate to itself.[37] Some have suggested that although its authoritarian and patrimonial aspects were beyond doubt, the regime was such an oddity as to defy classification.

Certain elements seem clear:

1. A highly skilled and astute politician, Stroessner ruled by controlling and perfecting the party–armed forces–government triad.
2. As the system's main beneficiary and guarantor, the armed forces (especially the army) held decisive power in the state but generally stayed behind the scenes.[39]
3. The Colorado party was the regime's main instrument of social control and its principal patronage funnel.
4. The regime legitimated itself by adopting and co-opting democratic forms and held power by selectively using repression and concession.
5. The regime immobilized, depoliticized, and "deactivated" civil society to such an extent that political opposition appeared as a discordant element in an apparently naturally harmonious system.
6. The regime attracted and retained supporters mainly by regulating access to wealth (including contraband).
7. Those who profited from officially sanctioned corruption and contraband trade became progressively more important within the regime.

8. The dictatorship functioned as much to keep the ruling group in line as the opposition.
9. The terror unleashed by the victorious Colorados during and after the 1947 civil war became a permanent feature of the Stroessner regime.

Torture, official terror, arbitrary arrest and detention, "disappearances," and abuse of human rights in Stroessner's Paraguay were as common as rain. During the 1950s and 1960s, captured guerrillas and Communists were subject to summary execution or worse, including being thrown alive from airplanes over the Chaco. One captured Communist leader was said to have been dismembered by chain saw. Torture was used routinely against anyone deemed to be a political dissident and became so routine that virtually any Paraguayan detained for whatever reason could be subject to it. Paraguay developed a macabre folkloric vocabulary for the various torture techniques, including "the cattle prod" (*la picana eléctrica*), "the swimming pool" (*la pilera*—a victim's head is plunged into a tub of water filled with excrement), "the crate" (*el cajón*—prolonged confinement in a box), "the fetus" (*el feto*—a person is forced to curl up in a fetal position for a prolonged period), "the bat" (*el murciélago*—the victim is hung upside down by his ankles), and so forth. Beatings and sexual abuse of women were also widespread. Two officials who bear much responsibility for these horrors are Edgar Ynsfrán, as interior minister, and Pastor Coronel, as chief of police investigations.[38]

THE WORM TURNS

The great socioeconomic changes of the 1970s and 1980s altered Paraguay's political and economic landscape. These decades coincided with the construction and completion of the giant Itaipú hydroelectric project and with the aging of Stroessner and his regime. As Fernando Masi has argued, by the beginning of the 1980s the Paraguayan economy had dropped nearly all its precapitalist vestiges and had ceased being dominated by the traditional logging, ranching, and commercial interests. The economy's focal point shifted and social relations were transformed. Paraguay had acquired a modern, capitalist, agricultural export sector increasingly dominated by Brazilians of German origin and by Japanese; a modern commercial-financial sector based on Itaipú money and financial manipulation; a rapidly expanding trade in contraband; and growing public investment in the economy.[40]

Divisions that appeared within the ruling group reflected the shifts of relative economic and social power that were taking place within

Paraguayan society. While industry remained backward (primarily con-
cerned with processing agricultural goods) and the peasantry became
increasingly marginalized and desperate, a new class of "kleptocrats"
emerged. The primary beneficiary of the Itaipú boom, this so-called
burguesía fraudulenta, included many army officers and high-level regime
functionaries (not to mention international investors) who became increasingly important social and political actors. Many technicians, professionals, and entrepreneurs unconnected with the regime also benefited
from the economic expansion, contributing to the depoliticization of
society as the regime expanded its clientilist base.[41]

In the end, the Stroessner model proved unsustainable in the face
of new economic and political realities and the dictator's failing health.
The economic downturn at the end of Itaipú construction posed insu-
perable problems for a regime whose economic legitimacy was based
on giving its supporters access to wealth. By the mid-1980s, Stroessner
had parceled out virtually all of Paraguay's state lands, some of them
several times over. Without access to other sources of funds, the regime
was forced to permit an increase in the scope of the contraband trade
and to shop for foreign loans. It found some particularly lucrative deals
in the ACEPAR (Acero Paraguayo) steel enterprise and the INC (Industria
Nacional de Cimiento) cement plants. Each of these Brazilian-backed
projects cost nearly half a billion dollars and provided a handy source
of rake-offs and graft.[42]

During the 1980s, foreign debt mushroomed (although it is still
puny by Brazilian and Argentine standards), inflation rose to 20–30
percent per annum, and the guaraní fell sharply against the U.S. dollar.
A looming crisis of political succession, manifested by intense political
maneuvering, soon overshadowed the backdrop of economic malaise,
while the growing uncertainty of future political arrangements contributed
to it. The Colorado party convention of August 1987 that nominated
President Stroessner for his eighth term brought to a head factional
fighting that finally destroyed party unity. The militant wing grabbed
control of the party's national committee from the traditionalists and
captured all the key political levers within the government.[43] The militants
had covert support from Stroessner, who was becoming sensitive about
his advancing age and his frustrated plans to engineer a succession of
power to his son, Gustavo.

The striking thing about this internal political clash was the cynicism
of the militants' tactics and the virulence of the internal party campaign.
To begin with, the militants prevented their rivals from even participating
in the convention by posting a double cordon of police in front of the
convention building. When some of the traditionalist leaders tried to
force their way through they were assaulted as though they were members

of the unrecognized opposition parties. During the period leading up to the convention, the verbal abuse that each faction heaped on the other was astounding, including epithets like hangers on, traffickers, embezzlers, drunks, drug addicts, fugitives from justice, lunatics, and delinquents, which may demonstrate just how thoroughly the corruption of the regime had compromised most of the Colorado delegates.[44] The entire show was broadcast to the country on national television.

Explicitly denouncing any discussion of a "post-Stronista" future for Paraguay, the militant leadership included most of Stroessner's closest collaborators, such as Mario Abdo Benítez (Stroessner's private secretary), Adán Godoy Jiménez (minister of public health and social welfare), J. Eugenio Jacquet (minister of justice and labor), and Sabino Augusto Montanaro (minister of the interior and president of the Colorado party). Although they declared themselves "absolutely loyal" to Stroessner, most militants were relative newcomers to the Colorado party, opportunists with unsavory reputations who had gained prominence and made their fortunes during the Itaipú boom. The militants felt especially threatened by any change in the status quo, as a new regime would likely deprive them of their privileges and of much of their access to wealth and power.[45] For them, the best person to replace the aging president was his son, Gustavo, an air force colonel and the man responsible for the family business.

The traditionalists, along with other reform-minded Colorado groups,[46] represented the Colorado party's old guard. They were aware that the party had existed before Stroessner and were beginning to think about the party's post-Stroessner future. Much compromised by years of unconditional support for the regime, they nonetheless realized that Stroessner's interests and those of the Colorado party were not identical. With Stroessner backing the militants, the outmaneuvered traditionalists were soon reduced to whimpering about the lack of internal party democracy.

THE FEBRUARY 1989 COUP

The crisis of the regime began a year later. In September 1988, Stroessner fell ill and went to hospital. On September 9, for several hours he was rumored to be dead.[47] Stroessner was not dead but his recovery was slow. He never regained his capacity for sustained periods of hard work. This episode convinced the militants (and perhaps Stroessner himself) of the need to put into place the machinery to ensure that questions about succession would not threaten their positions. The army hierarchy adamantly opposed the Gustavo succession scenario, a fact that encouraged the militants to use Gustavo as a wedge between

Stroessner and their military rivals for power. The militants wanted Gustavo to succeed his father, perhaps by filling a new constitutional post of vice-president. But their maneuvering was clumsy. With Stroessner operating at a much-reduced mental and physical capacity during the last months of 1988, their intrigues blew up in their faces.

Most military officers, including General Andrés Rodríguez, the commander of the First Brigade (Paraguay's largest, best equipped, and best trained army unit), mistrusted the militants. The political loyalty of the First Brigade is crucial to the Paraguayan state because the unit's barracks are right outside of Asunción. Years of indoctrination to remain loyal to the Colorado party left the army troubled after the August 1987 convention. Army officers feared what the new political lineup might mean for them. By and large, the army detested Gustavo Stroessner and his militant backers. They despised Gustavo as a social climber and an opportunist and derided him for being a homosexual, calling him "La Coronela" (a mocking, feminized version of "el coronel"—"the colonel") behind his back. The army officers were afraid the army would receive the same treatment at the hands of the militants as the Colorado party had. In fact, the militants indeed had to find some way to neutralize the army. General Rodríguez would never have moved against the dictator if Stroessner had been firmly "in the saddle." What was most disquieting was that the militants, not Stroessner, seemed to be calling the shots.

After much maneuvering behind the scenes, events began to speed up late in December 1988 and early in 1989.[48] As the guaraní plummeted against the dollar, the Central Bank announced the closure of Paraguay's *casas de cambio*, the unofficial nonbank exchange houses. Not coincidentally, General Rodríguez owned the largest *casa de cambio* in Paraguay.[49] On the following Monday, January 30, the defense ministry released a list of several dozen colonels who were being forced to retire early. The list included many officers who were known to be Rodríguez supporters yet were well below retirement age.

At this point the militants blundered. On Wednesday, February 1, Rodríguez was handed an ultimatum: either accept the post of minister of defense (and give up direct command of troops) or resign. But Rodríguez declined to be "kicked upstairs" and had no intention of resigning. Instead, on the next evening, he ordered his troops to arrest President Stroessner at the home of the latter's mistress, Ñata Legal.[50] But when Stroessner slipped out an unguarded entrance during a firefight that left several soldiers dead, Rodríguez attacked the Presidential Escort Regiment (next to the Defense Ministry), after hearing that Stroessner had holed up there with his son, Gustavo. The fight lasted a few hours, but Stroessner surrendered toward dawn on February 3.[51] On Sunday, February 5, Stroessner boarded an airplane and flew into exile in Brazil.

Workmen repairing damage at the Presidential Escort Regiment during the week following the February 3, 1989, coup. The black spots on the wall at the right are bullet holes.

Despite all the shooting, the coup had only claimed the lives of 40–50 soldiers and police.[52]

WHITHER PARAGUAY?

Observers of the post-Stroessner political scene in Paraguay are struck by the tremendous changes that have taken place on the surface of Paraguayan politics and by the toughness of the system's underlying structures. In the days following the coup, Stroessner critics must have felt gratified to see almost his entire government in exile or behind bars. Yet most members of the new Rodríguez government (including Rodríguez himself) had been close Stroessner associates before August 1, 1987 (the date of the traditionalist-militant split).

Stroessner critics could not have agreed, however, when former Supreme Court Justice Luís Maria Argaña, whom Rodríguez had just named foreign minister, said there were "32 or 33 years of great government" under Stroessner.[53] Rodríguez's refusal to call Stroessner a dictator at a February 6, 1989, news conference also raised eyebrows.

If Stroessner was not a dictator, why did Paraguay need democracy, and why did Stroessner have to be overthrown?

Nonetheless, Rodríguez was seemingly keeping his word to bring Paraguay "real democracy, not just a façade." Within days of Stroessner's fall, opposition newspapers were back on the streets of Asunción, independent radio stations were back in business, and formerly unrecognized political parties were allowed to hold mass demonstrations.[54] Rodríguez had explicitly named the need to take action for democracy, human rights, and better church-state relations as the motivating forces behind his coup. In addition, he announced his regime would crack down hard on drug smugglers.

Before one accepts President Rodríguez and his democratic-sounding pronouncements at face value, a large caveat is in order. After all, Rodríguez is Stroessner's most successful understudy, a man who prospered hugely under Stroessner's corrupt, dictatorial system. Long the number-two man in the army, Rodríguez cemented his relationship with Stroessner by having his daughter, Marta, marry the now-deposed dictator's youngest son, Alfredo. For years before the coup, many Paraguayans considered Rodríguez to be Stroessner's natural successor. The owner of one of Asunción's largest and most luxurious mansions, Rodríguez has sizeable interests in banking and currency exchange, brewing, flour milling, construction, manufacturing, ranching, real estate, and the import-export trade, and he controls key cigarette, luxury car, and aircraft import concessions.[55]

By the time of the 1989 coup, Rodríguez was one of the wealthiest men in Paraguay, with a fortune estimated by some at over $1 billion. A man so immensely rich may be governed by interests rather than the love of liberty and may have interests that conflict with the democratic prerogatives of the citizenry. However, Rodríguez's investments in Paraguay are so wide-ranging, diversified, and enormous that he obviously has a big stake in his country's future. What was once said about General Motors may be even more true of him: what is good for President Rodríguez may be good for Paraguay, and what is good for Paraguay may turn out to be good for President Rodríguez. Nonetheless, under Rodríguez, Paraguay is still caught in its classical bind: The essence of personalism in politics is that the nation's fate should depend so completely on the will and actions of a single man.

But one must gulp a larger, more sinister grain of salt when reading Rodríguez's speeches: Rodríguez owes his fortune to being Paraguay's most successful smuggler. Using his vast influence as the second-ranking general in the army, Rodríguez made a fortune during the 1960s and 1970s smuggling cigarettes and scotch whiskey. Moreover, despite his new-found enthusiasm about combating the drug trade, abundant evidence suggests that Rodríguez himself was deeply involved in trading illicit drugs, mainly heroin and cocaine, which may have produced his biggest profits.[56] The likely conduits for the trade in drugs were Rodríguez's control over landing strips in Hernandarias and his ownership of TAGSA, an Asunción air-taxi company.[57]

Proving the case that President Rodríguez made part of his fortune as a drug trafficker is next to impossible because the evidence is fragmentary, incomplete, and often circumstantial. Although witnesses consistently named Rodríguez as the chief Paraguayan backer of French heroin smuggler André Ricord—the mastermind of the "Latin Connection" heroin trade during the 1960s and 1970s—to U.S. prosecutors who handled the case during the 1970s, the evidence was judged insufficient to bring to trial. In the 1980s—the drug now was cocaine—fresh rumors surfaced to link Rodríguez with drug trafficking when his personal pilot, Juan D. Viveros, was captured in 1985 along with a plane carrying 43 kilos (95 pounds) of cocaine. According to reports published at that time, the cargo had been in the custory of Rodríguez's First Cavalry Regiment prior to the Viveros incident.[58] A year earlier, in 1984, Paraguayan customs agents seized 49,000 gallons of precursor chemicals used in cocaine production. The shipping papers listed the owner of the chemicals as General Eduardo Sánchez, who at that time was Rodríguez's chief of staff. After the coup, Rodríguez appointed General Sánchez chief of police.[59]

Despite the innuendo about his past, Rodríguez has proved an adept politician, saying and doing everything in relation to drugs and democracy that Washington and Western Europe expected of him. Now the question is, "Will he continue to deliver?" So far, Rodríguez has cooperated fully with U.S. government requests to intensify pressure on drug traffickers in Paraguay. A program to spray Paraguayan marijuana fields near the Brazilian border is one example of this cooperation. On the political side, Rodríguez has repeatedly promised to amend or scrap Stroessner's constitution to limit the number of consecutive presidential terms to one and to limit the president's ability to impose a state of siege. Paraguay's unusual electoral law still awards the plurality party an automatic two-thirds of congressional seats; this law was in effect for the May 1, 1989, elections. There is a reasonable chance, however, that the 1993 elections will feature proportional representation.

Yet Paraguay's two-party-plus political system still lacks other than the appearance of a separation of powers (including truly independent legislative, judicial, and electoral branches), alternation of parties in the presidency, or free elections. The May 1, 1989, elections were much fairer than any polling done under Stroessner, but they were not a completely fair contest.[60] The 1993 elections will better indicate how far the democratic opening may go. In short, post-Stroessner Paraguay is still being run by a general and Stroessner's armed forces–Colorado party–bureaucracy triad is still in place. Although it is undergoing an unprecedented period of liberalization and democratization, Paraguay in 1989 was somewhere between dictatorship and democracy.

In the end, the entire liberalization process depends on the army's continued goodwill and on the commitment that Rodríguez brings to the process. Before any real progress will occur, the army will have to retire from active politics, the Colorado party will have to agree to the divorce, and Paraguay's citizens and politicians will have to start playing by the rules of the game. This is obviously a transformation that could take years, not one that will happen overnight. Rodríguez faces very real and stubborn limits on how much reform he can introduce. For instance, he will have a hard time prosecuting those who benefited from corruption or practiced torture under the old regime,[61] for to do so would tend to implicate everyone who participated in that regime and thereby would undercut the entire fabric of Colorado party government. Thus it seems likely that corruption and contraband trade will continue, though possibly in modified forms. In addition, although he has promised to step down when his term is over, Rodríguez may find this difficult when the time comes. In 1993, the Colorado party may decide that its fortunes will be more secure by continuing with a military man at the controls. Will Rodríguez be in a position to refuse?

NOTES

1. Elman R. Service and Helen S. Service, *Tobatí: Paraguayan Town,* Chicago: University of Chicago Press, 1954, p. 129.

2. Frederic Hicks defines *caudillismo* as one-man rule and the suppression of dissent in an environment conditioned by a patrimonial division of wealth. Hicks, "Interpersonal Relationships and *Caudillismo* in Paraguay," *Journal of Inter-American Studies and World Affairs,* 13, 1971, pp. 89–111. In Latin America, a *caudillo* often is a military ruler.

3. Service and Service, *Tobatí,* p. 127. In the same way, people often "help" a certain store owner by always buying from him, even though prices may be lower elsewhere. Maintaining the personal relationship and the advantages it may offer later—such as easy credit—is more important than saving money by "shopping around."

4. The only comparable political party systems in Latin America are found in Colombia and Uruguay.

5. Rodríguez got about 75 percent of the votes cast (out-polling the Colorado party's parliamentary list by 5 percent) compared with 21 percent for his closest competitor, PLRA leader Domingo Laíno. An observer delegation from the National Democratic Institute concluded that although serious electoral irregularities had occurred, they did not change the result.

6. The PL had legal stature conferred in 1962; the PLR, in 1967.

7. About 1 percent of Paraguay's population (roughly 40,000 people) belong to an unassimilated Indian subculture (see Chapter 5).

8. Hicks, "Interpersonal Relationships and *Caudillismo* in Paraguay," pp. 89–111.

9. Ibid.

10. Ibid.

11. As many as 400,000 Paraguayans became refugees, mainly in Argentina (Paul H. Lewis, *Socialism, Liberalism, and Dictatorship in Paraguay*, New York: Praeger, 1982).

12. Ibid., pp. 225–230.

13. Epifanistas were followers of former police chief Epifanio Méndez-Fleitas, the president of Paraguay's Central Bank until 1955 and an admirer of the populist style of Argentine dictator Juan Perón; Democráticos were followers of former president Federico Chaves; and Guionistas were followers of J. Natalicio González (see Chapter 3).

14. His predawn ministerial meetings are legendary.

15. Lewis, *Socialism, Liberalism, and Dictatorship*, pp. 105–123.

16. In 1987, the number of senators was increased from 30 to 36 and the number of deputies was increased from 60 to 72. Senators must be at least forty years old; deputies must be at least twenty-five. Senators and deputies must be native-born Paraguayans and may not be active-duty members of the armed forces or members of the clergy.

17. Stroessner dissolved the legislature in 1959, when Colorado Democráticos gained control of Congress and censured Interior Minister Edgar Ynsfrán and Police Chief Ramón Duarte Vera.

18. These parties were derisively known as the "kept," "bought," or "rented" opposition.

19. Some MOPOCO members continued to live in Paraguay under Stroessner but kept a low profile to avoid persecution. After 1983, some PCP members returned as visitors under the tacit agreement that they would not be persecuted as long as they refrained from political activity.

20. *Zocateros* comes from *zoquete*, meaning "scrap of meat" or "handout." The PL and the PLR were variously known as *"Liberales Stronistas"* and the "rented" opposition.

21. Some Colorado party strategems for reducing the electoral impact of non-Colorados have included (1) recording names in indecipherable handwriting, (2) clandestine distribution of official voting passes and "losing" those passes for non-Colorado voters, (3) limiting media access for opposition parties and closing non-Colorado newspapers and radio stations, (4) making no provision for secret ballot in many locations, (5) allowing Colorados to vote more than once, and (6) not allowing non-Colorado party members to act as observers at polling places. The Central Electoral Commission usually ignored opposition grievances regarding these practices (Marcial Antonio Riquelme, "Reforma, ruptura o continuismo en el Paraguay: Dificuldades y perspectivas para una apertura democrática," Asunción: Fundación Friedrich Naumann, 1988, pp. 126–127 [mimeo]).

22. Colorado candidates often got 100 percent of the vote as reported officially; at times local candidates racked up more votes than there were registered voters.

23. Paraguay's ambassador to the United States has dismissed Laíno's allegations of brutal treatment and torture, calling Laíno "a liar." *The Merchant General* examined the career of Nicaraguan dictator Anastasio Somoza, who was assassinated by Argentine guerrillas in Asunción while he was a guest of Stroessner. The book also took a heavily anti-imperialist line, implying that the United States and Brazil were busily gobbling up Paraguayan economic resources.

24. Interview with Robert White, November 16, 1988.

25. The Alianza Popular Revolucionaria Americana (APRA), founded by Victor Raúl Hayade la Torre in Peru around 1925, espoused a non-Marxist revolutionary populism. After alienating the Peruvian military with its ill-considered, bloody uprising in Trujillo in 1930, APRA was kept out of power in Peru for 55 years, until Alán García became president in 1985.

26. Rodríguez recognized the PDC in time for the May 1989 elections.

27. Lewis, *Socialism, Liberalism, and Dictatorship*, pp. 220–221.

28. In March 1980, the government sent 1,000 troops against a few dozen peasants, armed with machetes and rifles, who had hijacked a bus and fired on police in frustration over land encroachments by officials and military officers. Thirty peasants were shot to death in the ensuing roundup; the survivors were sent to detention camps and their families were forcibly evicted from their land holdings (Richard F. Staar (ed.), *Yearbook on International Communist Affairs*, Stanford, Calif.: Hoover Institution Press, 1984, pp. 162–163; also see Latin American Bureau, *Paraguay: Power Game*, Nottingham, Eng.: Russell Press, 1980, pp. 58–59).

29. For example, Sabino Montanaro, Stroessner's interior minister who left Paraguay for exile in Honduras after the 1989 coup, and Francisco Brítez, the former Asunción police chief, each enjoy the rare distinction of being excommunicated from the church twice. Archbishop Aníbal Mena Porta excommunicated Montanaro and Brítez on October 23, 1969, for deporting a Spanish-born priest who was a naturalized Paraguayan citizen, but later lifted the order. Then, newly named Archbishop Ismael Rolón Silvero excommunicated the pair once more in March 1970 after a screaming mob at the Asunción airport attacked a Montevideo bishop who had been sent to investigate the arrest of an Uruguayan priest accused of being a contact man for the Tupamaro guerrillas. The guerrillas wreaked havoc in Uruguay's capital, Montevideo, during the late 1960s and early 1970s (Paul Lewis, *Paraguay Under Stroessner*, Chapel Hill: University of North Carolina Press, 1980, pp. 193–195).

30. The corruption associated with Itaipú funds had already sparked some serious disturbances in the countryside, as described in note 28 above.

31. *Patria* (the Colorado party organ) often told its readers, disingenuously, that the leader of both the MIT and the Bank Workers Federation, Victor Baez, made more money than a general in the Paraguayan army. The newspaper obviously was not counting the contraband and graft common among high-ranking military officers when making this claim.

32. Lewis, *Paraguay Under Stroessner*, pp. 189–198; see also *Keesing's Contemporary Archives*, number 27976, 1976.

33. More than 40 percent of the population is under age fifteen (James W. Wilkie, *Statistical Abstract of Latin America*, Los Angeles: UCLA Latin American Center Publications, 1987, p. 112). Some sources estimate that 70 percent of Paraguayans are under thirty.

34. Thomas E. Skidmore and Peter H. Smith, *Modern Latin America*, New York: Oxford University Press, 1984, pp. 46–69.

35. See, for instance, Hicks, "Interpersonal Relationships and *Caudillismo* in Paraguay."

36. Euclides Acevedo, "Aproximación a la realidad Paraguaya: Algunas ideas básicas para la transición," in *Sistemas electorales y representación política en Latinoamérica*, Madrid: Fundación Friedrich Ebert, 1986.

37. Fernando Masi, "Estado y régimen en el Paraguay," Asunción: Centro de Estudios de Economía y Sociedad (CEDES), 1988 (mimeo); Benjamin Arditi, "Estado omnívoro, sociedad estatizada. Poder y orden político en Paraguay," Asuncion: Centro de Documentación y Estudios (CDE), 1987 (pamphlet).

38. See Riquelme, "Reforma, ruptura o continuismo en el Paraguay," for a description of the Stroessner regime. For more information on the state of human rights under Stroessner, see "Report on the Situation of Human Rights in Paraguay," Organization of American States, Doc. 19, September 28, 1987; "Paraguay: An Amnesty International Briefing," London: Amnesty International Publications, February 1984; and "Paraguay: Repression in the Countryside," An America's Watch Report, New York, May 1988.

39. Police and political henchmen, rather than regular army soldiers, broke protesters' heads.

40. Masi, "Estado y régimen en el Paraguay," p. 19.

41. Riquelme, "Reforma, ruptura o continuismo en el Paraguay," p. 65.

42. The ACEPAR project sponsored the construction of a thoroughly uneconomic charcoal-burning steel mill outside of Asunción (see Chapter 4). Paraguay's forests, which are to provide charcoal in place of coking coal for the plant, are receding rapidly and the country has little or no exploitable iron ore and no coal deposits. Most important, it has no market for the steel.

43. Other factions have existed within the Colorado party during the 1980s, such as the *éticos* (led by Carlos Romero Pereira), the Movement for Colorado Integration (led by former interior minister Edgar Ynsfrán), the National Popular Movement (led by Leandro Prieto Yegros), and several others. However, only the traditionalists and the militants held high office during this period.

44. Riquelme, "Reforma, ruptura o continuismo en el Paraguay," pp. 76–80.

45. Ibid., pp. 69–74.

46. One such group is the Movimiento Independiente Colorado (MIC), led by Edgar Ynsfrán.

47. In fact, he underwent prostate surgery later in September.

48. As Ynsfrán revealed on national television after the coup, several coup dates had been scheduled and discarded for various reasons. The first coup date had been December 27, 1988.

49. Closing Paraguay's exchange houses immediately deprived Rodríguez of income (estimated by Western diplomats at $20,000 a day) from Cambios Guaraní, one of the largest *casas de cambio* in Paraguay. See Eugene Robinson, "Paraguay Calm Again After Military Takeover," *The Washington Post*, February 5, 1989, p. A29.

50. Ñata means "flatnose" in Guaraní. Her given name is Stella.

51. Stroessner and the militants had tried to keep the First Brigade short of ammunition, fuel, and spare parts, anticipating that its armor might be used against them. Some evidence exists that certain businessmen donated several million dollars to buy military equipment, fuel, and supplies in Argentina in the months prior to the coup to circumvent this strategy. At the very least, Stroessner and the militants seem to have committed a glaring intelligence error.

52. The number of dead is uncertain. Many news sources placed the death toll at 200–300 immediately after the coup.

53. "Paraguayan Chief Shakes Up Army," *New York Times*, February 8, 1989, p. A16. Many observers believe that Argaña will be the Colorado candidate for president in the 1993 elections.

54. The demonstration of Saturday, February 11, 1989, attracted tens of thousands of Liberal supporters and was the first one of its kind in decades. In a startling departure from the past, Domingo Laíno's speech was broadcast live on national television.

55. See James Brooke, "Paraguay Voting in Open Election," *The New York Times*, May 1, 1989, p. A3; Eugene Robinson, "Paraguayans Vote Today for President of New Era," *The Washington Post*, May 1, 1989, p. A19; "Tradition Won," *The Economist*, February 11, 1989; and John Barham, "The Ways of General Stroessner Linger On," *The Financial Times*, March 15, 1990, p. 7.

56. The newly "liberated" Asunción press is most reluctant to explore this topic.

57. See Paul H. Lewis, *Paraguay Under Stroessner*, Chapel Hill: University of North Carolina Press, 1968, pp. 131–139; Nathan M. Andrews, "The Hunt for André," *Reader's Digest*, March 1973, pp. 223–259; and Evert Clark and Nicholas Horrock, *Contrabandista!* New York: Praeger Publishers, 1973, p. 85. See also Chapter 7, this volume.

58. See Andres Oppenheimer, "Paraguay's New Ruler Had Disputes with Stroessner," *The Washington Post*, February 4, 1989, p. A19.

59. See Brooke, "Paraguay Voting in Open Election," p. A3.

60. Not only were the electoral lists full of the names of voters long since deceased, the May 1, 1989, elections could not have been truly fair because opposition had been severely repressed for forty years. No party possessed anything like the resources or organization of the Colorados, who enjoyed a giant head start. Although the government made significant gestures toward the opposition parties by granting them free television time and by recognizing all

except the Communists, the electoral law, which was inherited from Stroessner, contained major flaws: (1) it disallowed coalitions, (2) it awarded the winning party two-thirds of congressional seats regardless of electoral proportionality, and (3) it did not allow the opposition to participate in the work of the electoral commission.

61. In particular, Pastor Coronel, the former head of police investigations, has often been accused as Stroessner's chief torturer.

7

International Relations

Like Uruguay to the south, [Paraguay] is a buffer state separating Brazil and Argentina—the two largest countries in South America—and, like Bolivia to the west, it is landlocked. The circumstance of being landlocked has historically led the country alternately into isolationism and expansionism; its buffer status has underwritten its sovereignty. Paraguay's foreign policy traditionally aimed at striking a balance between the influence of its two large neighbors.
— Thomas C. Bruneau, "Government and Politics"

To preserve its own sovereignty, Paraguay needs to be able to swing between [Argentina and Brazil], and it goes wherever it gets more favorable treatment.
—Melissa Birch,
"Pendulum Politics: Paraguayan Economic Diplomacy, 1940–1975"

Squeezed between South America's two biggest countries, in the center of a vast continent, Paraguay's chief international concern has always been maintaining its independence. As the quotations at the beginning of this chapter indicate, Paraguay's leaders have, at turns, resorted to isolationism and expansionism to protect Paraguayan sovereignty. The country has survived largely because of its value to its giant neighbors as a buffer state. Another element is the largely invisible role played by the United States as a "balancer." Otherwise, given its history and geographic setting, Paraguay easily could have wound up a remote province of Brazil or Agentina. Balancing the influence of both countries for the benefit of Paraguay is a constant concern of Paraguayan diplomacy.

Throughout their history, Paraguayans have exhibited a ferocious nationalism that translated into a willingness to fight to the death when the future of their country was at stake. This element has been a key to their survival as a nation. Isolation is also a part of Paraguay's legacy. Pinned between the inhospitable Chaco to the north and west, the Mato Grosso to the north and northeast, and dangerous powers to the south and east, Paraguayans often have had to depend on their own resources.

141

Hazard often has saved Paraguay from annihilation. Argentine ineptitude and disunity as much as Francia's isolationism and noninterventionism preserved the country's borders in the early part of the nineteenth century. Argentine-Brazilian rivalry saved the country again after the 1864–1870 holocaust of the Triple Alliance War, when the victorious powers, mistrusting each other, declined to divide Paraguay between them.

Another element is the people's physical toughness, fortitude, and courage. Paraguayans have endured more than their share of adversity since colonial times, when Jesuit-led Indian armies drove back Portuguese marauders. Of the three major South American wars since 1820, two were fought mainly on Paraguayan soil.[1] Paraguayans defeated *porteño* military forces twice in 1811 and resisted the combined might of Brazil, Argentina, and Uruguay for more than five years, from 1864 to 1870. In the Chaco War (1932–1935), Paraguayans drove the better-armed and better-equipped Bolivian army from the field even though the Bolivians were more numerous and were trained and led by German officers.

A useful metaphor for Paraguay's international diplomacy since World War II, especially in economic affairs, is that of a pendulum swinging between the orbs of Buenos Aires and Brasilia.[2] By playing its giant neighbors against each other, Paraguay has been able to secure advantageous economic and political concessions. Paraguay's apparent official embrace of the Axis cause during World War II similarly brought it aid from a worried United States.[3]

Stroessner based his foreign relations on anticommunism and nonintervention in the affairs of other states. Nonetheless, he sent troops to the Dominican Republic in 1965 under the auspices of the Organization of American States (OAS) and offered to send troops to fight in Vietnam under U.S. command. The Stroessner regime maintained diplomatic relations with countries dominated by conservative politicians, such as Taiwan and South Africa. Except for Yugoslavia, Paraguay has not maintained relations with any communist country, including the People's Republic of China and Nicaragua after 1980. Paraguay broke ties with Cuba in 1959, before the United States did, after the Fidel Castro regime sent aid to guerrillas fighting to overthrow Stroessner.

INTERNATIONAL RELATIONS TO 1870

Paraguay's first dictator, José Gaspar Rodríguez de Francia, probably saved Paraguay's independence through his foreign policy of isolationism and noninterference in the affairs of neighboring states. Francia's critics have always delighted in accusing him of girdling Paraguay with a diplomatic "Chinese wall" by forbidding Paraguayans (or anyone else) to leave or enter the country. Yet Francia's policy of isolationism after 1811 was mostly forced on him by objective conditions and by the decisions of his neighbors.[4] Argentina and Brazil would not establish normal diplomatic relations with Paraguay because they refused to recognize Paraguay's independence. Argentina put Paraguay's survival at stake by invading the country in 1811 and, after being defeated, by choking off Paraguayan commerce at Buenos Aires. Meanwhile, the Brazilians were encouraging the local Indian tribes to cause problems for Paraguay on its northern border. Nor did Bolivia or any European powers make any explicit efforts to establish diplomatic ties.

Paraguay's isolation under Francia was not complete, however. Even during the grim 1820s, Paraguay's trade with Buenos Aires did not cease. The *porteños* continued to want Paraguayan yerba, tobacco, and hides, and Paraguay's government continued to need arms, munitions, books, ponchos, coffee, oil, vinegar, wine, salt, and iron. A large but informal trade continued with Brazil at the Alto Paraná port of Itapua, where tax receipts and fines on smugglers became an important source of tax revenues for Francia's government.[5] Yet Paraguay's isolation from the rest of the world was not without benefits for Francia himself, whose bizarre dictatorship would not have survived long in a setting more open to normal international exchange.[6]

Francia's habit of kidnapping or expelling foreign visitors was probably conditioned by his frustrations about gaining international recognition, notably from Great Britain. In addition, Francia's maltreatment of them may have been exaggerated.[7] The most celebrated kidnapping case was the 1821 arrest of Aimé Bonpland, a French botanist who had entered Paraguay despite Francia's refusal to grant him permission to visit. Bonpland was held in a state of benign detention for ten years, until 1831. The case attracted the attention of one of Bonpland's influential friends, Simón Bolívar, who threatened in 1823 to invade Paraguay from Bolivia if Francia did not release Bonpland. Francia ignored Bolívar, whose invasion never took place partly because of logistical difficulties and partly because Buenos Aires refused to approve the project.

Another novel but often overlooked policy of the period was Francia's willingness to grant asylum to many South Americans fleeing the endemic disorder, chaos, and civil war that raged on Paraguay's borders for decades after independence. The grant of this *derecho de asilo* was principled, in that Francia at times risked attack on account of it.[8] The most famous refugee to seek asylum in Paraguay was Uruguayan *caudillo* José Artigas, who escaped into Paraguay with 200 men during the 1820s after fleeing from his rebellious associate Francisco Ramírez. Although Artigas had himself earlier threatened to invade Paraguay, Francia gave

Artigas a farm and a pension but kept him very much at arm's length. Meanwhile, the military preparations that Ramírez was making to invade Paraguay came to nought.

After Francia's death, Carlos Antonio López took the inevitable steps to end Paraguay's twenty-six years of isolation. Brazil finally recognized Paraguay in 1844. López invited foreign physicians, engineers, and investors to settle in Paraguay; paid for students to study abroad; boosted exports; and sent his son, the future dictator Francisco Solano López, to Europe to buy guns. López retained Francia's mistrust of Brazil and Argentina but believed he could use diplomacy to protect Paraguay's interests abroad. He had some success at this, but López lacked the diplomatic virtuosity of Francia's earlier years as well as his caution. López narrowly averted a war with Buenos Aires by meddling in the affairs of a border province. But López also signed a treaty with Buenos Aires that finally recognized Paraguay's independence when Argentine dictator Juan Manuel de Rosas fell in 1852.[9] In quick succession, Paraguay signed treaties of friendship, commerce, and navigation with France and the United States, gaining diplomatic recognition from the United States, France, and Great Britain.

Despite this promising start, the reign of López I was marked by rising tensions with all of Paraguay's new international contacts, including the United States and Great Britain. López recklessly dropped Francia's key policies of neutrality (some would say indifference) and nonintervention without making clear where Paraguay's allegiances lay, especially with regard to his neighbors. López exposed Paraguay to outside forces without ever making the hard choices and compromises to decide his loyalties. He wanted better relations with Brazil and Argentina and tried to woo his big neighbors by tantalizing them with ambiguous navigational agreements and talk about border negotiations. At the same time, he wore his suspicion and disdain for them like a patriotic badge and allowed their territorial claims to fester. By seeming to promise much but offering little, he helped turn both countries into deadly enemies.

Brazil and Argentina had each tolerated Paraguayan independence because Paraguay served to check the expansionist tendencies of the other. Each was satisfied as long as the other could not dominate Paraguayan affairs. Each hesitated to threaten Paraguay, because doing so might provoke an alliance between Paraguay and the other. However, a Paraguay antagonistic to both Brazil and Argentina gave the two countries a reason to unite against it.

Francisco Solano López (López II) had an even worse effect on Paraguay's international relations, leading to a disaster that almost erased the country from the map. Among the thousands that López II executed were many foreign diplomats. Even the U.S. ambassador, Charles Washburn, almost fell victim to his bloody purges. But, though he was callous and cruel, López II should not get all the blame for the Triple Alliance War. As soon became clear once the fighting stopped, Brazil and Argentina both had coveted large areas of Paraguayan territory, which they quickly annexed.

RELATIONS WITH THE UNITED STATES

Diplomatic ties between Paraguay and the United States have grown and diminished intermittently, conditioned by policy issues external to Paraguay.[10] The two countries are far apart, and Paraguay is too small to attract much sustained interest in Washington, either political or economic. Most frequently, security concerns in the United States are what have overcome this habit of indifference.

The first official U.S. notice of Paraguay occurred in 1845, when President James K. Polk appointed Edward Augustus Hopkins as his special agent there. Carlos Antonio López was suspicious of the twenty-two-year-old Hopkins because the latter had no power to make treaties or to extend official recognition to the Paraguayan government. A colorful, controversial figure, Hopkins was mainly interested in using his diplomatic position to turn a profit, taking time out from his unsuccessful mediation effort with Buenos Aires to explore the Paraguay and Paraná rivers by canoe. He was soon embroiled in disputes with Carlos Antonio López that nearly caused a war with the United States.[11]

In 1854, López banished Hopkins, who was by then U.S. consul, canceling the various commercial monopolies that he had been granted. The López-Hopkins dispute was complicated by the arrival of the *Water Witch*, a U.S. naval vessel sent to carry out scientific investigations in the local rivers. In 1855, Paraguayan gunners fired on the *Water Witch*, killing a helmsman, after it proceeded on the upper Paraná against orders. With Hopkins egging it on, the U.S. Congress decided to "chastise" López in 1858 by sending a flotilla of nineteen ships and 2,500 men to Paraguayan waters. The ships left after López agreed to pay $250,000 to the helmsman's survivors, but López used the Hopkins affair to enhance his political position in Paraguay by claiming it as a diplomatic victory.

The 1877 U.S. mediation effort in Paraguay, that of President Rutherford B. Hayes, was successful from the Paraguayan point of view. In a treaty signed that year, Argentina agreed to give up its claim to a large chunk of the Paraguayan Chaco.[12] Paraguay approved the outcome and in appreciation named a city and one of the country's 19 departments after President Hayes.

The generalized concern of the United States for inter-American security involved it in Paraguay's main international crisis of the twentieth century: the Chaco War with Bolivia. The war ended with an international peace conference that convened in Buenos Aires in July 1935 with U.S. participation (see Chapter 3). Although Bolivian diplomats had signed agreements in 1879, 1887, 1894, and 1907 that ceded progressively larger areas of the Chaco to Paraguay, the boundary between Bolivia and Paraguay never had been delineated. Bolivia had several reasons for trying to seize the unpopulated region by stealth and by force. Partly, Bolivian politicians wanted to vindicate their country's national honor by winning new territory to compensate for that lost to Chile (during the War of the Pacific, 1879–1883) and Brazil. In addition, the growing value of cattle ranching and quebracho[13] exaggerated the Chaco's economic possibilities in Bolivian eyes. Landlocked like Paraguay since 1883, Bolivia was also looking for an outlet to the sea for its oil exports, which it imagined it would gain by pushing its border to the Paraguay River. Last, oil was rumored to underlie the entire border region. Bolivia's oil was controlled by a U.S. company, Standard Oil.

Unprepared for war, the Liberal government in Asunción sought to temporize even after a Paraguayan army major (later colonel and president) named Rafael Franco burned down Bolivia's Fort Vanguardia in the disputed area. Full-scale fighting erupted in 1932, and by 1935 the Paraguayans occupied positions in the foothills of the Bolivian Andes.[14] The war was costly in both blood and booty; most of the fighting took place in the western Chaco. Because this was far from Paraguayan and Bolivian population centers, however, economic disruption was minimal. Spruille Braden (later U.S. ambassador to Perón's Argentina) was the U.S. delegate to the peace conference, which finally produced a settlement in October 1938.

The outbreak of World War II intensified the security concerns of the United States and brought the two countries closer together. This was ironic because Morínigo's openly pro-Axis regime had made the country a hotbed of Axis spies and sympathizers. Alarmed by a surge of German activity and influence in the region and vexed by Argentina's pro-Axis leanings, the United States sought to wean Paraguay away from German and Argentine blandishments and to enhance its own presence. The State Department encouraged closer ties between Brazil and Paraguay, especially regarding Brazil's offer to finance a road project to help reduce Paraguay's dependence on Argentina. Along with many other Latin American countries, Paraguay became eligible for major economic assistance. During the war years, the United States donated to Paraguay large amounts of Lend-Lease funds and supplies,[15] loans for public works, and technical assistance in agriculture and health care.

But German influence in Paraguay was pronounced. South America's first Nazi party branch was formed in Paraguay in 1931. In addition, the German embassy worked effectively to transform Paraguay's extensive network of German immigrant schools, churches, hospitals, farmers' cooperatives, youth groups, and charitable societies into Axis tools. By 1939, these institutions were prominently displaying swastikas and portraits of Hitler throughout Paraguay. Large numbers of Paraguayan military officers and government officials were openly sympathetic to the Axis, among them the national police chief, who named his son Adolfo Hirohito after the leading Axis personalities. The director of the national police academy was active in Mussolini's Fascist party; the head of Morínigo's secret police was a confidant of the leading Nazi agents in the country; Morínigo's official secretary and the army's secret police director were Axis supporters; and the undersecretary of state was the attorney for several large German companies. By 1941, the official newspaper, *El País*, had taken an overtly pro-German slant. Pro-Allied labor unions were under strict government control, while Paraguayan police cadets were wearing swastikas and Italian insignia on their uniforms.[16]

With the outbreak of war between the Axis powers and the United States on December 7 and 8, 1941, the United States gained the leverage it needed to force Morínigo to commit himself publicly to the Allied cause. Morínigo officially severed diplomatic relations with the Axis countries in 1942. He hedged his bets by postponing a declaration of war against Germany until February 1945 and by refusing to act against German economic and diplomatic interests until the bitter end. In addition, Morínigo continued close relations with the pro-Axis Argentine military.

The benefits of an Allied victory did not seem as clear in Paraguay as they did in the United States; Paraguayan officials were reluctant to antagonize Germany while the outcome of the war was still in doubt. One reason was that a break with Argentina would have severely disrupted Paraguay's economy. In addition, Morínigo could hardly have afforded to hinder the economic activities of his German citizens, who were among Paraguay's hardest workers. Many Paraguayans believed their interests lay in economic expediency, viewing German-U.S. rivalry in South America simply as friction between great powers whose spheres of influence overlapped.

U.S. notice of Paraguay, which had lessened after V-E Day, increased sharply after Stroessner's 1954 coup. Appearing on the world scene at the high-water mark of the Cold War, Stroessner and his impeccable anticommunist credentials attracted attention in Washington, where policy makers were increasingly preoccupied with containing communism. Especially after the 1959 victory of Fidel Castro's revolution in Cuba,

Washington's principal regional concern was the hypothetical emergence of a left-wing Paraguayan regime that would provide a haven for radicals and a base for revolutionary activities around the hemisphere.[17] Naturally, these fears intensified when Castro helped finance and organize attempts to forcefully overthrow Stroessner.[18]

The coincidence of security interests between the two countries produced, by Paraguayan standards, a largess of U.S. military and economic aid. Between 1954 and 1975, the United States gave close to $200 million in bilateral aid to Paraguay.[19] From 1961 to 1966 alone, Stroessner received over $60 million in U.S. economic aid.[20] As a point of reference, the total Paraguayan state budget for 1959 was $21 million.[21] Although the U.S. Congress sharply cut military assistance to South America in 1977, the United States trained over 2,000 Paraguayan military officers in counterintelligence and counterinsurgency.[22] Stroessner owes the successes of his early years in power to the United States more than to other any foreign power.

In return for U.S. aid and support, which strengthened the regime and lent it international respectability, Paraguay became one of Washington's most dependable Latin American allies. The Paraguayan delegate regularly cast his vote in favor of U.S. policies in the United Nations and in the Organization of American States. Relations warmed, and Stroessner was once quoted as saying that the U.S. ambassador was like an extra member of his cabinet.[23] Richard Nixon praised the regime for its stand against communism during his controversial 1958 trip to South America. Stroessner sent troops to support the 1965 U.S. intervention in the Dominican Republic and offered in 1968 to send Paraguayan troops to fight in Vietnam. In addition, Paraguay signed the September 1965 Selden resolution passed by the U.S. House of Representatives, which authorized unilateral U.S. military intervention in Paraguay in the event of a direct or indirect threat from "international communism."[24]

The United States succeeded in forcing Stroessner to make some cosmetic changes to his regime in the early 1960s, using Alliance for Progress funds as a rather large carrot. The problem was that Washington really had no stick, as the United States feared that withholding the funds might destabilize Stroessner and bring in a less friendly regime. In any case, at that time stability still outweighed democracy as a goal of U.S. foreign policy in Latin America, and Paraguay still possessed very few of the attributes that make democracy possible, in terms of political culture, standard of living, and independent institutions. In 1965, Paraguay's contribution to the Dominican Republic intervention and new, pro-U.S. military governments in Brazil and Argentina helped improve United States–Paraguay ties.[25]

Paraguay's emerging notoriety as a drug entrepôt during the 1960s and 1970s began to undermine the relationship. A drug ring masterminded by August (André) Ricord used Paraguay as a privileged haven for running a lucrative heroin-smuggling business through Marseilles, France, smuggling into the United States heroin worth an estimated $2.5 million a year, or about one-third of the total U.S. supply. Obviously, Ricord counted on the connivance of high Paraguayan officials to protect his enterprise.[26] In 1972, President Nixon threatened to cut off U.S. aid if Stroessner would not agree to extradite Ricord. Stroessner stalled but ultimately gave in. Ricord was handed over to U.S. agents and flown to New York, where he was convicted, sentenced to fifteen years behind bars, and jailed on drug trafficking charges.[27] Smuggling of "hard" drugs from Paraguay apparently declined so much after the Ricord affair that the United States closed its Drug Enforcement Agency (DEA) office in Asunción in 1981.

The 1976 election of Jimmy Carter produced fundamental changes in U.S.-Paraguayan relations. Carter's emphasis on human rights and the decision by Congress to cut off military hardware deliveries in 1977 ended the decades of Washington's public near-silence on Paraguay's lack of political democracy. Thanks largely to the determined efforts of U.S. Ambassador Robert White, Stroessner released hundreds of political prisoners. In addition, White encouraged the opposition politicians who formed the National Accord in 1979 and was linked to Stroessner's 1983 decision to allow the return of political exiles. Even more dramatic changes came under President Ronald Reagan, who made a clean break with the past in May 1985 by lumping Paraguay together with Chile, Cuba, and Nicaragua as the region's last dictatorships.

With the arrival of Clyde Taylor, U.S. ambassador from 1985 to 1988, the United States openly began sponsoring efforts to bring about a democratic transition in Paraguay, by quiet pressure for reforms within the system and by increasing contacts with the opposition. With a regime like Stroessner's, this was a tricky game to play, as the embassy was not interested in destabilizing the regime, per se. Not surprisingly, Taylor's attempts to encourage a prodemocratic opposition immediately aroused intense suspicion and, rather than ignore Taylor, Stroessner opted to try to turn the situation to his advantage.

Stroessner had always treated anyone who doubted that the ruling Colorado party was trying to perfect "Paraguayan" democracy as a communist. Thus, Paraguayan officials could plausibly portray Taylor in the local media as a maverick who was pursuing his own agenda outside of Washington's knowledge and control. The low point in U.S.-Paraguayan relations probably occurred in February 1985, when Taylor was teargassed as a result of Stroessner's direct orders to the chief of police.[28] Taylor's

U.S. Ambassador Clyde Taylor (seated, left) and President Alfredo Stroessner (seated, right) at the National Palace in Asunción in November 1985, on the same evening that Taylor presented his credentials. Looking on are (standing, left to right) Lieutenant General and Chief of the Military Cabinet Guillermo Clebsch, Naval Captain Ignacio C. Moreno, and Air Force Colonel Alcibiades R. Soto. (Courtesy Clyde Taylor)

replacement, Timothy Towell, a political appointee who has had a diplomatic career, began his tour as ambassador in mid-1988.

During the late 1980s, the United States began to perceive that Paraguay had once again "joined the big leagues" in "hard" drug trafficking, this time by smuggling cocaine.[29] More than a ton of Bolivian cocaine annually was then estimated to be transiting Paraguay on its way to the United States.[30] Three events focused U.S. concern. One was the August 1987 seizure in Brussels of 114 kilograms (251 pounds) of cocaine hidden in a Lineas Aereas Paraguayas (LAP) shipment of coconut soap. The second incident was the September 19, 1987, crash of a small private plane in northern Argentina, which turned out to be carrying four Paraguayans and 200 kilograms (440 pounds) of cocaine.[31] The third incident was the May 1988 discovery of 34 kilograms (75 pounds) of "crystal pure" cocaine in a suitcase abandoned on the LAP luggage carrousel in the Miami airport.[32] In addition, U.S. officials suspected that Paraguay had become a major center for laundering drug money.

Evidently, several strands came together to cause Paraguay's drug problem. Increased pressure on Bolivian drug traffickers as a result of U.S. efforts to destroy drug laboratories had a "spillover" effect on Paraguay. In addition, drug dealers had identified Paraguay as a less hostile and less vigilant place to ply their trade. Third, although coca probably is not grown or processed within the country,[33] Paraguay's vast Chaco, a virtually unpatrolled wilderness with over 900 airstrips, provided an ideal base for planes to land and take off[34] (the Paraguayan Air Force has minimal radar capability in the Chaco). Fourth, Paraguayan law enforcement officials were poorly equipped to deal with sophisticated drug traffickers, both because they lacked training and because the law on drug-related crimes was out of date. Fifth, Paraguayan sentencing of drug traffickers was notoriously lax. Sixth, money that passed through Paraguay's exchange houses (casas de cambio) was impossible to trace.

Paraguay began to cooperate with U.S. drug control efforts during Stroessner's last years in power, after pressure was applied by the U.S. Embassy and by U.S. lawmakers.[35] In January 1988, the Stroessner government welcomed the reopening of the Drug Enforcement Agency's Asunción office.[36] With the help of U.S. legal experts, Paraguay redrafted its penal code to add tough, new antidrug provisions and Paraguayan drug enforcement officers received training from U.S. instructors. Paraguay also approved an aerial marijuana eradication program that was completed in the spring of 1989.[37] Another indication of Paraguay's seriousness in halting the drug trade is the many statements that President Rodríguez has made on the subject.[38]

The United States enjoys little leverage over Paraguay in trade, because neither nation produces anything truly vital in the other's economy. In 1987, for example, the United States suspended Paraguay as a beneficiary under the Generalized System of Preferences for Paraguay's failure to respect elementary trade union rights. This action cost Paraguay about $2 million a year in sugar exports. Although a major supplier of Paraguay's imports (accounting for 20–25 percent of the total), the United States buys few Paraguayan products in return and ran a bilateral trade surplus with Paraguay in 1988.[39]

In 1988, the largest U.S. program in Paraguay was the Peace Corps.[40] In addition, Partners of the Americas, with its U.S. Information Agency (USIA) and Agency for International Development (AID) subsidies, operates a highly active research and exchange program between Paraguay and the University of Kansas, which houses a large Paraguay research archive. In addition, USIA operates several binational cultural centers in Paraguay. The only military program that remains (one that has strong support from the U.S. State Department and from the Paraguayan military) is the $125,000 annual expenditure for the International Military Education and Training (IMET) program designed to increase the professionalism of the armed forces.[41]

The remaining levers of U.S. influence in Paraguayan economic affairs are some sizeable multilateral loans. For example, the Interamerican Development Bank approved $68 million in credits in February 1987 for an expansion of Asunción's water system. In addition, a U.S. firm controls construction of the joint Argentine-Paraguayan Yacyretá hydroelectric project several hundred miles downstream from Itaipú (with about half that plant's generating capacity), which is very slowly nearing completion. A U.S. firm will supply the turbines, although Argentina has guaranteed the loans; the Eximbank has provided $400 million for the project. Both loans were approved by U.S. representatives at the banks.

PENDULUM DIPLOMACY:
RELATIONS WITH ARGENTINA AND BRAZIL

Since the time of its origin in the sixteenth century, Paraguay's fortunes have been tied inextricably to its relations with its two giant neighbors, Argentina and Brazil. Although the United States has, at times and often at crucial points, played the role of balancer and arbiter behind the scenes, its influence on Paraguay will continue to diminish. For the moment, Brazil has replaced Argentina as Paraguay's lodestar. Since the 1960s Paraguay has tended to take more of its political, economic, and commercial cues from Brasilia than from Buenos Aires. This trend will likely continue until Argentina's leaders can halt and then reverse the progressive economic disintegration of their country set into motion by the first period of rule of Juan Perón (1946–1955).

Brazil and Argentina are by far Paraguay's biggest investors; combined, they are also Paraguay's largest trading partners. Together they accounted for two-thirds of Paraguay's $1.5 billion 1987 external investment total. In 1987, Brazilians owned 40.6 percent of all external investment in Paraguay; Argentines owned 23.7 percent.[42] The increasing stake of Brazil in Paraguay's political and economic affairs is a rather

Figure 7.1
Paraguayan Exports and Imports (1960)

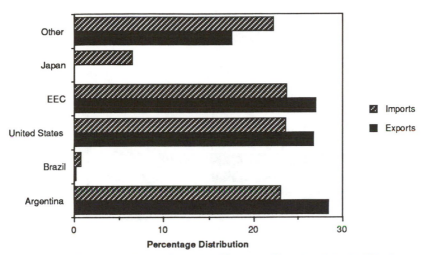

Source: *Boletín Estadístico*, Banco Central del Paraguay, Departamento de Estudios Económicos, Asunción, November 1988.

recent phenomenon. Since 1960, Brazil's share in Paraguay's external trade has jumped markedly, mostly at the expense of Argentina and the United States (Figures 7.1 and 7.2). For instance, in 1988 Brazil supplied nearly 30 percent of Paraguay's imports, while Argentina's share was less than 12 percent. But in 1960, Argentina provided more than 23 percent of Paraguay's imports while Brazil's share of the market was negligible (less than 1 percent). During the same period, the U.S. share in Paraguay's imports dropped from nearly 25 percent to just over 10 percent. In a similar manner, Brazil has outpaced Argentina and the United States as Paraguay's largest single export destination.

From colonial times until the 1960s, except for a few decades at the end of the nineteenth century, when a Brazilian-backed Colorado regime ruled in Asunción, Argentine influence predominated in Paraguay. Brazilian population centers were simply too remote and inaccessible from Asunción. But a cultural aspect was also at work. Educated Paraguayans in particular tended to emulate the cosmopolitan and sophisticated Argentines. What trade there was with Brazil went down the river to Buenos Aires first (a distance of about 1,200 miles) and then north along the seacoast to Brazilian ports on the South Atlantic. This situation lasted nearly 400 years, from colonial times until the 1930s and 1940s, when changing economic conditions and policies in

Figure 7.2
Paraguayan Exports and Imports (1988 estimates)

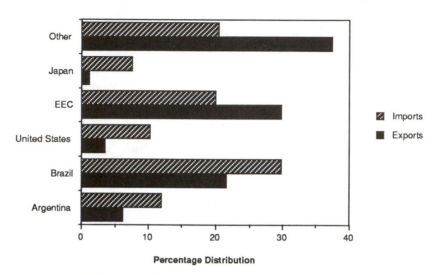

Percentage Distribution

Source: *Boletín Estadístico*, Banco Central del Paraguay, Departamento de Estudios Económicos, Asunción, November 1988.

the Southern Cone environment led successive Paraguayan governments to break Argentina's dominant position.

Tied to Paraguay by language and history, Argentina also controlled Paraguay's fluvial access to the sea (and to the outside world) by exercising authority over traffic along the Paraguay-Paraná river system. Argentine dominance was dealt a setback in the decades following World War II when Paraguay completed road links with Brazil, acquired a duty-free port on the South Atlantic Ocean at Paranaguá, and built the massive hydroelectric plant at Itaipú. Yet Paraguay adroitly balanced growing Brazilian influence by subsequently agreeing to build two more large hydroelectric plants with Argentina, at Yacyretá and at Corpus.

The massive land sales of successive Paraguayan governments after 1870 made Argentines the biggest landlords in the country after 1900. Entire departments, such as Amambay, were sometimes owned by a single company. Foreign interests, mostly Argentine, controlled entire industries and industrial sectors. These foreign intrusions caused resentment and finally became a political issue in the 1930s following the Paraguayan nationalist reaction to the Chaco War with Bolivia. The war, which had nationalist and economic causes, had pitted twolandlocked nations against each other. Paraguay's politicians became ever more aware of the nation's need for an alternative to its Argentine-controlled river route to the sea. In an explicit attempt to lessen Argentine influence, President Estigarribia signed agreements in 1939 to greatly improve road and rail links with Brazil. His successor, President Morínigo, continued the policy of strengthening ties with Brazil. Morínigo negotiated free port facilities for Paraguay at the South Atlantic port of Santos, to be linked to Paraguay by rail.[43]

The Paraguayan pendulum was to swing strongly toward Brazil during the next four decades, although the trend was not immediately apparent. Argentine president Pedro Ramírez granted Paraguay free port facilities at Buenos Aires and Rosario in 1943, and granted other trade concessions. In addition, he agreed to study the idea of forming a customs union. This idea appealed to Argentina since the war in the northern hemisphere had disrupted Argentina's traditional trade links with Great Britain and its sources of raw materials.

Preparations for the customs union continued through the 1946 election of Juan Perón as president and Paraguay's 1947 civil war. Paraguayan critics charged that Argentina was poised to take over economic control of Paraguay. In 1953, President Federico Chaves led Paraguay into the existing Argentina-Chile customs union, but Stroessner overthrew Chaves in 1954, before the treaty was ratified. Perón himself was overthrown thefollowing year. Stroessner never acted to ratify the customs union treaty. Relations between Buenos Aires and Asunción deteriorated after Perón's ouster because Stroessner granted Perón temporary asylum in Asunción. Even after Perón left Paraguay, Argentina's decaying political and economic picture throughout the 1950s and 1960s further removed Paraguay from Argentina's orbit. Nonetheless, with IDB financing, Argentina agreed to build a 90,000 kilowatt hydroelectric generator at Acaray Falls Dam that opened in 1969. The dam produced more power than Paraguay could use, so Paraguay became an energy exporter by selling its surplus back to Argentina.

Argentina's eclipse in Asunción was simultaneous with Brazil's rise. In 1956 and 1957 the Brazilian government under President Juselino Kubitschek signed a series of far-reaching transportation, trade, and investment agreements with Paraguay that greatly strengthened the ties between the two countries. The treaties included the following clauses:

1. Duty-free port facilities were granted to Paraguay on the Atlantic coast at Paranaguá and Brazil's duty-free privileges at Concepción were renewed.
2. Brazilian financing was approved for the construction of a bridge over the Paraná at Foz do Iguaçu.

3. Brazilian financial backing was guaranteed for an east-west highway linking Coronel Oviedo with the bridge at Foz do Iguaçu.
4. Brazilian investors were given the same status as native-born Paraguayans.
5. Import/export restrictions were removed on Brazil-Paraguay trade and payment both ways was allowed in Brazilian currency.
6. Brazilian financing was arranged for a road linking Concepción and Pedro Juan Caballero.
7. Brazilian fianancing was arranged to study the construction of hydroelectric dams in Paraguayan territory on the Acaray and Monday rivers.
8. Brazilian funding was provided for the construction of new buildings at the University of Asunción.

These accords together with the new roads, bridge, and port facilites—all mostly completed by the late 1960s—finally broke Paraguay's traditional dependence on Argentine goodwill for the smooth flow of its international trade. Argentina was not excluded as a major partner, however. In 1958, Paraguay and Argentina formed a joint commission to study the hydroelectric potential of the Paraná rapids at Yacyretá.[44]

All of these projects were soon dwarfed by a Brazilian proposal to build an enormous dam on the Paraná River at Itaipú[45] upstream from Foz do Iguaçu. Then as now, Paraguay obviously would not need more than a tiny fraction of the electricity generated, and it could not contribute financially to the project. But Paraguay's cooperation was essential to Brazil, which counted on the new dam to supply its growing electricity needs. In return for Brazilian financing of the multibillion-dollar project, Paraguay had to make controversial concessions regarding ownership of the construction site at Guairá falls[46] and the rates that Paraguay would receive for its share of the electricity. The two countries settled their differences over the ownership of the falls by signing the Acta Final in 1966, whose main provision was that Paraguay and Brazil would share equally the electricity produced by any dam at that location. Paraguay also got a valuable share of the construction contracts.[47]

Alarmed by these developments, Argentina tried during the 1970s to convince Paraguay to change its plans. First it complained that Itaipú might lower the water level of the Paraná River so much that Argentine ships might not be able to reach Asunción. When Paraguay rejected this, Argentina suggested that if Paraguay dropped the Itaipú project, the two countries could build an equally suitable dam at a different site a few miles downstream between Paraguay and Argentina. Paraguay also refused this proposal. A Paraguayan diplomat informed Argentina

Traffic on the Friendship Bridge linking Foz do Iguaçu (Brazil) and Puerto Presidente Stroessner (now renamed Ciudad del Este), Paraguay. Ciudad del Este is in the distance.

that "Paraguay will not involve itself in any project with any other country without the prior agreement of Brazil."[48]

Itaipú gave Paraguay's economy a great new source of wealth. Construction costs, estimated at $12 billion, produced a tremendous economic boom (see Chapter 4), as thousands of rural Paraguayans who never before had held a regular job went to work on the enormous dam. The construction of Itaipú demonstrated that Paraguay's relations with Brazil were more important than its relations with Argentina. Primary construction was completed in 1981. With an installed capacity of 12.6 megawatts, Itaipú is the world's biggest hydroelectric power plant, generating six times as much power as the Aswan Dam.

Stroessner played the pendulum game adeptly to reap benefits for Paraguay. Six months after the Itaipú treaty was signed with Brazil, in December 1973 Paraguay signed the Yacyretá treaty with Argentina. Progress on construction at Yacyretá has been much slower than at Itaipú, for various reasons, among them, Argentina's poor economic condition, and the subsequent discovery of oil and gas deposits on Argentine territory. The Yacyretá plant is not expected to generate electricity until the mid-1990s. Meanwhile, construction at Itaipú had begun in 1975. Another dam project, between Yacyretá and Itaipú at Corpus, has been deferred until the twenty-first century.

For all of its economic benefits, Itaipú was not an unalloyed economic or political blessing. Critics of the economic union with Argentina had once accused the government of agreeing to hand over control of Paraguay's economy to Argentina. Now they were blaming Stroessner for selling out to Brazil. Some charged that Itaipú was Paraguay's "Panama Canal." Brazil became Paraguay's main source for military equipment and training. The opportunites for graft and rake-offs in Itaipú-related contracts were mammoth and widespread on both sides of the project. A worldwide boom in commodity prices, particularly in soybeans and cotton (see Chapter 4), coupled with low prices for Paraguayan land and agricultural labor flooded Paraguay's eastern border region with 300,000–400,000 land-hungry Brazilian farmers. Portuguese suddenly replaced Spanish as the *lingua franca* in many areas and Brazilian currency replaced the guaraní as the medium of exchange.

Paraguay started to suffer from other Itaipú-induced economic and diplomatic problems. For instance, pressure from the opposition and from *ABC Color* in 1985 forced Stroessner to renegotiate the terms that Paraguay would sell electricity to Brazil. In addition, Paraguay's mounting debt was partly due to ACEPAR (Acero Paraguayo), an ill-conceived joint venture with Brazil to produce steel (see Chapter 4). Access to the Brazilian economy increased the opportunities for smuggling and contraband trade in ways that Brazil did not always find congenial: An estimated half of Paraguay's vehicles are stolen from Brazilian motorists. In 1988, Brazilian teamsters threatened to block the Friendship Bridge to protest the killing by car thieves of Brazilian drivers who had resisted the theft of their trucks. Brazil also accused Paraguay of forcing Brazilian farmers to leave. By the mid-1980s, 75,000 Brazilian families had moved back to their side of the border. In 1988, Brazil forced the recall of Justo Eres Almada, Paraguayan consul at Paranaguá and close Stroessner crony, for his alleged involvement in contraband and narcotics trafficking operations.[49]

The election of Radical party leader Raúl Alfonsín as president of Argentina in 1983 caused waves in Asunción. Alfonsín permitted Paraguayans in Argentina to demonstrate against Stroessner and sent messages of support to Stroessner's opposition. Paraguay ignored Argentine requests to extradite Argentine officers accused of human rights violations during the "dirty war" of the late 1970s. Likewise, it ignored requests for information about missing children from that era, most of whom had been adopted by Argentine couples who had settled in Paraguay.

In 1985, Brazil began a transition to democratic government that boded ill for Stroessner; Brazil sent its first nonmilitary ambassador to Asunción in twenty years. Although Brazil refrained from an openly critical policy, it agreed with the Argentine government in 1986 that a new program for economic integration in the Río de la Plata region would only be open to democratic nations.[50]

Despite the strains, relations with Brazil remain close. The Brazilians, who have much political and financial capital invested in Paraguay, obviously regard Rodríguez as a friend and a known quantity. The Brazilian high command greeted the Rodríguez coup and the fall of Stroessner with equanimity, expressing confidence that it would lead to "no changes in the internal politics or the external relations" of Paraguay.[51] Shortly after the coup, Brazil renegotiated hundreds of millions of dollars of Paraguayan debt, but on terms less favorable to Paraguay than those that Brazil was seeking from its own international creditors (see Chapter 4).

RELATIONS WITH SOUTH AFRICA, ISRAEL, AND THE FAR EAST

Until Pope John Paul II came to Paraguay in 1988, no head of state had visited Paraguay since the head of Argentina's military government visited Paraguay ten years before. As more and more countries began to look askance at Paraguay's peculiar political system during the 1970s and 1980s, Stroessner began to court states, such as South Africa, Israel, Rhodesia (before it became Zimbabwe in 1980), and Taiwan, that had fallen out of favor at the United Nations. In addition, Paraguay has maintained important ties with South Korea and Japan.

This policy saved Paraguay from total isolation during the last years of Stroessner's tenure and produced sources of useful services to the Paraguayan state. For instance, Israeli technicians are responsible for inspecting and servicing the airplanes of Paraguay's national airline, LAP. Taiwan, where Stroessner's extreme anticommunist stance struck a receptive chord, for years has maintained a Chinese Cultural Center in Asunción (complete with a public statue of Chiang Kai-shek). In addition, Taipei gave Stroessner a rare invitation for a state visit in 1988, which he turned down because of poor health. Thousands of Chinese, mostly from Taiwan, operate import-export businesses in Ciudad del Este (formerly Puerto Presidente Stroessner).

Relations between Paraguay and its circle of outcast states were mutually beneficial. Stroessner's 1974 visit to South Africa was the first by a non-African head of state in twenty years. During 1974–1975, the South Africans granted Paraguay significant financial concessions, including construction of several expensive new government buildings (such as the Palace of Justice and a foreign ministry building). Military links between the two countries were strong: The South African military presence in Asunción was second only to that of Brazil. General Andrés Rodríguez toured South African military installations during the late 1970s, and Paraguay helped divert shipments of embargoed arms to South Africa. In addition, Paraguay helped Rhodesia evade the embargo on its tobacco exports.[52]

Paraguay's relations with Japan have a longer history. As a result of a 1919 treaty that allowed Japanese to emigrate to Paraguay, a group of Japanese farmers arrived in 1936 and founded an agricultural settlement at *La Colmena*[53] between Asunción and Villarrica. By 1989, about 30,000–40,000 Japanese farmers and their descendants lived in few scattered agricultural colonies in Paraguay.[54] Japan was grateful for the welcome that Paraguay extended to Japanese settlers during the depression years of the 1930s; in return, the Japanese have been generous to Paraguay. A symbol of the goodwill between the two countries is the recently completed $15 million Paraguayan-Japanese Center in Asunción, where the principal activity is the teaching of English. One of the city's most imposing structures, the Paraguayan-Japanese Center is far more impressive than the local U.S. equivalent. In addition, the Japanese are financing a $200 million international airport at Ciudad del Este, following the World Bank's rejection of the project as unnecessary.[55] During the last years of Stroessner's tenure, the Japanese often ruffled U.S. feathers by refusing to join the United States in trying to influence Stroessner to begin a political evolution toward a more democratic regime. One Japanese ambassador to Asunción had the habit of joining Colorado party members in singing the Paraguayan national anthem in public and even spoke at events in honor of Stroessner, acts that Washington viewed as showing needless public support for a corrupt and repressive regime.

About 15,000 South Korean citizens also live in Paraguay. Holders of Paraguayan passports, many of these "immigrants" are actually looking for an easier way of entering the United States: South Korea's annual U.S. quota is always filled, but Paraguay's is not. But many South Koreans wind up staying in Asunción permanently, where they operate businesses such as jewelry stores, hotels, restaurants, and neighborhood grocery stores. South Korea recently built an attractive new embassy in Asunción. But the South Korean government began to distance itself from Stroessner in 1987. In particular, the South Koreans began spending their modest annual grant of $200,000 on computer software and language training instead of on nonlethal military assistance.

The Paraguayan-Japanese Center is one of the most imposing buildings in Asunción.

LOOKING AHEAD

Geopolitics will likely continue to drive Paraguayan foreign policy; the pendulum process, orienting Asunción to Buenos Aires and Brasilia, will continue. In turn, the internal stability of the Southern Cone states will determine the dynamics of the region's foreign relations. Continued democratization in Paraguay may improve Paraguay's chances of being included in any regional economic integration schemes in the 1990s. Certainly, Paraguay's fluvial resources make it a natural partner in any wider regional economic plan.[56] But Paraguay's prospects of attracting outside investors are not good, given the absence of attractive natural resources and of advantageous geographical locations for assembling or manufacturing. Paraguay's relative geographical isolation discourages large-scale investment.

Brazil will continue to exert enormous, if benign, influence in Paraguay. Some reasons for this are extensive Brazilian land holdings in Paraguay, Brazil's continuing economic and security interests in Itaipú, the highly permeable border between the two countries, and Brazil's grants of trade and transportation preferences to Paraguay that are critical for the latter's linkages to the outside world.

This does not mean that Argentina will not attempt to subtly counterbalance Brazil's presence and influence. The new government of President Carlos Menem in Argentina may try to resurrect the historical ties between the Peronist movement and Paraguay in coming years. Geography and politics will inevitably drive Argentina to seek ways to maintain, and expand, its hesitant presence in Paraguay. Most other South American states (the exception is Bolivia) probably will not give priority to Paraguay. But presently even Bolivian-Paraguayan relations appear to be on hold.

The United States will continue to be preoccupied with a secure democratic transition and with drug trafficking in Paraguay. President Carter began the emphasis on a transition to democracy, which continued into the 1980s under Reagan and will continue under Bush. The 1989 election of General Rodríguez with opposition participation will buy time for the Colorado party. But the opposition inevitably will continue to press for greater freedom and guarantees that future elections will be completely free regardless of their outcomes. In the 1990s, Paraguay may begin to feel the same internal and external pressures to liberalize that Mexico is now encountering. An entrenched elite in Mexico, in the Institutional Revolutionary party (PRI), is as reluctant to yield power as are the stalwarts of the Colorado party in Paraguay. In both cases a constellation of forces is emerging that may force a continued, tortured accommodation to civil liberties and civilian rule. One thing working in favor of U.S. policy in Paraguay is an apparently widespread pro-U.S. feeling among Paraguayans. The drug issue is the number two priority of the United States in Paraguay and throughout the Western Hemisphere. Washington will continue to focus on ending the trans-shipment of narcotics through Paraguay. Although the United States may join forces with Brazil in seeking to neutralize Paraguayan drug smuggling, the likelihood of eliminating the smuggling is doubtful as long as the Colorados and the armed forces run Paraguay. The wealth generated by narcotics is too tempting and too useful for Paraguay's narrow power structure to reject it wholeheartedly. Only if Colorado and military power decrease will a successor regime be able to reduce the attractions and the rewards of the drug trade.

Paraguay will probably not get much priority from the United States or from its neighbors unless it becomes destabilized and its internal strife threatens to spill over or it decides to become involved in foreign adventures as was the case under El Mariscal López in the mid-nineteenth century. As neither possibility seems likely, Paraguay probably will remain a small regional player in Southern Cone geopolitics. It will continue to have little global projection and minimal regional presence, but no more than that formally dictated by its membership in a broad array of hemisphere and international organizations.

NOTES

1. These were the Triple Alliance War (Paraguay vs. Brazil, Argentina, and Uruguay [1864–1870]), the War of the Pacific (Chile vs. Peru and Bolivia [1879–1883]), and the Chaco War (Paraguay vs. Bolivia [1932–1935]).

2. Melissa Birch, "Pendulum Politics: Paraguayan Economic Diplomacy, 1940–1975," Darden School of Business Administration, University of Virginia at Charlottesville, 1988 (mimeo).

3. Michael Grow, *The Good Neighbor Policy and Authoritarianism in Paraguay*, Lawrence: Regents Press of Kansas, 1981, pp. 70–84.

4. John Hoyt Williams, "Paraguayan Isolation Under Dr. Francia: A Reevaluation," *Hispanic American Historical Review*, 52:1, February 1972, pp. 102–122.

5. Ibid., pp. 106–107.

6. John Lynch, *The Spanish American Revolutions, 1808–1826*, New York: W. W. Norton, 1973, pp. 111–112.

7. Some of Francia's victims were the Scottish trader John Parish Robertson and J. R. Rengger and Marcel Longchamps, the Swiss doctors who were held against their will in Paraguay (José Antonio Vázquez, *El Doctor Francia visto y oído por sus contemporaneos*, Buenos Aires: Editorial Universitaria de Buenos Aires, 1975, pp. 110, 196, 197, 254). In addition, John Hoyt Williams pointed out that many Europeans lived unmolested in Paraguay during Francia's rule (Williams, "Paraguayan Isolation Under Dr. Francia," pp. 118–121).

8. In 1839, an entire company of Brazilian troops defected at Ytapua (Williams, "Paraguayan Isolation Under Dr. Francia," pp. 120–121). Stroessner later perverted the tradition of asylum when he granted Nazi war criminal Jozef Mengele refuge and a passport in the 1960s.

9. In fact, the *porteños* never got around to ratifying this treaty.

10. Riordan Roett, "Paraguay After Stroessner," *Foreign Affairs*, 68:2, Spring 1989, pp. 124–142.

11. For more on Hopkins, see Harold F. Peterson, "Edward A. Hopkins: A Pioneer Promoter in Paraguay," *Hispanic American Historical Review*, 22:2, May 1942, pp. 245–261.

12. Argentina had already annexed two large pieces of Paraguayan territory in 1872, between the Bermejo and Pilcomayo rivers and between the Uruguay and Paraná rivers. Brazil had also annexed a slice in the north, between the Branco and Apa rivers. Paraguay lost nearly as much territory in these annexations as was contained in its final boundaries.

13. Quebracho (literally, "break axe") is reputed to be the hardest wood in the world, grows abundantly in the Paraguayan Chaco, and is a natural source of tannin, which is needed to cure hides for leather.

14. Leslie B. Rout, *Politics of the Chaco Peace Conference, 1935–1939*, Austin: University of Texas Press, 1970, In particular, see pages 28 and 40 for the

boastful comments of Bolivia's president and commander-in-chief (a German soldier named Hans Kundt) and an insight into Bolivian motivation.

15. Lend-Lease was a U.S. program, begun in 1940, to funnel materiel and financing to countries fighting the Axis powers. Great Britain was the first recipient of Lend-Lease equipment.

16. Grow, *Good Neighbor Policy and Authoritarianism in Paraguay*, pp. 59–70. Also see Harris Gaylord Warren, *Paraguay: An Informal History*, Norman: University of Oklahoma Press, 1949.

17. Upon reaching Asunción during his 1958 tour of Latin America, Vice-President Richard M. Nixon praised Stroessner's Paraguay for opposing the communist "threat" more strongly than "any other nation" in the world (Virginia M. Bouvier, *Decline of a Dictator: Paraguay at a Crossroads*, Washington, D.C.: Washington Office on Latin America, 1988, pp. 8–9). See also R. Andrew Nickson, "Tyranny and Longevity: Stroessner's Paraguay," *Third World Quarterly*, 10:1, January 1988, pp. 237–259.

18. Paul H. Lewis, *Paraguay Under Stroessner*, Chapel Hill: University of North Carolina Press, 1980, pp. 180–181.

19. During the same period, the World Bank, the IMF, and other public international funding organizations (such as the Interamerican Development Bank) provided over $260 million to Paraguay in grants and loans. Also during this period, private U.S. citizens invested $60 million in Paraguay (Latin American Bureau, *Paraguay: Power Game*, Nottingham, Eng.: Russell Press, 1980, pp. 44–45). See also Bouvier, *Decline of a Dictator*.

20. These figures refer to aid disbursements, not allocations. Part of the U.S. aid money spent in Paraguay during the 1950s and 1960s had been allocated before Stroessner came to power.

21. All official Paraguayan economic figures are subject to the caveat that they often take no account of contraband trade and illegal financial transactions.

22. Bouvier, *Decline of a Dictator*, pp. 8–9. As the source for her United States–Paraguay foreign aid figures, Bouvier cites K. Larry Storrs and Diane Rennack, *U.S. Bilateral and Military Assistance to Latin America and the Caribbean: Fiscal Years 1946 to 1987*, Washington, D.C.: Congressional Research Service, July 31, 1987, p. 33.

23. Richard Bourne, *Political Leaders of Latin America*, Hammondsworth: Penguin Books, 1969, p. 121.

24. Latin American Bureau, *Paraguay: Power Game*, p. 45. See also House Resolution 542, August 28, 1965, "International Communism in the Western Hemisphere."

25. Ibid., pp. 121–123; Paul H. Lewis, *Socialism, Liberalism, and Dictatorship in Paraguay*, New York: Praeger, 1982, pp. 172–176, 182; Edwin Lieuwin, *Arms and Politics in Latin America*, New York: Praeger, 1960, pp. 228, 240.

26. Paul Lewis and Nathan Adams have identified Andrés Rodríguez, now president of Paraguay, as Ricord's chief backer, and General Patricio Colmán and secret police boss Pastor Coronel as subsidiary supporters (Lewis, *Paraguay Under Stroessner*, p. 136; Nathan M. Adams, "The Hunt for André," *Reader's Digest*, March 1973, pp. 223–259). See also Evert Clark and Nicholas Horrock,

Contrabandista! New York: Praeger, 1973. Allegations linking Rodríguez to drug traffickers persist ("Paraguay Coup Leader Called Drug Kingpin," *Atlanta Constitution,* February 4, 1989, p. 1C).

27. Ricord was released early, in 1985, due to failing health. He returned to Paraguay on a Paraguayan passport and died there the same year.

28. The incident occurred at a dinner for 300 at a private home that was organized by a group called Mujeres por la democracia (Women for Democracy—see Chapter 5). During the party, Paraguayan police arrived and lobbed a tear gas grenade over the wall, which landed near Taylor's feet. After the incident, the Colorado party media resorted openly to name-calling, labeling Taylor a "treacherous and caustic big-mouth" and a "defamer and blasphemer with a diplomatic sinecure." Even worse things were said about Taylor in Guaraní on the Colorado party radio station ("U.S. Drug-Trade Allegations Anger Top Paraguayans," *Washington Post,* March 31, 1988, p. A33).

29. J. Millard Burr, "Narcotics Trafficking in Paraguay: An Asunción Perspective," U.S. Department of State, Bureau of Intelligence and Research, Office of Terrorism and Narcotics Analysis, 1988 (mimeo).

30. According to a 1989 U.S. Department of Justice report, the amount of cocaine traveling through Paraguay was estimated at 500–700 kilograms (1,200–1,550 pounds) a month and was primarily for distribution in Europe.

31. In this incident, President Stroessner dispatched a Paraguayan Air Force plane to retrieve the remains of two of the victims who had close connections to his family.

32. These seizures are significant because LAP, the official state airline, operates under the auspices of the Paraguayan Defense Ministry with pilots who are Paraguayan Air Force officers ("Drug Probe Blocked to Shield Top Paraguayans," *Atlanta Constitution,* November 13, 1988, p. 23A; and "Florida Lawmaker Vows 'Bitter Fight' to Expose Paraguayan Link to Drugs," *Atlanta Constitution,* December 18, 1988, p. 18A). See also "Fugitive in Miami Cocaine Case Is Son of Paraguayan Dictator's Pal," *Miami News,* November 4, 1988, p. 4A; "U.S. Presses Paraguay To Fight Drug Trade," *Washington Post,* March 7, 1988, p. A28; "U.S. Drug-Trade Allegations Anger Top Paraguayans," *Washington Post,* March 31, 1988, p. A33; "Something Rotten in Paraguay," *Washington Post,* June 14, 1988, p. A23.

33. To date, no cocaine processing plants have been discovered in Paraguay, although large quantities of cocaine precursor chemicals and equipment used in cocaine laboratories have been seized.

34. The 1989 Department of Justice report specified that drug traffickers preferred private aircraft to ferry cocaine; their number two choice was thought to be commercial aircraft.

35. Specifically, these pressures took the form of growing sentiment in the U.S. Congress to decertify Paraguay's eligibility as an aid recipient from multilateral institutions in which the United States has veto power. Decertification also could have meant an end to all U.S. aid programs, including the Peace Corps, or trade sanctions. The Reagan administration had opposed decertifying Paraguay, claiming that it would be contrary to the U.S. national interest because

of Paraguay's importance in the fight against drugs. Nonetheless, a 1988 bill sponsored by U.S. Representative Larry Smith (D-FL) to reject President Reagan's finding came close to becoming law ("Florida Lawmaker Vows 'Bitter Fight' ").

36. Apparently Stroessner had opposed the closing of the office in 1981. Paraguayan officials repeatedly requested afterward that the office be reopened. From 1981 to 1988, Paraguay was covered, albeit irregularly, out of the Buenos Aires DEA office.

37. Marijuana grown in Paraguay's eastern border region is destined for Brazil, not the United States.

38. In his February 3, 1989, acceptance speech, Rodríguez said, "Drug trafficking is one of the worst scourges of mankind. My government will wage a firm and intransigent struggle against drug trafficking, and will make the laws even more strict and stronger in order to repress it. International cooperation will obviously be invaluable for the attainment of these objectives" (Foreign Broadcast Information Service, "Reports from Latin America," week of January 30–February 5, 1989).

39. *FY 91 Commercial Activities Report, Paraguay,* U.S. Department of Commerce, 1989. Leather, coffee, and sugar are the principal U.S. imports while exports to Paraguay include computers, tape recorders, large tractors and heavy equipment, TVs, radios, cigarettes, and cameras. Many of these items are sold "in transit" to Brazil or Argentina, as tourists from those countries buy the products in Asunción. Brazil, followed by Netherlands, Argentina, and Switzerland, is Paraguay's main export market. If contraband trade were included, Paraguay's official trade figures would probably double.

40. With close to 200 volunteers in 1989, the Peace Corps remained highly popular with Paraguayans and Americans.

41. Since 1986, IMET funds have been spent almost exclusively in the United States. The purpose of the program is to give military officers a greater appreciation for U.S. democratic values by having them attend courses given in English. Less that 10 percent of IMET funds are spent in a program of naval courses in Panama.

42. In contrast, U.S. and Japanese investors each held about 5 percent of Paraguay's 1987 external investment total ("Paraguay: Estimated Foreign Investment by Country of Origin, 1987," U.S. Department of Commerce, 1987).

43. Birch, "Pendulum Politics," pp. 7–8.

44. Ibid.

45. Itaipú means "the stone that sings" in Guaraní. The word referred to a small island in midstream that appeared and disappeared with the seasonal ebb and flow of the river. At the point in its course proposed for the dam, the Paraná makes a sharp turn and falls 55 yards (50 meters) ("The Colossus of Brazil," *GEO*, 3:11, November 1981, pp. 70–86).

46. Paraguay had always considered the Guairá Falls (which Itaipú obliterated) to be Paraguayan territory. A boundary commission formed at the end of the Triple Alliance War was never able to agree exactly where the border lay. Brazil had claimed the eastern end of the falls and occupied the area with troops in 1965 to underscore the seriousness of its claim. Obviously, if the falls

were wholly in Paraguay, Brazil would have had no claim to the electricity produced by a dam.

47. The text of this agreement was considered so potentially controversial that it was not released until two months after the Itaipú treaty was signed in April 1973, although this may be deemed typical of both governments' attitudes toward the public's "need to know."

48. Lewis, *Paraguay Under Stroessner*, p. 162.

49. Thomas C. Bruneau, "Government and Politics," in Sandra W. Meditz and Dennis M. Hanratty (eds.), *Paraguay: A Country Study*, Washington, D.C.: U.S. Government Printing Office, 1990.

50. Ibid.

51. February 5, 1989, EFE dispatch that quotes the *Jornal do Brazil*.

52. Latin American Bureau, *Paraguay: Power Game*, pp. 42–43.

53. *La colmena* means "the beehive."

54. Information supplied by the Paraguayan Embassy in Washington.

55. Still in the initial phase of construction, the new airport did not seem practical to the World Bank for several reasons. In the first place, Paraguay (a nation of 4 million) already has a modern international airport in Asunción. Second, two other international airports with 10,000-foot runways already exist just over the river from Paraguay, at Foz do Iguaçu in Brazil and Puerto Iguazú in Argentina. Despite Paraguayan assurances that the airport was intended to boost "tourism," speculation was rife that, in fact, the airport would boost the trade in contraband. For more on the contraband trade see Roger Cohen, "Paraguay Provides a Haven for Smugglers," *Wall Street Journal*, December 23, 1988, p. A8.

56. Efforts toward achieving a broader conception of River Plate integration focused on Argentina, Brazil, and Uruguay in the 1980s.

Acronyms

ACEPAR	Acero del Paraguay
CDE	Centro de Documentación y Estudios
CEDES	Centro de Estudios de Economía y Sociedad
CEP	Paraguayan Episcopal Conference
CEPES	Centro Paraguayo de Estudios Sociológicos
CNT	National Workers Confederation
CONAPA	National Coordinating Committee for Small Farmers
CORP	Regional Workers Central of Paraguay
CPT	Paraguayan Confederation of Workers
CPTE	Paraguayan Confederation of Workers in Exile
EEC	European Economic Community
GDP	gross domestic product
ICFTU	International Confederation of Free Trade Unions
IDB	Interamerican Development Bank
ILO	International Labor Organization
IMF	International Monetary Fund
INC	Industria Nacional de Cemento
LAC	Christian Agrarian Leagues
LAP	Paraguayan Airlines
LIBOR	London inter-bank offer rate
MCP	Paraguayan Peasant Movement
MDP	Democratic and Popular Movement (Movimiento Democrático y Popular)
MIC	Movimiento Independiente Colorado
MIT	Inter-Union Movement of Workers (Movimiento Intersindical de Trabajadores)
MOPOCO	Movimiento Popular Colorado
OAS	Organization of American States
ONAC	National Peasant Organization
ORO	Republican Workers Organization
PCP	Paraguayan Communist party

PDC   Christian Democratic party (Partido Democrático Cristiano)
PL   Partido Liberal
PLR   Partido Liberal Radical
PLRA   Authentic Radical Liberal party (Partido Liberal Radical Auténtico)
PRF   Partido Revolucionario Febrerista (Revolutionary Febrerista party)

Selected Bibliography

Abente, Diego. "Constraints and Opportunities: External Factors, Authoritarianism, and the Prospects for Democratization in Paraguay." *Journal of Inter-American Studies and World Affairs*, 30:1, Spring 1988, pp. 73–104.

————. "The War of the Triple Alliance: Three Explanatory Models." *Latin American Research Review*, 22:2, 1987, pp. 47–69.

Acevedo, Euclides. "Aproximación a la realidad Paraguaya: Algunas ideas básicas para la transición." In *Sistemas electorales y representación política en Latinoamérica*. Madrid: Fundación Friedrich Ebert, 1986.

Adams, Nathan M. "The Hunt for André." *Reader's Digest*, March 1973, pp. 223–259.

Arditi, Benjamín. "Estado omnívoro, sociedad estatizada. Poder y orden político en Paraguay." Asunción: Centro de Documentación y Estudios (CDE), 1987.

Arens, Richard. *Genocide in Paraguay*. Philadelphia: Temple University Press, 1976.

Arnold, Adlai F. *Foundations of an Agricultural Policy in Paraguay*. New York: Praeger, 1971.

Baer, Werner, and Melissa Birch. "The International Economic Relations of a Small Country: The Case of Paraguay." *Economic and Cultural Change*, 35:3, April 1987, pp. 601–627.

————. "Expansion of the Economic Frontier: Paraguayan Growth in the 1970s." *World Development*, 12:8, 1984, pp. 783–798.

Baer, Werner, and Luis Breuer. "From Inward to Outward Growth: Paraguay in the 1980s." *Journal of Inter-American Studies and World Affairs*, 28:3, Fall 1986, pp. 125–139.

Bareiro, Line. "Situación de la mujer en el Paraguay." Asunción: Centro de Documentación y Estudios (CDE), 1987 (mimeo).

Barrett, William E. *Woman on Horseback*. New York: Frederick A. Stokes Company, 1938.

Benítez, Luís G. *Historia diplomática del Paraguay*. Asunción: N.p., 1972.

Birch, Melissa. "Pendulum Politics: Paraguayan Economic Diplomacy, 1940–1975." Darden School of Business Administration, University of Virginia at Charlottesville, 1988 (mimeo).

Bourne, Richard. *Political Leaders of Latin America*. Hammondsworth: Penguin, 1969.

Bouvier, Virginia. *Decline of a Dictator: Paraguay at a Crossroads*. Washington, D.C.: Washington Office on Latin America, 1988.

Box, Pelham Horton. *The Origins of the Paraguayan War*. New York: Russell & Russell, 1967 (original printing, University of Illinois, 1930).

Britos de Villafañe, Margarita. *Las épocas históricas de Paraguay*. Asunción: N.p., 1982.

Bruneau, Thomas C. "Government and Politics." In Sandra W. Meditz and Dennis M. Hanratty (eds.). *Paraguay: A Country Study*. Washington, D.C.: U.S. Government Printing Office, 1990.

Burr, J. Millard. "Narcotics Trafficking in Paraguay: An Asunción Perspective." U.S. Department of State, Bureau of Intelligence and Research, Office of Terrorism and Narcotics Analysis, 1988 (mimeo).

Burton, Richard F. *Letters from the Battlefields of Paraguay*. London: Tinsley Brothers, 1870.

Canese, Ricardo, and Luis Alberto Mauro. *Itaipú: Dependencia o desarrollo*. Asunción: Editorial Araverá, 1985.

Caraman, Philip. *The Lost Paradise*. London: Sidgwick & Jackson, 1975.

Cardozo, Efraím. *Breve historia del Paraguay*. Buenos Aires: Editorial Universitaria de Buenos Aires, 1965.

———. *Vísperas de la guerra del Paraguay*. Buenos Aires: El Ateneo, 1954.

———. *Paraguay independiente*. Tomo 21 de *Historia de América y de los pueblos Americanos*. Barcelona: Salvat Editores, 1949.

Chaves, Julio César. *El supremo dictador*. Madrid: Ediciones Atlas, 1964.

———. *Historia de las relaciones entre Buenos Aires y el Paraguay*. Asunción and Buenos Aires: N.p., 1959.

Clark, Evert, and Nicholas Horrock. *Contrabandista!* New York: Praeger, 1973.

Cooney, Jerry W. "The Destruction of the Religious Orders in Paraguay, 1810–24." *The Americas*, 36:2, October 1979, pp. 177–198.

———. "Paraguayan Independence and Dr. Francia." *The Americas*, 28:4, April 1972, pp. 407–428.

Corvalán, Graziella. *Lengua y educación: Un desafío nacional*. Asunción: Centro Paraguayo de Estudios Sociológicos, 1985.

Corvalán, Graziella, and German de Granada (eds.). *Sociedad y lengua: Bilingüismo en el Paraguay*. Asunción: Centro Paraguayo de Estudios Sociológicos, 1983.

Economist Intelligence Unit. *Uruguay, Paraguay: Country Profile, 1989–90*. London: *Economist* Intelligence Unit, 1989.

Einhorn, David, and Stela Ortiz Einhorn. "A Choice of Words." *The Americas*, 41:1, 1989, pp. 42–47.

Encuentro Nacional de Mujeres. *Por nuestra igualdad ante la ley*. Asunción: R. P. Ediciones, 1987.

Escobar, Tito. *Una interpretación de las artes visuales en el Paraguay* (two volumes). Asunción: Centro Cultural Paraguayo Americano, 1982.

Ferguson, J. Halcro. *The River Plate Republics: Argentina, Paraguay, Uruguay*. New York: Time Inc., 1965.

Garner, William R. *The Chaco Dispute: A Study of Prestige Diplomacy.* Washington, D.C.: Public Affairs Press, 1966.

Gillespie, Francis. "Comprehending the Slow Pace of Urbanization in Paraguay Between 1950 and 1972." *Economic Development and Cultural Change,* 31:2, January 1983, pp. 355–375.

Gillespie, Francis, and Harley Browning. "The Effect of Emigration upon Socioeconomic Structure: The Case of Paraguay." *International Migration Review,* 13, Fall 1979, pp. 502–518.

González, J. Natalicio. *Proceso y formación de la cultura Paraguaya.* Asunción: Editorial Cuadernos Republicanos, 1988.

Graham, R. B. Cunninghame. *Portrait of a Dictator.* London: William Heinemann, 1933.

———. *A Vanished Arcadia.* New York: Dial Press, 1924.

Grow, Michael. *The Good Neighbor Policy and Authoritarianism in Paraguay.* Lawrence: Regents Press of Kansas, 1981.

Hicks, Frederic. "Interpersonal Relationships and *Caudillismo* in Paraguay." *Journal of Inter-American Studies and World Affairs,* 13:1, January 1971, pp. 89–111.

———. "Power, Politics, and the Role of the Village Priest in Paraguay." *Journal of Inter-American Studies and World Affairs,* 9:2, April 1967, pp. 273–282.

Hobsbawm, Eric. "Dictatorship with Charm." *New York Review of Books,* October 2, 1975, pp. 22–24.

Kolinski, Charles J. *Independence or Death! The Story of the Paraguayan War.* Gainesville: University of Florida Press, 1965.

Kostianovsky, Pepa. *Nuevas entrevistas para este tiempo.* Asunción: Ediciones Ñandutí Vive, 1988.

———. *28 entrevistas para este tiempo.* Asunción: Universidad Católica, 1985.

Latin American Bureau. *Paraguay: Power Game.* Nottingham, Eng.: Russell Press, 1980.

Lewis, Paul H. "The Origins of Paraguay's Traditional Parties." New Orleans, La.: Tulane University, 1988 (mimeo).

———. *Socialism, Liberalism, and Dictatorship in Paraguay.* New York: Praeger, 1982.

———. *Paraguay Under Stroessner.* Chapel Hill: University of North Carolina Press, 1980.

———. *The Politics of Exile: Paraguay's Febrerista Party.* Chapel Hill: University of North Carolina Press, 1968.

———. "Leadership and Conflict Within the Febrerista Party of Paraguay." *Journal of Inter-American Studies and World Affairs,* 9:2, April 1967, pp. 283–295.

Lieuwen, Edwin. *Arms and Politics in Latin America.* New York: Praeger, 1960.

López, Adalberto. *The Revolt of the Comuñeros, 1721–1735.* Cambridge, Mass.: Schenkman Publishing Company, 1976.

Lott, Leo B. *Venezuela and Paraguay: Political Modernity and Tradition in Conflict.* New York: Holt, Rinehart and Winston, 1972.

Lynch, John. *The Spanish American Revolutions, 1808–1826.* New York: W. W. Norton, 1973.

McNaspy, C. J. *Conquistador Without Sword*. Chicago: Loyola University Press, 1984.

Masi, Fernando. "Paraguay: Crisis del régimen autoritario tradicional, alternativas de transición y papel del Partido Colorado." Asunción and Buenos Aires: Consejo Latinoamericano de Ciencias Sociales (CLACSO), 1989 (mimeo).

_____. "Estado y regimen político en el Paraguay." Asunción: Centro de Estudios de Economía y Sociedad (CEDES), 1988 (mimeo).

Maybury-Lewis, David, and James Howe. *The Indian Peoples of Paraguay and Their Prospects*. Peterborough, N.H.: Cultural Survival, 1980.

Meditz, Sandra W., and Dennis M. Hanratty (eds.). *Paraguay: A Country Study*. Washington, D.C.: U.S. Government Printing Office, 1990.

Melià, Bartomeu. *Una nación, dos culturas*. Asunción: R. P. Ediciones, 1988.

Méndez, Epifanio. *Diagnosis Paraguaya*. Montevideo: Impreso en los Talleres Prometeo, 1965.

Meyer, Gordon. *The River and the People*. London: Methuen, 1965.

Miranda, Aníbal. *Desarrollo y pobreza en Paraguay*. Rosslyn, Va.: Inter-American Foundation, 1982.

Nichols, Byron Albert. *The Role and Function of Political Parties in Paraguay*. Unpublished doctoral dissertation, Johns Hopkins University, 1969.

Nickson, R. Andrew. "Tyranny and Longevity: Stroessner's Paraguay." *Third World Quarterly*, 10:1, January 1988, pp. 237–259.

_____. "Brazilian Colonization of the Eastern Border Region of Paraguay." *Journal of Latin American Studies*, 13:1, May 1981, pp. 111–131.

Nowell, Charles E. "Aleixo Garcia and the White King." *Hispanic American Historical Review*, 26:4, November 1946, pp. 450–466.

O'Donnell, Guillermo, and Philippe C. Schmitter. *Transitions from Authoritarian Rule: Tentative Conclusions About Uncertain Democracies*. Baltimore, Md.: Johns Hopkins University Press, 1986.

Pendle, George. *Paraguay: A Riverside Nation*. London: Royal Institute of International Affairs, Oxford University Press, 1967.

Peroni, Guillermo F., and Martín Burt. *Paraguay: Laws and Economy*. Asunción: Editora Litocolor, 1985.

Peterson, Harold F. "Edward A. Hopkins: A Pioneer Promoter in Paraguay." *Hispanic American Historical Review*, 22:2, May 1942, pp. 245–261.

Phelps, Gilbert. *Tragedy of Paraguay*. New York: St. Martin's Press, 1975.

Pincus, Joseph. *The Economy of Paraguay*. New York: Praeger, 1968.

Plá, Josefina (trans. B. C. MacDermot). *The British in Paraguay: 1850–1870*. Richmond (Surrey): Richmond Publishing Co., 1976.

Poppino, Rollie E. "Paraguay." In Witold S. Sworakowski (ed.). *World Communism: A Handbook, 1918–1965*. Stanford, Calif.: Hoover Institution Press, 1973, pp. 355–356.

_____. *International Communism in Latin America*. Toronto: Free Press at Glencoe, 1964.

Raine, Philip. *Paraguay*. New Brunswick, N.J.: Scarecrow Press, 1956.

Redekop, Calvin. *Strangers Become Neighbors: Mennonite and Indigenous Relations in the Paraguayan Chaco*. Scottdale, Penn.: Herald Press, 1980.

Rengger, J. R., and Marcel Longchamps. *The Reign of Doctor Joseph Gaspard Roderick de Francia in Paraguay.* Port Washington, N.Y.: Kennikat Press, 1971 (original printing, London: T. Hurst, E. Chance, and Company, 1827).

Riquelme, Marcial Antonio. "Reforma, ruptura o continuismo en el Paraguay: Dificuldades y perspectivas para una apertura democrática." Asunción: Fundación Friedrich Naumann, 1988 (mimeo).

Rivarola, Domingo M. "Politica y sociedad en el Paraguay contemporaneo: El autoritarismo y la democracia." Asunción: CEPES (Centro Paraguayo de Éstudios Sociológicos), September 1988 (mimeo).

———— (ed.). *Los movimientos sociales en el Paraguay.* Asunción: CEPES (Centro Paraguayo de Éstudios Sociológicos), 1986.

Roa Bastos, Augusto Antonio (trans. Helen Lane). *I, the Supreme.* New York: Alfred A. Knopf, 1986.

Rodríguez Alcalá, Guido. *Ideología autoritaria.* Asunción: R. P. Ediciones, 1987.

Roett, Riordan. "Paraguay After Stroessner." *Foreign Affairs,* 68:2, Spring 1989, pp. 124–142.

Roett, Riordan, and Amparo Menéndez-Carrión. "Paraguay." In Gerald Michael Greenfield and Sheldon Maram (eds.). *Latin American Labor Organizations,* Westport, Conn.: Greenwood Press, 1987, pp. 595–606.

Roett, Riordan, and Richard S. Sacks. "Authoritarian Paraguay: The Personalist Tradition." In Howard J. Wiarda and Harvey F. Kline (eds.). *Latin American Politics and Development* (third edition). Boulder, Colo.: Westview Press, 1990.

Romano, M. A. "Paraguay: Situación económica reciente." Washington, D.C.: Interamerican Development Bank, May 17, 1989 (mimeo).

Romano, M. A., and J. Dinsmoor. *Informe socioeconómico: Paraguay.* Washington, D.C.: Interamerican Development Bank (GN-1646), March 1989.

Rona, José Pedro. "The Social and Cultural Status of Guaraní in Paraguay." In William Bright (ed.). *Sociolinguistics.* The Hague: Mouton, 1966, pp. 277–298. (A Spanish version of this article is contained in Corvalán and Granada, *Sociedad y lengua.*)

Rout, Leslie B. *Politics of the Chaco Peace Conference, 1935–1939.* Austin: University of Texas Press, 1970.

Rubin, Joan. *National Bilingualism in Paraguay.* The Hague: Mouton, 1968.

Seiferheld, Alfredo M. *Nazismo y fascismo en el Paraguay: Los años de la guerra, 1939–1945.* Asunción: Editorial Histórica, 1986.

————. *Nazismo y fascismo en el Paraguay: Visperas de la II guerra mundial (gobiernos de Rafael Franco y Félix Paiva).* Asunción: Editorial Histórica, 1985.

————. *Los judíos en el Paraguay: Inmigración y presencia judías (siglo XVI–1935)* (Vol. 1). Asunción: El Lector, 1981.

———— (ed.). *La caída de Federico Chaves: Una visión documental norteamericana.* Asunción: Editorial Histórica, 1987.

Selser, Gregorio. "Paraguay: Octavo mandato presidencial de Alfredo Stroessner." Unpublished manuscript presented to the Latin American Studies Association Conference, New Orleans, La., March 1988.

Service, Elman R. *Spanish-Guaraní Relations in Early Colonial Paraguay*. Westport, Conn.: Greenwood Press, 1971 (original printing, Ann Arbor: University of Michigan Press, 1954).

———. "The *Encomienda* in Paraguay." *Hispanic American Historical Review*, 32:1, February 1952, pp. 230–252.

Service, Elman R., and Helen S. Service. *Tobatí: Paraguayan Town*. Chicago: University of Chicago Press, 1954.

Shoumatoff, Alex. "The End of the Tyrannosaur." *Vanity Fair*, 52:9, September 1989, pp. 230–304.

Skidmore, Thomas, and Peter H. Smith. *Modern Latin America* (second edition). New York: Oxford University Press, 1989.

Stewart, Norman R. *Japanese Colonization in Eastern Paraguay*. Washington, D.C.: National Academy of Sciences, 1967.

Valdés, Luis. "Stroessner's Paraguay: Traditional vs. Modern Authoritarianism." San Germán, P.R.: CISCLA, 1986.

Vázquez, José Antonio. *El Doctor Francia visto y oído por sus contemporaneos*. Buenos Aires: Editorial Universitaria de Buenos Aires, 1975.

Warren, Harris Gaylord. *Rebirth of the Paraguayan Republic, 1878–1904*. Pittsburgh: University of Pittsburgh Press, 1985.

———. *Paraguay and the Triple Alliance: The Post-War Decade, 1869–1878*. Austin: Institute of Latin American Studies, University of Texas Press, 1978.

———. "Political Aspects of the Paraguayan Revolution, 1936–1940." *Hispanic American Historical Review*, 30:1, February 1950, pp. 2–25.

———. *Paraguay: An Informal History*. Norman: University of Oklahoma Press, 1949.

Washburn, Charles A. *The History of Paraguay* (in 2 vols.). New York: AMS Press, 1973 (original printing, Boston: Lee and Shepard, 1871).

Whigham, Thomas. "Some Reflections on Early Anglo-Paraguayan Commerce." *The Americas*, 44:3, January 1988, pp. 279–284.

———. "Cattle Raising in the Argentine Northeast: Corrientes, c. 1750–1870." *Journal of Latin American Studies*, 20, pp. 313–335.

———. "The Iron Works of Ybycui: Paraguayan Industrial Development in the Mid-Nineteenth Century." *The Americas*, 32:2, October 1978, pp. 201–218.

Whigham, Thomas Lyle, and Jerry W. Cooney. "Paraguayan History: Manuscript Source in the United States." *Latin American Research Review*, 18:1, 1983, pp. 104–117.

White, Richard Alan. *Paraguay's Autonomous Revolution, 1810–1840*. Albuquerque: University of New Mexico Press, 1978.

Wilkie, James W., and David Lorey (eds.). *Statistical Abstract of Latin America*. Los Angeles: UCLA Latin America Center Publications, 1987.

Williams, John Hoyt. "Paraguay's Stroessner: Losing Control?" *Current History*, 86:516, January 1987, pp. 25–28, 34.

———. *The Rise and Fall of the Paraguayan Republic, 1800–1870*. Austin: Institute of Latin American Studies, University of Texas Press, 1979.

———. "Política paranóica: Paraguay, 1800–1870." Latin American Studies Association (LASA), 1976 (mimeo).

———. "Race, Threat, and Geography—The Paraguayan Experience of Nationalism." *Canadian Review of Studies in Nationalism*, 1:2, Spring 1974, pp. 173–191.

———. "Governor Velasco, the Portuguese and the Paraguayan Revolution of 1811: A New Look." *The Americas*, 28:4, April 1972, pp. 441–449.

———. "Paraguayan Isolation Under Dr. Francia: A Re-evaluation." *Hispanic American Historical Review*, 52:1, February 1972, pp. 102–122.

Wood, Bryce. *The United States and Latin American Wars, 1932–1942*. New York: Columbia University Press, 1966.

Ynsfrán, Pablo Max. *The Epic of the Chaco: Marshall Estigarribia's Memoirs of the Chaco War, 1932–1935*. New York: Greenwood Press, 1969 (original printing, Austin: University of Texas Press, 1950.)

Zook, David H. *The Conduct of the Chaco War*. New Haven: Bookman Associates, 1960.

Index